# Mac
## migration

### *Additional Books Written by Jason R. Rich*
### *and Published by Entrepreneur Press*

The following books are now or will soon be available wherever books are sold, or can be ordered from the EntrepreneurPress.com website. For more information about these and other books written by bestselling author Jason R. Rich, visit his website at JasonRich.com.

Smart Debt

202 High-Paying Jobs You Can Land Without a College Degree

202 Things You Can Buy and Sell for Big Profits, 2nd Edition

Click Start: Design and Launch an Online E-Commerce Website in One Week

*Entrepreneur Magazine's Personal Finance Pocket Guides*

Buying or Leasing a Car: Without Being Taken for a Ride

Dirty Little Secrets: What the Credit Bureaus Won't Tell You

Get That Raise!

Mortgages & Refinancing: Get the Best Rates

Mutual Funds: A Quick-Start Guide

Why Rent? Own Your Dream Home

*Entrepreneur Magazine's Business Traveler Series*

Entrepreneur Magazine's Business Traveler Guide to Chicago

Entrepreneur Magazine's Business Traveler Guide to Las Vegas

Entrepreneur Magazine's Business Traveler Guide to Los Angeles

Entrepreneur Magazine's Business Traveler Guide to New York City

Entrepreneur Magazine's Business Traveler Guide to Orlando

Entrepreneur Magazine's Business Traveler Guide to Washington, DC

FOREWORD BY KASPER JADE, EDITOR-IN-CHIEF, *APPLEINSIDER.COM*

# Mac

# migration

## The Small-Business Guide to
# Switching to the Mac

- *Choose the Right Mac for Your Business*

- *Easily Move Files from Your PC to Your Mac*

- *Increase Productivity with Cutting-Edge Office Software, Tools, and Applications*

Entrepreneur
Press

Jason R. Rich

Editorial Director: Jere L. Calmes
Cover Design: Kaochoy Saeteurn
Production and Composition: Eliot House Productions

This publication is designed to provide accurate and authoritative information in regard to the subject matter covered. It is sold with the understanding that the publisher is not engaged in rendering legal, accounting, or other professional services. If legal advice or other expert assistance is required, the services of a competent professional person should be sought.

Apple logo ©Vagu Ariel/Shutterstock

**Library of Congress Cataloging-in-Publication Data**
   Rich, Jason.
     Mac migration/by Jason R. Rich.
     p.   cm.
     ISBN-13: 978-1-59918-271-1 (alk. paper)
     ISBN-10: 1-59918-271-8
     1. Macintosh (Computer)—Programming. 2. Business—Data processing. I. Title.
   HF5548.4.M32R53 2008
   004.165—dc22                         2008020617

Printed in Canada
12 11 10 09 08                        10 9 8 7 6 5 4 3 2 1

# Contents

# Acknowledgments

T HANKS TO JERE CALMES, COURTNEY THURMAN, AND RONALD YOUNG AT Entrepreneur Press for inviting me to work on this project. This book is also possible because of the fine editing and design work of Karen Billipp and everyone at Eliot House Productions.

Thanks also to everyone at Apple, Microsoft, and all of the third-party companies that provided me with the information needed to create this book and make it a comprehensive resource for anyone interested in switching from a PC to a Mac. Bravo to Apple's advertising agency for creating the "Get a Mac" series of television ads, which served as a partial inspiration for this book.

My never-ending love and gratitude goes out to my lifelong friends—Mark, Ellen (and Ellen's family), and Ferras (FerrasMusic.com), who are all extremely important people in my life—as well as to my close friends Garrick Procter, Christopher Henry, Chris Coates, and Kiel James Patrick.

I'd also like to thank my family for all of its support and give a shout-out to my Yorkshire terrier Rusty (MyPalRusty.com). Yes, he has his own website, so please check it out! To visit my website, point your web browser to Jason Rich.com.

# Foreword

## by Kasper Jade, Editor-in-Chief, AppleInsider.com

I F JASON WOULD HAVE COME TO ME TEN YEARS AGO AND ASKED IF I'D WRITE THE PREFACE to his book about migrating small businesses to the Mac, I would have thought he'd damn near lost his marbles.

In a world then dominated by Microsoft's marketing prowess, the Windows operating system reigned supreme and "switching to Mac" was a foreign concept for most. The general consensus those days was that you'd have to be overly courageous, or downright crazy, to sideline your mainstream PC and invest in one of the few running the Mac OS.

Lucky for me, switching was never an option. I was essentially born into the Apple family. My uncles, aunts, and cousins all heralded the Mac, and when I was 13 my parents finally bit the bullet and purchased one of their own as an investment in my education. It was one of the single greatest moves they ever made. I still remember that day like it was yesterday because it would forever change my life and springboard me into a career comprised of all things Apple.

In the years that followed, both Apple and the Mac would face some turbulent times. The Mac OS was growing long in the tooth, as it lacked some modern technologies that were making their way into versions of Windows, and its underlying architecture proved increasingly resistant to extensibility. At the same time, Apple's fundamentals as a company were being brought into question, the Mac's share of the PC market slowly began to dwindle, and the mainstream media ran rampant with headlines predicting the company's ultimate demise almost daily.

Now, fast forward about ten years. Today, it's Microsoft's fundamentals and software that are falling under the microscope as Windows users, frustrated with a lack of progress in recent years, are fleeing the platform in clumps. Many are finding solace in the Mac, as are first-time buyers who've never owned a computer before.

According to Apple, more than 50 percent of Mac purchases at its international retail chain are by consumers who are transitioning from Windows or choosing the Mac over a Windows machine as their first computer. In general, sales of Macs are now growing at more than three times their Windows-based peers, and the number of Mac users worldwide was estimated at more than 22 million even before the first copies of Mac OS X Leopard hit store shelves in late 2007.

In just over a decade, Apple has staged the most extraordinary comeback in Silicon Valley history, and arguably one of the greatest recoveries in all of corporate America. Now the envy of many of its peers, I've had the pleasure of following this international icon through its resurgence, documenting the company's daily progress on AppleInsider.com, an online publication I founded 11 years ago purely out of love for the once ailing Mac.

Though many factors played into Apple's return to stardom, one undeniable catalyst was the advent of the Mac OS X operating system in March of

2001—about six months prior to Microsoft's Windows XP. A modern-day replacement to the Mac OS of old, Apple built the new software atop a powerful and versatile UNIX core. It then wrapped the entire system in an elegant interface called Aqua, which allowed even the most novice of users to harness its strengths.

Since then, Apple has gone on to polish Max OS X with five major upgrades, the latest of which is Leopard. (During that same time, Microsoft managed to push out just one major upgrade to its malware- and virus-ridden operating system dubbed Windows Vista.) This rapid progress on Apple's part has helped Mac OS X earn praise as the world's most advanced operating system, which in turn has helped the Mac reemerge as one of technology's healthiest brands.

Within weeks of reading this book and familiarizing yourself with all a Leopard has to offer, I'm sure you'll agree with pundits like the *Wall Street Journal*'s Walt Mossberg and myself in finding that the latest version of the Mac OS is faster, more stable, and far easier to use than any version of Windows Microsoft has ever brought to the table.

In fact, I'm willing to bet you'll find the Mac to be one of those most intuitive and inviting pieces of technology right out of the box. That's a direct result of Apple's complete autonomy over the platform in that it's the only personal computer manufacturer to develop both its own software and the hardware to run it. There are no blue screens of death, quirky configuration files, or missing drivers. Instead, most services are pre-configured to work out of the box, and there are clear and concise visual setup assistants included as part of Leopard for those that aren't.

In the little time it takes you to conquer the shallow learning curve of the Mac, you'll also find that you've have unwittingly opened your doors to the remainder of Apple's multifaceted product matrix. Though a hardware company at face value, Apple's a software company at its core, and Mac OS X is its strongest and most vital asset. In addition to the Mac, Mac OS X can also now be found at the heart of every iPhone, Apple TV, and even the latest iPods.

In addition to its growing presence in consumer markets and small business, for which your very interest in this book is a testament, the Mac has also regained its stride in education, recently overtaking Dell as the most purchased notebook brand by U.S. universities for use by their students. This movement by influential markets away from Windows PCs and toward Macs has even started to spill over into big businesses. Many Fortune 500 companies, including Intel, are said to have recently initiated pilot programs by which their employees are being afforded the opportunity to opt for a Mac as their primary work machine, even if in these early stages that means plunking down some of their own change to make it happen.

Over at AppleInsider.com we recently reported on an internal pilot program under way at IBM to study the possibility of moving a significant number of its staff to Mac. The first phase saw 24 MacBook Pros distributed to researchers at different sites within the company's research division. After the four-month test period, the 14 research scientists, 8 software engineers, a director, and a vice president were asked to provide feedback on their experience.

Of the 22 who responded, 18, or a resounding 81 percent, said that the Mac offered a "better or best experience" compared to their existing Windows-based ThinkPad computer. What's more telling, however, is that when asked if they would rather keep their MacBook Pro or return to using their familiar ThinkPad, only three chose the ThinkPad, with the the rest electing to cling tight to their new Mac. IBM now plans successive phases of the program that will see even more of its employees equipped with Macs.

Given its recent momentum, it's only natural to ponder the Mac's prospects given another ten years. With that in mind, I invite you to enjoy this guide out of the dark side and toward a more productive and rewarding career as a member of the Apple family, in which you can leave behind all the trials and tribulations of the Windows platform. Oh, and if by the slim chance you'll have the intermittent urge to use one of your existing pieces of Microsoft software, you'll find some comfort in knowing that Macs now runs Windows, too.

—Kasper Jade, Editor-in-Chief,
AppleInsider.com

# Preface

S O, YOU'RE A BUSINESSPERSON OR ENTREPRENEUR WORKING IN CORPORATE America, and you're thinking about making the switch from a PC that runs Windows to an Apple Mac. Well, you're not alone! In recent years, Apple has gained a fast-growing market share among both desktop and notebook computer users by offering easy-to-use, sleekly designed, powerful, stable, reliable, and highly functional computers that set themselves apart from PC-based computers in many ways.

For years, Apple was known for offering computers useful to students and to creative people who dealt with graphics, animation, music, and images. However, with an ever-growing lineup of popular business-oriented applications now available for the Mac, including Microsoft Office, these computers are now in demand by businesspeople working in all jobs and industries.

Apple and the companies developing software for Mac OS–based computers have begun to focus heavily on compatibility issues, making it extremely easy for Mac users to transfer and share files and data with PC users running similar applications. Macs can also be used in conjunction with office networks, and they're now capable of running Windows XP or Windows Vista (along with Windows applications) in conjunction with Mac applications and the Mac OS X Leopard operating system.

If the newest and most advanced Apple Mac computers have caught your attention and you've become interested in migrating from your unstable PC (which is prone to viruses and spyware, for example) to a more reliable Mac, *Mac Migration: The Small Business Guide to Switching to the Mac* will provide all of the information you need to make the transformation quick, effortless, and trouble free, regardless of your level of technical expertise.

This book will help you choose a Mac desktop or notebook computer that's best suited to your needs and budget, help you configure your new computer, select and install the most suitable Mac software to meet your needs, transfer your critical PC data to the Mac, and then quickly teach you to become proficient and highly productive using your Mac OS–based computer for all of your work-related and personal computing needs.

# Introduction

I'S IMPOSSIBLE TO WATCH PRIME-TIME NETWORK TELEVISION THESE DAYS AND NOT SEE the ongoing series of incredibly clever "Get a Mac" Apple ads. If you're not familiar with the ads, point your web browser to apple.com/geta mac/ads/, and see how pop culture and ingenious marketing have allowed Apple to dramatically increase its market share in both desktop and notebook computer sales.

The premise of these ads is simple. There are no fancy sets. No special effects and no catchy jingles. Most of the ads feature just two guys standing side by side in front of a sterile white background. The guy who stands on the right (actor/comedian Justin Long) is dressed casually, typically in jeans and a T-shirt, and introduces himself by saying, "Hi, I'm a Mac." The second guy, dressed in a business suit (actor/comedian John Hodgan), says, "and I'm a PC." Each ad in the series then focuses, in a comical way, on one or more reasons why Macs are superior to PCs.

These ads have been running for a while now. Have they captured your attention as a PC user? After seeing these ads, have you wondered what you're missing out on by not doing your computing on a Mac? Have you found yourself having problems with your PC running Windows Vista, for example, and agreeing with the anti-Windows sentiments communicated in the Apple TV ads?

Well, since you're reading this book, chances are something about Apple Macs has captured your attention, and you're now seriously considering giving up your PC and migrating to a Mac. Perhaps you've already finalized your decision. The good news is, you're not alone!

To be perfectly honest, you're reading this book because of how successful the Apple "Get a Mac" ads are. Since the 1980s, when PCs first started to become commonplace in America's homes and offices, I have been a dedicated and hardcore PC user. Until these ads started to run on TV, never in my wildest dreams would I ever have imagined switching to a Mac. I just never took these machines seriously.

About two years ago, my PC-based notebook computer that ran Windows XP suddenly and unexpectedly crashed. Needless to say, I wasn't happy. During the time I spent visiting computer retailers and consumer electronics stores shopping for a new PC-based notebook computer, I kept seeing those "Get a Mac" ads, and they piqued my interest. So, I visited a local Apple Store, played around on a MacBook for a while, and ultimately took one home.

I still relied heavily on my desktop PC to do my writing and computer work, but while I was on the go, I used my Mac and found that transferring data between the two computers was relatively easy. About a year later, I had to upgrade my desktop PC. Needless to say, my first stop this time was my local Apple Store, where I tried out one of the sleek-looking iMac desktop computers. Again, I was hooked.

Because I wanted to purchase a custom configuration for my new iMac, I wound up ordering it from the Apple.com website. Within a week, I gave up my remaining PC-based computer and have never looked back or regretted the decision.

As I sit in my office writing *Mac Migration: The Small Business Guide to Switching to the Mac*, the book's manuscript is being written using Microsoft Word 2008 on my iMac desktop computer as well as on my brand-new MacBook Pro notebook computer. After attending MacWorld in January 2008, I sold my original MacBook and upgraded to the MacBook Pro. Sitting on my desk, connected to the iMac, are my iPhone and iPod.

So as you've probably guessed, within a two-year period, I have given up on PCs running Windows XP or Windows Vista altogether. In all seriousness, however, one of the things that really influenced my decision to switch to Macs (in addition to the clever TV ads) was that I became totally fed up when I needed to get in touch with the technical support department for my former Windows-based notebook computer's manufacturer.

While I was still using my Windows-based notebook computer, I needed to call the technical support department and wound up sitting on hold for several hours trying to resolve my problem. Each time my call was transferred overseas, and I was connected to someone who spoke virtually no English and was totally unhelpful. It was a frustrating experience. I vowed at that point that my next computer would come from a company that offered much better technical support and customer service—something Apple has.

As you'll discover when you buy a new Mac and invest in the optional AppleCare Protection Plan, you receive three years' worth of free technical support and repair services from any Apple Store where you can obtain support on a face-to-face basis after making an appointment or via a toll-free phone number speaking directly with an Apple expert who is helpful and knowledgeable. Only minimal time on hold is required for telephone help.

In addition to the superior technical support assistance from Apple, the Mac computers offer a sleek, ergonomic design. The operating system that all Macs use (Mac OS X Leopard) is also far more stable than Windows XP or Windows Vista. Furthermore, you don't have to worry about your computer getting screwed up by viruses or spyware, nor worry about making sure you have the latest drivers in order to use specific peripherals such as a printer or scanner. The Mac OS X Leopard operating system is easier and more intuitive than any version of Windows. In a nutshell, all of the software and peripherals work well and work together.

Yet another reason migrating to a Mac is easy is that many of the most popular PC applications, including Microsoft Office, Quicken, and Photoshop CS3, and countless others, are also available for the Mac. There are literally thousands of Mac applications currently available, and more are constantly being released.

In cases where a Mac version of a popular PC program is not available, chances are the data from that PC application can be imported into a similar Mac application, giving you the same or better functionality. On the off chance you rely on a PC application that isn't available for the Mac and has no adequate alternatives, a Mac is now capable of running Windows and Windows applications.

Oh, and just about everything you need to get your new Mac up and running comes within the box.

## Millions Have Already Done It . . . The Mac Migration

While you might decide to migrate from a PC to a Mac as a result of those "Get a Mac" TV ads, chances are you already know someone who has made the switch and loves her Mac. In fact, independent market research shows that Apple is quickly gaining market share in both the desktop and notebook computer categories.

Sales figures from June 2007 show that Apple had a 17.6 percent market share in notebook computer sales within the United States, according to data from the research firm IDC. In 2007, Apple had a 5.9 percent market share in the overall PC market. It grew to 6.6 percent by early 2008. This growth trend shows no signs of slowing down.

In April 2008, Fox Business reported that worldwide shipments of personal computers totaled 71.1 million units in the first quarter of 2008. According to the market research firm Gartner Inc., that number represented an increase of 12.3 percent over 2007 PC sales. During that period, Dell Inc. held a 31.4 percent market share in PC sales, followed by Hewlett-Packard's 25.0 percent, are Acer's 9.1 percent. Apple had a 6.6 percent market share.

These statistics show that Apple is growing in popularity. And it's not just growth among computer enthusiasts and home computer users but in the business computing arena as well. As you'll discover from this book, businesspeople and entrepreneurs are now seeing Macs as a viable and welcome computing alternative to PCs that run Windows.

# Who Should Consider Migrating to a Mac

A few years ago if someone asked whether he should give up his PC computer in favor of a Mac, the response would probably have been no unless that person was a student, artist, graphic designer, photographer, musician, or someone in an artistic field. For years, Macs were known for being superior for artistic applications: music or video editing, page layout, photo editing, or graphic arts work, for example. They were not, however, considered serious business tools in corporate America.

The capabilities of all Macs have increased dramatically over the past few years! Today, Macs can handle a wide range of applications in demand by business professionals and entrepreneurs in most industries. The latest Mac computers are jam-packed with features and functionality not found on PCs, and the Mac OS X operating system has proven itself to be more stable and reliable than Windows.

Given these recent improvements in Apple Macs, the target audience for these computers has expanded to include just about anyone who is looking for a computer that can handle the most complex of applications yet provide a user-friendly, reliable, and powerful user interface.

Businesspeople, entrepreneurs, sales professionals, teachers, students, artists, photographers, graphics designers, website designers, IT professionals, accountants, lawyers, doctors, homemakers, and retired people are all now turning to Macs to meet their computing needs, so the number of those migrating is growing fast.

Because data and files are now so easily transferrable between PCs and Macs, even when your place of employment still replies primarily on Windows-based PCs to handle its computing needs, you'll be able to connect to the office network, communicate with co-workers, exchange files, and handle all of your computing needs with an Apple desktop or notebook computer running the Mac OS X Leopard operating system.

## What This Book Offers

The primary focus of *Mac Migration: The Small Business Guide to Switching to the Mac* is on helping business professionals and entrepreneurs who have been using PC-based computers (running Windows) easily and quickly switch to a Mac—without compromising their productivity, the capabilities of their computer, or their ability to handle whatever computer-related tasks are required of them.

This book will help you decide if switching to a Mac is right for you. Chapter 1 helps you choose which Mac system is best suited to your needs and budget. You'll also learn about the AppleCare Protection Plan and discover some of the many sources of Apple-related information available to you in the form of magazines, websites, and user groups.

Once you've purchased your Mac, Chapter 2 helps you unpack it, and get it up and running quickly and efficiently. You'll also learn how to customize the look of your Mac's desktop screen and screen saver, and how to install additional software.

Chapter 3 of *Mac Migration* offers an introduction to the Mac OS X Leopard operating system and helps you, as a former Windows user, become accustomed to interacting with your new computer. There are differences between a PC and a Mac from an operational standpoint that you'll need to understand and get used to.

From Chapter 4, you'll learn about how to pick and choose what additional software to install onto your Mac in order to fully customize your new computer so it is capable of handling all of your personal and work-related computing needs. Once you've gotten your computer running with your choice of software applications installed, Chapter 5 helps you transfer your essential PC data, files, and folders to your new Mac.

If you absolutely must continue to utilize a Windows-based application, Chapter 6 focuses on how to run Windows XP or Windows Vista, and Windows-based applications on your Mac. For the first time this is a viable alternative for Mac users.

Chapters 7, 8, and 9 help you become comfortable using many of the software applications that come bundled with your Mac and the popular optional software packages of interest to business professionals and entrepreneurs. You'll learn how to navigate around popular Mac applications and how to access the most commonly used commands and features of these various applications. These chapters are written specifically for former PC users who are still more comfortable and proficient using Windows-based applications.

Chapter 10 features details about 14 popular Mac applications that are of particular interest to business users. This chapter offers a preview of the many Mac programs available and provides advice on how to choose the applications that best meet your personal and business computing needs.

Regardless of what type of computer you use, who manufactures it, or what applications you'll be running, it's absolutely essential that you back up your important data. In Chapter 11, you'll discover some of the different ways of maintaining a current and reliable backup of your Mac applications, files, folders, and data.

At the end of this book, there are two appendixes. The first offers a record-keeping worksheet that will help you to easily keep track of important information pertaining to your new Mac, its peripherals, and all installed software. Using this worksheet, important information such as serial numbers can be kept in one handy location.

In Appendix B, you'll discover there are alternatives to purchasing genuine Apple Mac computers. These computers are capable of running the Mac OS X Leopard operating system.

Throughout this book, you'll find dozens of Mac Tips, important bits of information designed to help you save time, save money, and avoid common mistakes, and to bring important Mac-related facts to your attention. As you read each chapter, you'll be provided with additional resources, including specific website addresses, for obtaining more information about relevant topics.

Keep in mind that *Mac Migration: The Small Business Guide to Switching to the Mac* is not in any way associated or affiliated with Apple or any third-party software developers. The information within this book is designed to provide an unbiased resource for people interested in switching from a PC to a Mac. Any products, services, or companies featured within this book have been included to enhance this resource, but their inclusion should in no way be considered an endorsement. Before investing in any product, software application, or peripheral mentioned here, do your own research to determine if its functions and capabilities are best suited to meet your unique computing needs.

Just before this book was published, Apple announced plans to expand it's popular .Mac online service and rename it to "Mobile Me." In addition to the functionality of this service that's described throughout this book, chances are the revamped service will offer additional functionality for sharing and backing up data online. Be sure to check out the Apple.com website for details.

Finally, the one problem with writing book about computers or technology in general is that new developments and breakthroughs are constantly taking place, which means that technology that's available today will most likely be outdated within just a few months. So, by the time you read this book, it's very possible that more recent versions of the Mac OS X Leopard operating system as well as the various applications will be available. Thus don't be surprised if you discover changes and improvements to hardware system configurations or software features as you begin to shop for your new Mac and various software applications.

Regardless of who you are or what you do for a living, within a week or so after making the switch from a PC to a Mac, you'll probably wonder why you didn't make the switch much sooner. It's my belief (which is supported by millions of other Mac users) that Mac systems truly offer a better, more robust, more reliable, better designed, and easier-to-use computing experience than PCs running any version of Windows.

So, if you're a businessperson who has already purchased your new Mac, congratulations! If you're about to make the switch, have faith in yourself and in Apple, and know you're probably making the right decision.

—Jason R. Rich (JasonRich.com)

# CHAPTER 1

# Finding Your Inner Mac

APPLE HAS DEVELOPED SEVERAL UNIQUE COMPUTER PRODUCT LINES THAT APPEAL to users with vastly different needs, preferences, and budgets. The MacBook computers are Apple's line of battery-powered notebook computers. As of mid-2008, several MacBook products were available, including the MacBook, the MacBook Pro, and the ultrathin and lightweight MacBook Air. All are favorites among a growing number of businesspeople and entrepreneurs.

If you're looking for a full-size Mac-based desktop computer, your options include the economical *Mac Mini*, the standard *iMac,* and the *Mac Pro*, which is best suited for business users and others who require extra computing power and faster processor speeds.

A handful of system configurations are available for each Mac system. These configurations change every few months as newer, more powerful processors and other technology become available. In each new generation of Mac computers, larger hard disk sizes are often incorporated into the hardware for added storage, and hardware prices tend to drop. Also, the system configurations available to you will vary depending on where you purchase your Mac.

The Apple Stores and most authorized Apple dealers offer only preconfigured Macs. The Apple.com website (apple.com), however, allows customers to custom configure their computer and have it shipped directly from the factory, usually within three to seven business days.

As a Mac newbie, it's important to understand that all of Apple's latest Mac computers run the same Mac OS X Leopard operating system. Chapter 3 offers an introduction to this operating system, which is quickly growing in popularity. In addition to being more intuitive and easier to use, the Mac OS X Leopard operating system offers many technological advantages over Windows XP or Windows Vista, as you'll soon discover.

## Mac Tip

Depending on what you plan to use your new Mac for, you may find that running Windows isn't necessary, as Mac OS X versions of many popular third-party software packages, including Microsoft Office 2008, are available.

Thanks to the Intel chipset powering the newer Mac computers, the Apple desktop and notebook computers can now also run the Windows XP or Windows Vista operating system (as well as Windows-compatible programs). Chapter 6 focuses specifically on running Windows and Windows-compatible applications on your Mac.

This chapter focuses on finding your inner Mac, making the Mac migration, and choosing the best Mac OS–based computer to purchase and use, based on your unique computing needs and budget. After pinpointing your needs, this chapter explores your system options and will help you determine the best place to purchase your Mac.

You'll also learn about the optional AppleCare Service available to protect your computer purchase, plus the various technical support options that Apple offers, mainly through its chain of retail stores and a toll-free phone number. One of the reasons why Mac owners love their computers is because if a question or problem arises, knowledgeable, English-speaking Apple support specialists (referred to as "Geniuses") are available by appointment at all Apple retail stores to help you.

The AppleCare service plan costs extra, but it's an excellent investment not just because it ensures you'll receive technical support when you need it, but because it also covers repairs if your computer breaks or malfunctions.

## Defining Your Computing Needs

Simply by asking yourself a handful of questions, evaluating your past computing needs, and determining what you'll most likely be doing with your new computer in the future, you can narrow down your computer options and decide which Mac is best for you. The most important question to ask yourself as you get started in your search for a new computer is, "Do I want to invest in a Mac or a PC-based computer?" As you kick off your computer shopping, you'll discover that Macs typically cost more than comparable PC-based computers, but as this book explains, there are some definite advantages that Macs offer over PCs. For many people, these advantages are well worth the added financial investment.

In the Introduction, you learned some of the reasons why so many people are migrating to Macs. Because you've purchased this book, I'll assume you've already determined that you, too, are interested in purchasing a new Mac.

Now, the big question is, Do you want a desktop or laptop computer? Once you've made this decision, you'll need to choose a system configuration for your new computer. The more computing power you incorporate into your Mac (in terms of the microprocessor's speed, hard disk size, and amount of RAM memory, for example), the higher the cost of the system will be, but the better performance you'll experience, no matter what applications you'll be running.

The decision about whether to buy a desktop or notebook computer should depend on a number of factors, including what you'll be doing with your computer and where you'll be doing it. Start by answering these questions:

- Where will you be doing the majority of your computing?
- What applications will you be running?
- How many applications will you typically run at once?
- How important is speed and overall performance?
- What size monitor will work best for you?
- How much hard disk (storage space) will you need within the computer?
- Is portability important?
- What's your budget?

Once you've considered your answers to these questions, you can visit any Apple Store or authorized Apple reseller and have a salesperson help you choose a specific Mac computer to meet your computing objectives.

Remember, regardless of which system you choose, it's possible to run Microsoft Windows XP or Windows Vista on your Mac system, as well as programs specifically designed for the Windows operating system. These same Mac computers can also run all programs designed for the Mac OS operating system.

## (<sup></sup>) Mac Tip

Some of the primary advantages of using a desktop computer include a full-size keyboard, a large display (20 inches or 24 inches with an iMac or up to a 30-inch flat-screen Cinema display for a Mac Pro), and the ability to have more computing power at your fingertips, for less money, when compared to a comparable Apple notebook computer.

## Mac Desktop Computers

When it comes to Macs, a desktop computer (the Mac Mini, iMac, or Mac Pro) allows you to experience the Mac OS Leopard operating system and all of your programs on a large display. You interact with the computer itself using a full-size (corded or wireless) keyboard

**Mac Tip**

> While a notebook computer offers the same basic functionality as a desktop computer, it's battery powered and portable (weighing between 3 and 6.5 pounds). The MacBook, MacBook Pro, and MacBook Air systems tend to be a bit more costly than a comparable desktop system (from a technological standpoint). You'll also have a smaller display and keyboard. However, the Mac OS–based notebook computers have been ergonomically designed to provide comfort and usability.

and the Apple Mighty Mouse. All of the Mac desktop computers are known for their sleek, ultramodern design and built-in features.

If you'll be working in an office environment (including a home office) or the Mac will be your primary computer, opting to go with a desktop computer makes sense because of the additional computer power, larger display, and lower price (compared to a comparable Apple notebook computer).

While any size USB monitor can be used with a Mac Mini (Figure 1.1) or Mac Pro (Figure 1.2), iMacs (Figure 1.3) offer either a 20- or 24-inch widescreen display. For the Mac Pro, an optional 30-inch Apple Cinema HD display is available.

Of course, like any desktop computer, a Mac Mini, iMac, or Mac Pro needs to be plugged into an electrical outlet to operate. Peripherals, such as a printer, can be connected via USB cables, or in many cases by using wireless Bluetooth technology. The internet connection for the computer can be via Wi-Fi, Ethernet (using a cable), or optional dial-up modem.

When choosing a customized iMac or Mac Pro configuration, some of your options will include the amount of internal memory (RAM) the computer will possess. The more RAM you add, the more applications you'll be able to run simultaneously and the faster your applications will run. Typical configurations include 1GB, 2GB, or 4GB of RAM memory. At least 2GB is suitable for most business users.

*Figure 1.1*

The Mac Mini is considered the perfect "starter" Mac. It's priced starting at $599, but does not come bundled with a monitor, mouse, or keyboard. These necessary accessories are sold separately. *Photo courtesy of Apple.*

 **Mac Tip**

Keep in mind that the retail prices and system configurations described throughout this book for Mac OS–based desktop and laptop computers are subject to change every few months. Thus, when you start shopping for your Mac, you'll probably find systems with more powerful system configurations for the same or less money.

*Figure 1.2*

The Mac Pro is the ideal desktop computer for business users who need fast processing speed, a lot of hard disk storage space, and the most computer power possible to run multiple applications simultaneously. The retail price of a Mac Pro starts around $2,799. *Photo courtesy of Apple.*

You can also choose the amount of internal storage space your computer will possess, by determining the size of the computer's hard drive. Again, you have several options (which are subject to change), including 250GB, 320GB, or 500GB. An unlimited number of external hard drives can be connected to your computer to add additional space at any time. These external drives connect via a USB or Firewire cable. If given the option to upgrade to a faster hard drive, do so because this will enhance your computer's performance.

Yet another decision you'll need to make in addition to the size of your iMac or Mac Pro computer's display is the type and speed of optical drive installed in the machine. At the time this book was written, the Apple SuperDrive allowed for DVDs and CDs to be read or written at various speeds (up to 7,200 rpm). By the time you purchase your new iMac or Mac Pro, new

*Figure 1.3*

The iMac desktop computer is the most popular of the Macs. It's powerful, versatile, and sleek looking. Priced starting at $1,199, it's capable of running the Mac OS X Leopard operating system and the Windows XP or Windows Vista operating system, as well as thousands of third-party software applications. Hundreds of peripherals and accessories are also compatible with these Macs. *Photo courtesy of Apple.*

optical drive technologies and options may be available, including drives capable of playing Blu-ray discs.

All of Apple's desktop and notebook computers come bundled with the Mac OS X Leopard operating system, the iLife suite of software applications, and a working demo version of the iWork suite of applications, which is similar to Microsoft Office in terms of functionality.

Likewise, all Mac-based desktop computers have many features already built in, including multiple USB ports, a Firewire port, a video graphics card (although this can be upgraded), two stereo speakers (plus a built-in audio microphone and headphone jack), an Ethernet port, AirPort Extreme wireless internet capabilities, a Bluetooth 2.0+EDR (Enhanced Data Rate) module, an iSight video camera, and mini-DVI output port, to connect additional video-related products, such as an LCD projector. Much of this built-in functionality can also be found in the Mac notebook computers.

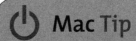 **Mac Tip**

Apple offers a wireless, 500GB hard drive for automatically backing up your data, called the Time Capsule ($299), which works seamlessly with the Time Machine data backup application built into the Mac OS Leopard operating system. See Chapter 11 to learn more about backing up your computer.

## Mac Notebook Computers

For people on the go who want a fully functional Mac-based computer available to them virtually anywhere, a MacBook notebook computer (Figure 1.4) is probably the way to go. Depending on your needs, there's the basic MacBook (ideal for casual computer users), the MacBook Pro (which offers extra computing power that's ideal for business users), and the MacBook Air (which when it was released was the thinnest laptop computer in the world).

The MacBooks run using a built-in rechargeable battery, or they can be plugged into an electrical outlet (or another power source). One potentially limiting feature of the MacBooks (or any notebook computer) is the size of their screens. The MacBook and MacBook Air both offer a 13.3-inch display, while the MacBook Pro offers the choice of a 15- or 17-inch display. The keyboards are also smaller than those used with a desktop computer; however, a lot of computing power has been packed into these relatively small and compact notebook computers.

If you're an international traveler, the Apple notebook computers come with an AC power adapter with interchangeable plugs (sold separately), so you'll be able to easily plug in and use (or charge) your computer virtually anywhere in

*Figure 1.4*

The MacBook is the entry-level notebook computer from Apple. It's priced starting at $1,099 and comes in several different system configurations. This computer is most popular in its white outer case. Higher-end MacBooks are also available in solid black. *Photo courtesy of Apple.*

the world. Other adapters, which are sold separately, allow you to plug your computer into the cigarette lighter of a vehicle or the power adapter available aboard some airplanes.

## The MacBook

The MacBook is considered Apple's entry-level laptop computer. It's used by students, entrepreneurs, and businesspeople alike. It's sleekly designed and offers a variety of built-in features and software. The retail price of a MacBook ranges from $1,099 to $1,499, depending on the system configuration. The processor speed, amount of RAM memory, optical drive type, and the hard drive size determine the price of the unit.

Like the iMac, the MacBook has a built-in iSight camera, along with a microphone and speakers, so it can be used for web-based videoconferences, video blogging, and other multimedia applications. For example, you can run Skype (skype.com) and make extremely inexpensive international or domestic calls over the internet, without having to add extra hardware. The MacBook will act as a speaker phone (or video phone). The system can also play DVDs and is fully compatible with all iTunes downloadable content, so the computer can serve as a full-featured entertainment system while you're on the go.

Of course, the MacBooks also run a vast number of software applications. You can do word processing, surf the web, handle spreadsheets or databases, make a presentation, and perform any number of other tasks—simultaneously if you desire.

The MacBook with a 13.3-inch screen weighs 5 pounds and measures 12.78 inches (width) by 8.92 inches (depth) by 1.08 inches (height). The battery life is about four and a half hours when the system is configured to conserve power and minimal optical drive usage is required. If you'll be watching a DVD a two-hour battery life is more typical.

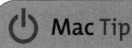

**Mac Tip**

At the time this book was being written, rumors were rampant on the internet about Apple releasing new notebook computers that would feature a titanium casing. So, by the time you read this book, additional models of the MacBook may already be available.

## MacBook Air

Priced starting at $1,799, the MacBook Air computer (Figure 1.5) was introduced at MacWorld Expo in early 2008, and at the time was the thinnest laptop computer on the market.

Boasting a battery life of over five hours, this unit is ideal for Mac users who already use a Mac desktop computer. In order to shrink the size of this unit, features like an internal optical drive were left out. And, the unit has fewer USB and other ports built in a MacBook or MacBook Pro. Software and data can, however, be transferred between a desktop Mac and the MacBook Air via a wireless connection. An external optical drive is available as an optional add-on.

MacBook Air has a 13.3-inch display and comes bundled with 2GB of RAM memory, a 1.6GHz microprocessor, and a 80GB hard drive. This system

*Figure 1.5*
The MacBook Air is an ideal second Mac computer for savvy Mac users on the go. It's more expensive than a basic MacBook, but it's also lighter and thinner, and has a much longer battery life. *Photo courtesy of Apple.*

configuration can be upgraded. Just one of many improvements made to the MacBook Air (compared to a MacBook) is the multitouch trackpad (which replaces a mouse). It accepts what Apple refers to as multifingered gestures to interact with the computer in much the same way as the iPhone touch screen is used. This feature has also been incorporated into the latest MacBook Pro notebook computers.

The MacBook Air weighs just 3 pounds and when shut measures 2.8 inches (width) by 8.94 inches (depth) by .76 inch (height). Because of its power-efficient display and lack of optical drive, average battery life is up to five hours per charge.

## MacBook Pro

For anyone running high-end or graphic-intensive software, such as artists, video editors, or power business users, the MacBook Pro (Figure 1.6) is the ideal

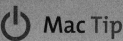

## Mac Tip

MacWorld Expo (not to be confused with *MacWorld* magazine) is an annual computer show that focuses exclusively on Apple computers and related products. It's open to computer enthusiasts, Mac owners, and anyone working in the computer industry. Traditionally, Apple makes major new product announcements for the upcoming year at this show. To learn more, visit macworldexpo.com.

portable computing solution. These systems are priced starting around $2,000, and offer faster processing speeds, more RAM, and larger hard drives than the basic MacBooks.

The souped-up MacBook Pro ($2,799), for example, offers a 17-inch LED backlit display (compared to the MacBook's 15-inch display) and incorporates a full-size, backlit keyboard and the multitouch trackpad that replaces the traditional mouse. The trackpad gives you additional ways to interact with your computer by using your fingers to perform tasks like scrolling, rotating, swiping, and dragging on-screen items.

The MacBook Pro with a 15-inch display weighs 5.4 pounds, and measures 14.1 inches (width) by 9.6 inches (depth) by 1 inch (height). The model with a 17-inch display weighs 6.8 pounds and measures 15.4 inches (width) by 10.4 inches (depth) by 1 inch (height). The battery life of these systems is between four and a half and five hours when configured to conserve power and when minimum optical drive usage is required.

## Creating and Ordering the Perfect System Configuration

If you visit any Apple Store or an authorized Apple dealer, you'll discover the retail locations offer each Mac system in the most popular configurations. For

*Figure 1.6*
For many businesspeople and entrepreneurs, the MacBook Pro is the ideal notebook computing solution. It offers the multitouch trackpad that replaces the traditional mouse. *Photo courtesy of Apple.*

basic computing needs, such as surfing the web or word processing, basic system configurations will work fine for the majority of users.

By upgrading to a customized configuration, however, you can select a faster microprocessor, extra RAM memory, a larger and faster hard drive, a more powerful optical drive, and upgrade the graphics card (of some models) in order to truly soup up the system so it can better handle more complex computing applications and run simultaneous applications faster. These are upgrades that are best done at the time of purchase and are typically not upgrades that computer users can later do on their own (with the exception of adding RAM).

By first determining what applications (or types of applications) you'll be running, you'll be better equipped to custom-configure your new Mac system accordingly. In addition to your computer, focus on what accessories, peripherals, and software you'll need right from the start. For example, if you're purchasing a notebook computer, you'll definitely want to purchase a custom-fitted and padded case to protect your investment. You might also opt to purchase an external (full-size) mouse and keyboard for when you're using your notebook computer at home or the office. If you'll be connecting a printer or another accessory, chances are you'll need to purchase a USB cable separately.

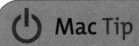 **Mac Tip**

If you'll be doing a lot of photo, audio, or video editing or playing graphic-intensive games, for example, upgrading the processor, RAM, graphics card (when applicable), optical drive speed, and hard drive size is definitely recommended.

Of course, you'll also want to purchase whatever software you plan to use. While some software, like Microsoft Office or iWork, comes on a CD and requires that you purchase a retail version, many other applications can be purchased online and downloaded directly to your computer.

# How and Where to Purchase or Order Your New Mac

When it comes to shopping for your new Mac, you can visit a local Apple Store (a chain of retail stores owned and operated by Apple) or an authorized Apple reseller (an independently owned and operated computer store). Many Best Buy stores are now authorized Apple resellers, for example. You can find authorized Apple resellers listed in your local Yellow Pages.

To custom-configure a Mac, you'll need to order it from the Apple.com website. You can also order any Apple first-party and many third-party Mac-compatible products (including accessories, peripherals, and software) from the Apple website. While you're shopping online, Mac Advisors are available to answer your questions by telephone (800-MY-APPLE) or via live online chat (from the Apple website). Free ground shipping is offered on all purchases over $50, and local sales tax will apply.

> ### ⏻ Mac Tip
>
> If you'll be a shopping at an Apple Store, consider visiting on a weekday. The stores tend to get very crowded on weekends and evenings. To ensure you receive personal attention, sign up for free, one-on-one, personal shopping services simply by making an advance appointment, which can be done online by visiting apple.com/retail/personalshopping.

Another option is to purchase a used or refurbished Mac. If you purchase a refurbished computer from the Apple.com website or from an authorized Apple reseller, it comes with a warrantee and meets original factory specifications. You can find money-saving offers on refurbished Mac products by clicking on the "Special Deals" icon located on the lower-left side of the Apple Store's homepage (http://store.apple.com) or by clicking "Store" at the Apple.com homepage. You'll find savings up to 25 percent off retail prices if you purchase a refurbished Mac. However, supplies are limited and available inventory changes constantly.

If you opt to save even more money and purchase a used computer from a private seller, you'll want to ensure the system's configuration is for a current model and that the computer itself is in full working order. eBay.com and Craigslist.org are ideal resources for tracking down used Mac computers. Mac of All Trades (813-925-1181/macofalltrades.com) is one of the country's top resellers of used (pre-owned) Mac computers.

## Technology Is Constantly Changing: Make Your Purchase and Don't Look Back!

Every few months, major technological advancements take place that allow computer manufacturers, including Apple, to create more powerful computers for less money. Thus, the system capabilities of new Mac OS–based computers tend to improve at least once per year (usually more often). So, within a few months after purchasing whatever computer you wind up with, you can count on it being outdated or replaced by newer technology. This doesn't mean, however, that the computer you purchase today will be useless. The Mac computer you buy now will most likely last you for several years, even though newer, more powerful, faster, and less expensive hardware will no doubt be released.

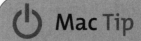 **Mac Tip**

Prices for Mac computers remain constant, whether you shop at an Apple Store, an authorized reseller, or use the Apple.com website, so there's no need to shop around for the best prices. Instead, focus on purchasing the best computer possible to fit your needs. You can rely on the free assistance and advice offered by Apple's Shopping Assistants (in the retail stores) or Mac Advisors (by calling 800-MY-APPLE).

Whether you purchase a PC or a Mac, there's really never a perfect time to make that purchase. Technology is always changing and evolving. Every year, Apple tends to make important new product announcements at the MacWorld trade show. However, significant changes to hardware configurations can be released almost anytime during the year, often with little or no advance notice.

When purchasing a new computer, focus on your computing needs today and what you anticipate your needs to be over the next year or so. Consider purchasing the most powerful and technologically advanced computer you can afford. Then, once you've made your purchase, don't look back or try to second-guess yourself by playing what-if games in your mind.

In the future, you can upgrade the computer you purchase, by adding more memory, external hard drives, or other peripherals. Then, a few years down the road, you'll probably want or need to buy a new computer altogether. So, the best you can do right now is address your current wants and needs with your computer purchase, and then be proud of yourself for switching to a Mac.

# Independent and Unbiased Mac Websites

To read the current, independent product reviews for Mac products, pick up the latest issue of *Macworld* or *MacLife* magazine at any newsstand, or visit one of these websites:

- Apple Insider—appleinsider.com
- Mac Review Zone—macreviewzone.com/index.php
- MacLife—maclife.com
- MacRumors Buyer's Guide—buyersguide.macrumors.com
- Macworld—macworld.com

# Service and Support from Apple Offers Much More Than Peace of Mind

All of the advice you need from Apple to help you decide which Mac computer to buy is available from Apple Stores, by phone, or online. Once you purchase your computer, however, Apple stands behind its products by offering top-notch support (but for an additional fee that's well worth the investment).

## *AppleCare Offers Comprehensive Service and Support Coverage*

After the initial 90 day's worth of free technical support you receive (plus one-year warranty coverage for your hardware), regardless of where you buy your Mac or which system you purchase, for an additional fee, you can purchase one of several support plans, all of which give you access to English-speaking, friendly, and knowledgeable Mac experts.

For that additional fee, which varies depending on which Mac system you purchase, the AppleCare Protection Plan is like purchasing insurance for your hardware investment. For three years from the purchase date of your computer, this service and support plan offers:

- *Unlimited telephone technical support.* Answers to any questions about how to use your Mac system are just a phone call away.
- *Global repair coverage.* If your computer breaks, repair services are provided either from any Apple Store or by sending your computer to Apple. On-site repair services are available for desktop computers.
- *Web support.* The Apple website offers a vast resource for obtaining support.
- *In-store technical support and minor repairs.* All Apple Stores offer in-store support and can handle minor repairs and hardware upgrades. An advance appointment is required.

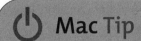

**Mac Tip**

While AppleCare covers your computer should it require repairs within a three-year period, this is not insurance that covers loss or theft.

AppleCare (apple.com/support/products) is priced between $169 and $349 for the three-year coverage. It should be purchased in conjunction with a new computer system and then activated online. The coverage is transferable if you sell your used equipment; however, the coverage is not renewable after the three-year period.

If you decide against purchasing the AppleCare service and protection plan, should a problem arise with your computer and it requires repair, you'll be forced to pay extremely high fees on a per-incident basis. A single repair could wind up costing you much more than the service plan.

## Genius Bar

Sometimes, it's faster to visit a local Apple Store and get your Mac-related questions answered in person. For hands-on technical support, offered for free, simply make an appointment to meet with an Apple Genius. You can make an appointment online at apple.com/retail/geniusbar/, or you can register for an appointment while in an Apple Store (pending availability). If you use this later option, expect a wait. Each one-on-one session with an Apple Genius will last approximately 15 minutes.

## Workshops

All Apple Stores offer an ongoing series of free workshops that can be registered for in advance. These workshops are open to everyone, and each lasts about one hour. Visit the following web page for your local Apple Store (apple.com/retail/workshops/) to access the current workshop schedule.

For new Mac users, some of the workshops you might be interested in include:

- *Mac OS X Leopard Workshop.* A hands-on introduction to Apple's Mac OS X operating system.
- *Getting Started Workshop.* This workshop will help you learn about the features and functionality of your new Mac-based computer.
- *PC to Mac Workshop.* Ideal for former PC users, this workshop will help acclimate you to your new Mac and allow you to address personal questions not answered in this book.
- *iLife Workshop.* Learn about the iLife suite of applications and how to best utilize them.
- *iWork '08 Workshop.* For business users, this workshop introduces you to the iWork suite of work-related applications.
- *iPod and iTunes Workshop.* Learn how to download music, TV shows, and movies using iTunes and transfer them to your iPod, iTouch, or iPhone, or watch/listen to this content on your Mac.

In addition to these workshops, many Apple Stores offer more in-depth workshops focusing on specific software applications, such as Aperture, Final Cut, FileMaker Pro, iMovie (and iDVD), Logic Pro, and Adobe Photoshop. More about these and other popular applications used by business professionals can be found in Chapter 10.

## One to One

Apple Stores limit your one-on-one time for technical support to about 15 minutes per session. If you're new to computers and want more extensive and personalized instruction on your new Mac, for $99 per year you can register for Apple's One to One service. This allows you to make an advance appointment

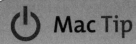
## Mac Tip

Whether you're computer savvy or not, by following the steps in Chapter 2, unpacking and setting up your new Mac will take under 30 minutes. However, custom-configuring your new system, installing your new software, and then transferring all of your data from your old computer could take several hours, so plan accordingly. This is time you'll need to invest just once to get your computer set up and working properly.

for unlimited one-on-one support and training that's customized to your needs and knowledge level. Each appointment can last up to one hour. Appointments can be booked up to 14 days in advance.

## *ProCare*

For $99 per year, the ProCare service is another way to obtain ongoing, in-person support for your Mac at your local Apple Store. Right when you purchase your computer, you can register to have a Genius help you set up your new system and even transfer your data from an older system (another Mac or a PC). This service also provides yearly computer tune-ups and gives you priority access to Geniuses at the Genius Bar in Apple Stores. For in-store repairs, ProCare members also receive expedited service, and help backing up essential data.

## *Online Support*

Available free of charge to all Mac users, the Apple Support website (apple.com/support) offers a vast database of technical support and how-to articles, answers to commonly asked questions, online video tutorials, the ability to download the latest updates to software, plus the ability to download user's manuals for all Mac hardware.

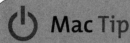

## Mac Tip

Once the computer is set up and fully operational, give yourself time to become acclimated with the Mac OS X operating system, which uses a slightly different interface than Windows XP or Windows Vista. Expect to experience a slight learning curve as you discover how to navigate your way around the Mac OS X operating system and learn to use your new computer, and be patient.

### Telephone Support

If you can't get to a local Apple Store to meet with a Genius in-person, for the first 90 days you own your computer (or for up to three years if you purchase AppleCare), you have unlimited access to Apple's telephone technical support service. To speak with an English-speaking Mac Specialist without experiencing an outrageously long hold time (it's usually 15 minutes or less), simply call (800) APL-CARE. This service and support line is available 7 days per week, at least 12 hours per day (hours are increased during busy periods).

The Mac expert you speak with will walk you step by step, through any problem or technical issue, answer your questions, and can recommend software, accessories, peripherals, or upgrades you might want for your computer.

## Making the Switch

Choosing the right Mac is only the first step toward making the Mac migration. Once you've purchased your new computer, you'll need to transfer all of your data from your older PC, and learn all about the differences between your former Windows-based computer and your new Mac.

The next chapter focuses on the key differences between Macs and PCs, introduces you to the Mac OS X Leopard operating system, and helps you unpack your new Mac and get it set up, configured, and ready to use.

# CHAPTER 2

# Setting Up Your
# New Mac

O NCE YOU HAVE YOUR NEW MAC COMPUTER IN HAND, YOU ARE READY TO
unpack it, set it up, and begin using it. This chapter will help
you get started. You'll learn how to use the Mac OS X's Setup
Assistant, plus how to personalize your Mac, install additional
software, and add peripherals, such as a printer. In Chapter 3, you'll then
learn more about how to use the Mac OS X operating system.

Many of the concepts involved with using a Mac computer are similar to using a PC-based computer running Windows XP or Windows Vista.

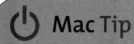

## Mac Tip

Once the computer is initially set up, you can connect any optional accessories or peripherals, such as a printer or external hard disk drive.

Both operating systems use graphic icons and allow you to navigate around the computer using the mouse. There are subtle differences, however, between a Mac and PC that you'll need to become accustomed to.

# Unpacking Your New Mac

You're new Mac comes nicely packaged in an Apple box and contains your computer, AC adapter, manual, and system discs. Upon opening the box, you'll find your computer neatly wrapped in a paper-like package, surrounded by Styrofoam.

Gently remove the computer from its packaging, and place it on a flat surface, such as your desk. When opening the packaging, do not use sharp objects that could accidentally scratch the computer or damage any of the box's contents.

Check out the first few pages of your new manual. You'll see a section called "What's in the Box." Perform a quick inventory to make sure your new Mac is equipped with all of the parts and accessories it's supposed to have.

If you've purchased a desktop computer, you'll first want to attach the keyboard and mouse using the USB ports on the back of the computer, as well as the Ethernet internet cable (unless you'll be using a wireless internet connection) before plugging it in and turning it on. For notebook computer users,

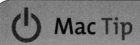

## Mac Tip

If you've purchased an Apple notebook computer (a MacBook, MacBook Pro, or MacBook Air), the battery comes partially charged, but it's essential that you plug in the computer and allow the battery to fully charge before operating the computer on battery power. While the computer is first charging, however, you can use it, as long as it's plugged in using the supplied MagSafe Power Adapter.

simply connect the unit's AC adapter to the computer and plug it in once all of the packaging has been removed.

Be sure to keep all of the computer's packaging. If you qualify for any rebates, you'll need the bar code and serial number sticker on the outside of the box. Later, if you ever need to ship your computer anywhere, being able to reuse the original packaging will help protect the computer during shipping.

# Turning On Your Mac for the First Time

Once you've plugged your new Mac in using the supplied Power Adapter, you're ready to turn the computer's power on. The very first time your computer is powered up, you need to configure your user account using the Mac OS X's Setup Assistant and then set your computer's preferences.

If you're using a notebook computer, as soon as you plug the MagSafe Power Adapter into your computer, the small light on the piece that plugs into

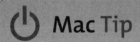

## Mac Tip

If you're using a laptop, you'll notice that instead of a mouse, your computer is equipped with a trackpad located just below the keyboard. By moving your index finger around on the touchpad's surface, it will move the on-screen cursor. The button below the touchpad has the same function as the Mac's single mouse button. Depending on the circumstance, you'll use the mouse button to click once or double-click on various icons, hyperlinks, and other on-screen elements. If you're using a MacBook Pro or MacBook Air, your touchpad offers Apple's multitouch technology, which allows you to use various two-finger movements (using your thumb and index finger) on the trackpad to rotate, swipe, drag, and zoom in on various items. If you're more comfortable using a mouse, however, you can plug an Apple Mighty Mouse into the USB port of any Apple notebook computer.

the computer will light up. A red light means the computer's battery is charging. A green light means the computer's battery is fully charged. There is no indicator light on the power supply for Mac desktop computers.

Before turning on the computer for the first time, connect the Ethernet internet cable into the computer (unless you'll be using a wireless internet connection). Early on in the initial setup process, the new computer will need to access the Apple website in order to download the latest version of the Mac OS X operating system.

With the AC power and internet cable (if applicable) connected, you're now ready to power up your new Mac for the first time. On an iMac, the power button is located on the back of the display, in the lower-left corner. In a MacBook or MacBook Pro, for example, the circular power button is located next to the keyboard, on the upper-right corner. To turn on the computer, briefly press the power button once. It might take a second or two for you to notice the computer powering up.

It's now time to set up your computer using the Mac Setup Assistant. This process only needs to be done once, the first time you turn on the computer.

## Using the Setup Assistant to Configure Your New Computer

Within seconds after powering up your new computer, you should hear a brief musical tone. On the display, the Apple logo will appear as the computer boots up for the first time. This process could take up to 30 seconds, so be patient. Follow these steps to navigate your way through using the Setup Assistant:

1.   When prompted, select the main language you'll want to configure the computer using. English is the default option. Once English is highlighted on the menu, click the mouse on the round right-pointing arrow icon in the lower-right corner of the language selection window to continue. The screen will go black for a few moments, before a special "Welcome" video is played.

2.   When the Welcome window appears on the screen after the short animated video plays, you'll need to select the country or region you're in.

The default option is United States; however, Canada, United Kingdom, Australia, New Zealand, and Ireland are among your other main choices. (For additional country selections, use the mouse to place a checkmark in the Show All box that's located under the country list, and then select your country or region from the more extensive listing.) From this point forward, your new Mac will actually talk you through the setup process. Select your country and click the mouse once on the Continue icon located at the bottom of the Welcome window.

3.  The next Setup Assistant window that appears asks you to select your keyboard layout. Primary options will be United States or Canadian English. But again, you can use the mouse to add a checkmark to the Show All box and access additional options, if necessary. The default option (the one highlighted in blue) will be United States. When ready, use the mouse to click on the Continue icon to proceed to the next step.

4.  The Do You Already Own a Mac? window now appears. This part of Setup Assistant allows you to quickly and easily transfer programs and data from an older Mac to your new Mac. (This transfer assistant only works from Mac to Mac, not from PC to Mac. So, if you need to transfer data from a PC, see Chapter 5.) For now, choose the Do Not Transfer My Information Now menu selection, and then use the mouse to click on the Continue icon.

5.  The Enter Your Apple ID screen will now appear. If you're a first-time Apple owner/user, you'll need to set up your Apple ID account. This allows you to register your equipment with Apple and keep track of serial numbers and other important information online. If you already own an iPod, iPhone, or another Mac, chances are you've already set up an Apple ID account. If so, enter your Apple ID (username) and Password now, and then use the mouse to click on the Continue icon. If you do not yet have an Apple ID account set up, use the mouse to click on the Continue icon.

6.  If you need to set up a new Apple ID account, the Registration Information screen will appear. You'll be prompted to use the keyboard to enter

your First Name, Last Name, Address, City, State, Zip Code, E-Mail Address, Phone Number, and Company/School. Click on the Continue icon to proceed.

7.  When the A Few More Questions screen appears, you will be asked additional questions, including "Where will you primarily use this computer?" and "What best describes what you do?" There are pull-down menu options you can use to select your responses. When you've selected your answers, once again use the mouse to click on the Continue icon to proceed.

8.  Every person who uses your new computer has the ability to create a unique, password-protected account. This account will keep track of each user's personalized settings and keep his or her data documents in unique folders. From the Create Your Account screen, enter your Full Name, Short Name, and Password. You will be asked to verify your selected Password by entering it a second time. Within the Password Hint box, type any information that will help you remember your password. It's important that you do not forget it! Anytime in the future that you need to add or change programs to your computer, or update the operating system, you will be prompted for this password. The Short Name you select on this screen will be the name of the main folder where all of your personal documents are stored. It cannot be changed later, but an unlimited number of sub-folders can be created. After the necessary information is entered using the keyboard, use the mouse to click on the Continue icon. It will take up to 30 seconds for the computer to activate your account.

9.  The Select a Picture for This Account screen will now be displayed. Using the computer's built-in iSight camera, you can take a snapshot of yourself. Or, you can choose a photo from the picture library. Make your selection and click the mouse on the Continue icon to proceed.

10. The setup process is almost complete. You are now given the option to Complete Your Mac Experience by signing up for the Mobile Me online service. If you've already purchased your optional membership, choose "I've purchased a Mobile Me box and want to enter the activation key." If you want to sign up for a one-year membership (a $99.95 fee applies),

select the "I want to sign up for a one-year 99.95 USD Mobile Me membership" option. If you're already a Mobile Me member, select the "I'm already a Mobile Me member" option, or if you want to skip this step for now, select "I don't want to purchase Mobile Me right now." For more information about the Mobile Me service, see Chapter 9.

11.  Once you've completed the necessary steps using the Setup Assistant, the Thank You screen will appear. Your computer is now ready to operate using the Mac OS X Leopard operating system. Figure 2.1 shows the basic Mac OS X desktop screen with the Finder window open. At this point, only the operating system software and the iLife suite of applications are installed on your new computer. If you purchased a custom-configured Mac, you might have ordered iWork or other software to come pre-installed on the computer. If this is the case, you'll discover that software is ready to begin using. It's now necessary to customize your preferences and start installing software onto your new Mac.

12.  Exit the Setup Assistant by clicking on the Continue icon. The main Mac OS X Leopard Desktop will appear on the screen. At the bottom of this screen (your Desktop) will be the Dock—icons representing some of the software currently installed on your computer, including Dashboard, Mail, Safari, Chat, Address Book, iCal, Preview, iTunes, iPhoto, iMovie, GarageBand, Spaces, Time Machine, and System Preferences.

13.  It's not important that you become acquainted with the Mac OS X Leopard operating system in order to begin fully using your new computer. While many of the key concepts behind navigating your way around the computer and interacting with

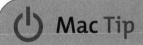

**Mac Tip**

Once your computer is set up and connected to the internet, one of the first things you'll want to do is register it with Apple and activate your optional AppleCare service and protection plan by following the directions that came in the AppleCare packaging.

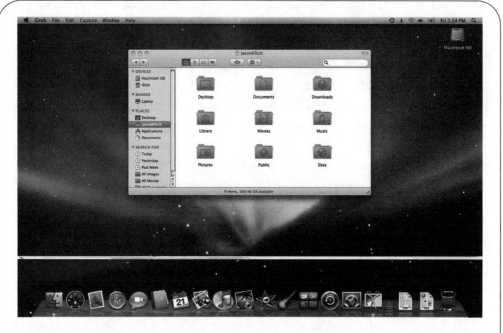

*Figure 2.1*

This is the basic Mac OS X Desktop screen, complete with the program icons located along the
Dock at the bottom of the screen and the Menu Bar pull-down menus across the top of the screen.
From the Finder window (shown in this figure), you can launch software applications, access your
data, and open or move file folders, for example. Later in this chapter, you'll discover how to customize this main screen as well as personalize other features of your new Mac.

programs is very similar to using a PC, there are a bunch of subtle differences that you'll need to get used to. Chapter 3 offers an introduction to the Mac OS X Leopard operating system.

# Updating Your Mac OS X Software

If your computer is connected to the internet, within a few minutes of completing the steps involved in using the Setup Assistant, a new, blue, circular icon
will appear and start bouncing at the bottom of the screen along the Dock.
This is the Software Update icon. Using the mouse, click on this icon so that

your new computer can download and install important operating system software updates from the Apple.com website. When you click on the Software Update icon, a new window will appear stating, "Software updates are available for your computer. Do you want to install them?"

Click on the Install and Restart icon to continue. Every time Apple releases updates to the Mac OS X operating system or any Apple first-party software, this icon will appear and you will be prompted to install the new software updates. It's important that your operating system software stay up-to-date to ensure the security and stability of your computer.

When you instruct the computer to download the software updates, a new window will appear on the screen that says, "Software Update requires that you type your password." In the Name box will be the name you initially selected when using the Setup Assistant (see Step 8 of "Using the Setup Assistant to Configure Your New Computer"). You must also enter in the personal password you selected in order to continue. Once you've read the software licensing agreement that appears, click on the Agree icon to continue. Follow the prompts to continue the software update procedure, which will involve the computer automatically restarting. This process could take several minutes, so be patient.

## ⏻ Mac Tip

At this point, if you're ready to take a break or wish to turn off your computer, from the main Mac OS X Desktop screen, move the mouse to the upper-left corner of the screen to the Apple logo icon, click on that icon to reveal the pull-down menu, and then select the "Shut Down . . ." option. Your computer will then power down (turn off). It's important that you shut your computer off by choosing the Shut Down option, as opposed to simply pressing the power button on your computer. If you're using a notebook computer, you can simply shut the computer (fold down the screen) to put the computer in hibernation mode, but this is different from shutting down the computer.

# Configuring Your New Mac and Installing Software

Now that your new Mac is ready to use, it's time to connect your printer and other peripherals, as well as install the additional first- and third-party software you'll be using. But first you can customize your computer and personalize it a bit by clicking on the System Preferences icon located on the Dock.

Figure 2.2 shows the main System Preferences window that will appear. From here, you can change the appearance of your screens, select a screen saver,

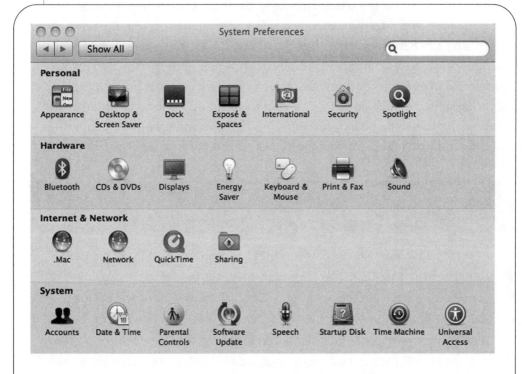

*Figure 2.2*

From this System Preferences window, you can handle a bunch of different customization and system maintenance tasks. For example, you can customize your desktop image by clicking on the Desktop & Screen Saver option.

and customize a handful of system maintenance procedures. For now, we'll focus on the Desktop & Screen Saver" and Dock options.

# Desktop & Screen Saver Options

By clicking on the Desktop & Screen Saver icon found in the System Preferences window, you can quickly change the background image of your computer's main Desktop screen. You can select one of the many patterns and images built into the Mac OS X operating system. You'll notice that the image called "Aurora" is the default. On the left side of the Desktop & Screen Saver window (Figure 2.3) are a handful of sub-directories containing desktop images you can select. They are divided into categories such as Nature, Plants, Black & White, and Abstract. Using the mouse, click on the image you want to be your main desktop image.

By clicking on the plus (+) icon located under the file folders (see Figure 2.3), you can add your own photo and transform it into your desktop image. The easiest way to do this is to first copy the desired photo into your Mac's Pictures folder. Once you select your image, the default Aurora desktop will be replaced with the image you select.

Next, you can select and customize your Screen Saver. From the Desktop & Screen Saver window (Figure 2.3), click the mouse on the Screen Saver icon located in the upper-center portion of the window. The Screen Saver Preview window will now appear (Figure 2.4).

On the left side of the Screen Saver window is a listing of screen saver options built into the Mac OS X operating system. The default is the Flurry screen saver, but you can choose any one of them or download your own from the internet. The Apple.com website (apple.com/downloads/) is just one source for obtaining additional screen savers.

After selecting your favorite screen saver, you can determine how quickly the screen saver will activate as a result of nonuse. The Start Screen Saver gauge (found under the Preview window, Figure 2.4) can be adjusted using the mouse. You can set the screen saver to automatically activate never, after three minutes, or select a time interval up to two hours. Depending on the screen saver you select, you can click on the Options icon (found under the Preview

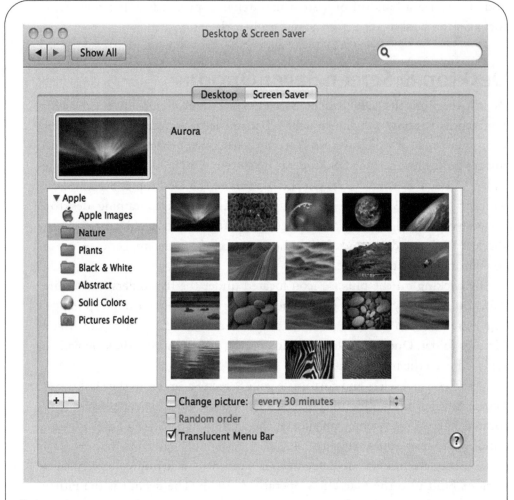

*Figure 2.3*
From the Desktop & Screen Saver window (found under System Preferences) you can customize the Desktop image and screen saver that will be used on your computer.

window) to make more personalized adjustments. To determine what the screen saver will actually look like once activated, click the mouse on the Test icon, also found under the Preview window.

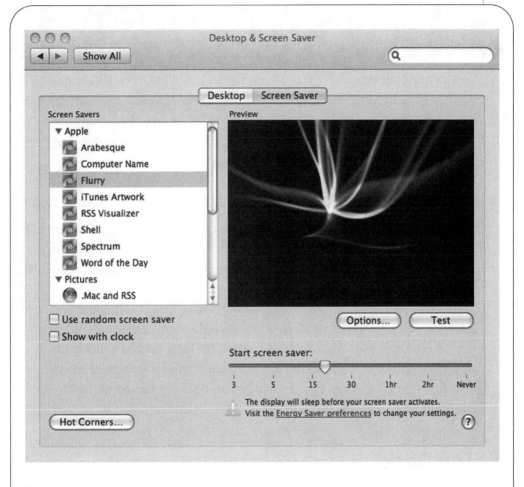

*Figure 2.4*
From the Desktop & Screen Saver window, you can select your favorite screen saver, that is, what will automatically appear on the screen after a predetermined time in which the computer is not used but is left turned on.

From the Desktop & Screen Saver window, you can revert back to the System Preferences window by clicking the mouse on the Show All icon, located in the upper-right corner of the window (see Figure 2.3). To exit out of System Preferences altogether, move the mouse to the upper-left corner of the

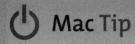

## Mac Tip

When choosing a screen saver, you can select Pictures folder and create a slide show of your own digital photographs to be used as your screen saver. First, however, you'll need to transfer a handful of digital photos into the appropriate Pictures folder of your new Mac. More information about transferring data and files from your old computer to your new Mac can be found in Chapter 5.

screen to where it says System Preferences. Click on this pull-down menu and select Quit System Preferences. This will exit you out of System Preferences and return you to the main Desktop, which now showcases the new Desktop image you selected.

As with any Mac OS program, simply clicking on the red dot in the upper-left corner of the Desktop & Screen Saver window will make the window disappear, but it will not exit the application. Clicking on the yellow dot in the upper-left corner of the Desktop & Screen Saver window will minimize the window (causing a thumbnail of the window to now appear along the Dock), but the application will still be running.

## The Dock

The Dock, found on the Mac OS X's main Desktop screen, offers a customizable collection of icons, each of which represents a software application that can quickly be launched with a click of the mouse. The program icons on your Dock can be rearranged and customized, so the Dock can be adjusted to only display the applications you most commonly use.

For programs installed on your Mac that are not displayed as part of your Dock, you can launch them by clicking on the Finder icon, selecting Applications on the left side of the window that appears, and then by scrolling up or down, left or right (as appropriate) to find the icon representing the program you wish to launch. To launch the application, click on the appropriate program icon.

## *The Default Dock Icons*

The first time you turn on your new computer and the Mac OS X operating system displays your main Desktop and your Dock, the following application icons will appear (from left to right): Finder, Dashboard, Mail, Safari, Chat, Address Book, iCal, Preview, iTunes, iPhoto, iMovie, GarageBand, Spaces, Time Machine, and System Preferences. On the lower-right corner of the screen will be an icon representing the most recent document and files you've accessed and used on your computer. Between this icon and the Trash icon will be the Downloads icon. When you click your mouse on this icon, a window will appear displaying all of the files and programs you've recently downloaded from the internet.

The Trash icon, found in the lower-right corner of the Dock, is where you can drag programs and files that you want to delete from your computer. Like a real garbage can, the files placed in the trash remain there until you physically empty the trash, which permanently deletes the files. To empty the trash, click on the Trash icon to open the Trash window. Next, move your mouse to the

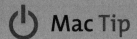

## Mac Tip

When you click on the Finder icon (or the Hard Drive icon on your Desktop), the Finder application opens in its own window on the Desktop. Using Finder, you can launch applications found in your Applications folder, or access a file or folder stored on your computer's hard drive (or on another drive connected to your computer). Using Finder, you can quickly access specific folders or files, like Movies, Documents, Pictures, Music, and Applications, which are listed on the left side of the window, along with icons representing additional drives connected to your Mac (if applicable). The Search field in the upper-right corner of the Finder window can be used to quickly find any file, folder, application, or document, for example, by entering a keyword or search phrase.

upper-left corner of the screen and click on the Finder pull-down menu. Click on the Empty Trash feature to permanently delete the files in your Trash.

As you install new applications onto your Mac, you'll want to store the applications themselves within the Applications folder. You can then determine what separate data folder(s) you want files related to that program to be stored in. For example, if you install Microsoft Word (the word processor that is part of Microsoft Office) onto your Mac, the Microsoft Word application would be installed into your Applications folder. You can then instruct Microsoft Word is save your document files in specific subdirectories (subfolders) you create within your main Documents folder.

## Adding Program Icons to Your Dock

If there's a program you'll be using often that you wish to add to your Dock, first click on the Finder icon to open the Applications folder. Next, find the icon that represents that program. Click the mouse once on that icon to highlight it, and then hold down the mouse button and drag the icon down to the Dock. The program icon will now appear where you place it within your Dock.

You can move program icons around on your Dock by clicking and holding down the mouse button on that icon and then dragging it either left or right. To remove a program icon from your Dock (such as a program you seldom or never use), simply drag it to the extreme right, onto the Trash icon. It will then disappear from your Dock, but remain installed on your computer. (You can later access that program from Finder, under the Applications window.)

To customize your Dock's appearance, click on the System Preferences icon (on your Dock), then click on the Dock icon. Figure 2.5 shows the Dock window. From this window, use the mouse to adjust the size of the program icons that appear within your Dock. Sliding the Size bar to the left will make the icons smaller. Sliding the Size bar to the right will increase the size of the program icons within the dock.

The Magnification icon determines how large the icons will appear on your Dock when you pass the mouse cursor over each icon. You can also determine the position on your Desktop screen where the Dock will appear. The default

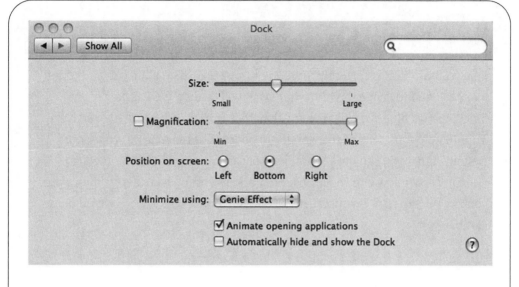

*Figure 2.5*

The Dock that appears on your Desktop can be fully customized, based on your personal preferences. For example, you can determine if it will appear along the bottom edge, or along the left or
right side of the screen.

is at the bottom of the screen; however, you can adjust the Dock to appear vertically along the left or right side of the screen.

When you have a program window or file window open on your Desktop
and then choose to close or minimize it, how the window disappears or reposi-
tions itself on the screen will be determined by the Minimize Using option you
select. You can determine what this animation will look like by choosing either
Genie Effect or Scale Effect. This is a personal preference and does not impact
the functionality of the computer.

At the bottom of the Dock window (Figure 2.5) you can add a checkmark
to the Animate Opening Applications icon to make the program icons bounce
on the screen when you open the application. The Automatically Hide and
Show the Dock option, if checked, will cause the Dock to disappear when it's
not being used. As a new Mac user, keep the Dock visible (by leaving this

## Mac Tip

Any program that is currently running on your Mac, even if an icon for it does not permanently appear within your Dock, will be displayed as part of your Dock. A small blue dot will appear below that icon to indicate it is an actively running program. One of the wonderful benefits of the Mac OS X operating system is that you can have multiple applications running simultaneously. Even if the window within which a program is running has been minimized, as long as the program is running, the icon will remain on the Dock with a blue dot below it.

option unchecked) until you're more familiar with using the Mac OS X operating system.

At the bottom-right corner of the Dock window you'll notice a round icon with a question mark within it. Anytime you see an icon like this (anywhere within the Mac OS X operating system environment), you can click on it to reveal a detailed help window that will explain each menu option available to you.

## Installing New Software Onto Your Mac

Your computer comes with a bunch of applications already installed on it. However, you'll want and need to install additional applications. There are several ways to load new software into your Mac. The directions offered within this book are valid for all Mac computers, except for the MacBook Air, which is slightly different in some cases. If using a MacBook Air, see the owner's manual for the computer to learn how to install software.

The main options you have for installing new software onto your Mac include:

1. Transferring the Program files from another Mac using the Migration Assistant found under the Utilities folder (under Applications)

2. Loading the new software from a program CD

3. Downloading the software from the internet and installing it. You can purchase and download thousands of applications from the Apple.com website (apple.com/downloads/). You can also purchase and download Mac applications directly from the websites operated by many third-party software developers.

If you have a program CD in hand, simply insert it into your Mac's optical drive. Within a few seconds, the software should begin an auto-install process. If this doesn't happen, you will notice a CD icon appear on your Desktop. Click on this CD icon, and then click on the program icon that references program installation. Anytime you attempt to install new software, you'll be asked for your Account Password. You'll also be asked to confirm where you want the software installed on your computer's hard drive. If you're installing an application, choose the Application folder. Follow the installation prompts provided by the software.

If you'll be downloading a software application from the internet, once the application is loaded it will be in the form of a [filename].dmg file. Click on this file when it appears in the Finder window to begin the installation process. You may be asked to "agree" to the licensing terms of the software and/or to drag the program icon into the Application folder icon of your computer. Follow the prompts offered as the program installs.

When a new program gets installed onto your computer, it will appear within the Applications folder. You can then drag the program icon to your Dock if it's an application you'll be using often. To access the Applications folder, click on the Finder icon (found on your Dock), then choose Applications from the choices on the left side of the window that appears. When the Applications window

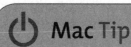

## Mac Tip

Details about iWork and Microsoft Office, both popular suites of business-oriented software applications, can be found in Chapters 8 and 9. For information about 14 other popular business-oriented applications available for the Mac, see Chapter 10.

opens, double-click the mouse on the appropriate program icon to launch the program.

Only install one program at a time. Once the new application is installed and you're ready to run it for the first time, be sure to select the Check for Updates menu option, which is almost always found under the program name pull-down menu of the Menu bar (found at the top of the screen, next to the small Apple logo) or under the Help pull-down menu. This will ensure you have the very latest version of the software installed on your computer before you begin actually using it.

## Connecting a Printer and Other Peripherals to Your Mac

The next major step in setting up and customizing your computer is to connect whatever peripherals you'll be using with the computer—your printer or external hard drive for data backup and additional storage purposes, for example. Most of these devices will be connected to your computer via a USB cable. Your Mac is equipped with one to five USB ports. By adding an optional USB hub, you can connect additional USB devices to your computer.

You can plug in a peripheral using a USB cable at anytime (whether the computer is turned on or off). Because these peripherals are typically "plug-and-play," as soon as the peripheral is plugged into the computer (and an electrical outlet, if applicable) and turned on it will become available to you through the computer. For example, if you plug an external USB hard drive into your computer via a USB cable, an icon for that hard drive will appear on your Desktop within a few seconds. You can then store or retrieve files from that hard drive.

When connecting a printer for the first time, you may need to install special software. If applicable, the printer will come with a CD containing the necessary application(s) needed to properly use it with your computer. In most cases, you should connect the printer to the computer first (following the directions provided with the printer) and then load the necessary drivers. If you don't have the required software on CD, you can almost always download it

> ⏻ **Mac Tip**
>
> After you've connected an external hard disk drive or thumb drive to your computer as well as certain other devices, such as a memory card reader, and are ready to disconnect that drive without shutting down the computer, you must first "eject" the drive, which can be done by highlighting the drive icon on your Desktop and dragging it to the Trash at the bottom of the screen. Or, you can highlight the drive icon on your Desktop and then under the File pull-down menu at the top of the screen, select the Eject Drive command. Doing this ejection procedure will ensure that none of the data stored on the external drive or memory card is accidentally corrupted or deleted.

from the printer manufacturer's website and then install it onto your computer in a matter of minutes.

In addition to using USB cables to connect popular peripherals, you can use wireless Bluetooth technology (if the peripheral supports this) or sometimes Firewire, which also requires a connection cable, but is usually much faster than USB for transferring data between the computer and the connected device. Your Mac is compatible with USB, Bluetooth, and Firewire technology.

Once you've installed the software applications you plan to use, and have properly connected and installed whatever peripherals you'll be using with the computer, you're ready either to begin using your new Mac as the powerful business and personal computing tool that it is or you can transfer your data and files from your old PC or Mac computer to the new computer by following the steps outlined in Chapter 5.

## Get Further Acquainted with Your New Mac

The next chapter provides a more in-depth introduction to the Mac OS X Leopard operating system and will help you become more familiar with your new computer. However, one quick way to jump-start your learning process is to participate in the free Getting Started on a Mac and/or the PC to Mac workshop offered at your local Apple Store. For details and to reserve a spot for one of these one-hour workshops, point your web browser to apple.com/retail/workshops/.

# Introduction to Mac OS X Leopard

PC–BASED COMPUTERS USED BY BUSINESSPEOPLE TYPICALLY OPERATE USING THE Windows XP or Windows Vista operating system from Microsoft. It's primarily a graphical interface incorporating clickable icons and pull-down menus that allows users to interact with pro- grams, manipulate data, and handle their computing needs using the mouse and computer keyboard.

Mac OS X Leopard, the operating system created by Apple for its Mac computers, is very similar to the Windows operating system in many

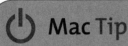

## Mac Tip

As you read this book, follow along with your computer turned on when appropriate. This helps you become better acquainted with the layout and design of your new Mac, the Mac OS X operating system, and whatever applications you are running on it.

ways. It is, however, designed to be more intuitive, crash less, run faster, and make the computing experience more productive. This chapter offers a brief introduction to the Mac OS X Leopard operating system to help you become familiar with your new Mac system as you get it up and running.

Unlike Windows Vista (which has four separate editions: Basic, Home Premium, Business, and Ultimate), there is only one current edition of the Mac OS X Leopard operating system, and it comes preloaded on all new Mac computers. When you combine the capabilities of this operating system with the other software applications you ultimately install onto your Mac, chances are, all of your computing needs will be met.

## Benefits of the Mac OS X Operating System

In addition to creating a highly functional, yet intuitive interface that allows Mac users to interact with their computer, the Mac OS X Leopard operating system offers a wide range of built-in applications and tools designed to make you more productive. For example, the Time Machine application built into the operating system automatically backs up all of your important programs and data onto an external hard drive, so you have the added peace of mind knowing that if something should happen to your computer, all of your data is safely backed up.

Without installing any additional software to your computer, some of the many tools and applications built into Mac OS X Leopard will help you:

- Manage e-mail (using Mail)
- Surf the web (using Safari)
- Keep track of your contacts (using Address Book)
- Manage your busy schedule (using iCal)

- Store, edit, and view your digital images and photos (using iPhoto)
- Chat in real time with friends and co-workers (using iChat)
- Download, store, listen to, and/or view digital audio and video (using iTunes)
- Back up critical programs and data (using Time Machine)
- Watch DVD movies (using DVD Player)
- Perform quick mathematical calculations (using Calculator)
- Do basic text editing (using TextEdit)

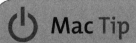

**Mac Tip**

Because the Mac OS X Leopard operating system is extremely robust, consider investing in a full-length how-to book for new users if you don't consider yourself to be too computer savvy. You can also participate in the free, one-hour workshops offered at any Apple Store to learn the basics.

As you'll discover, when you add the iLife suite of applications (see Chapter 9), which works seamlessly with Mac OS X and comes bundled with all new Macs, the functionality of your computer increases dramatically. Before you can start really utilizing your computer, however, it's important to become familiar with how to navigate your way around the Mac OS X operating system so you can open and close programs, find and access files, and customize your computing experience.

# Mac OS X Leopard: The Basics

If you're already familiar with Windows XP or Windows Vista, the biggest challenge you'll face operating your new Mac will be getting used to the interface. Everything happens from the Mac OS X's main Desktop screen (Figure 3.1). Let's take closer look at each section of the Desktop.

## *Seven Things Your Mighty Mouse Can Do*

Like Windows XP or Windows Vista, the Mac OS X operating system allows users to interact with their computer using the mouse to move around the

*Figure 3.1*
This is the main Mac OS X Desktop. From here, you can access all of your programs and files, plus navigate your way around your new Mac using the mouse and keyboard.

on-screen cursor. Mac desktop computers come bundled with Apple's Mighty Mouse, a one-button, ergonomic mouse that has a scroll ball and two additional squeeze side buttons built in. One of the biggest challenges former PC users face is getting used to the design of Apple's Mighty Mouse or the functionality of the touchpad built into their MacBook, MacBook Pro, or MacBook Air. What's missing is the ability to right-click, which is a necessity when using a mouse on a PC running Windows.

The Mighty Mouse can be connected to the computer (or to a Mac keyboard) via a USB cable; however, an optional wireless Bluetooth version of the Mighty Mouse is also available ($69). The same Mighty Mouse can also be connected to a MacBook, MacBook Pro, or MacBook Air if you want the full functionality and feel of the mouse, as opposed to using the built-in trackpad.

Apple MacBook computers are equipped with a one-button trackpad that's located below the keyboard. The MacBook Pro and MacBook Air offer a multi-touch trackpad, which gives the user even more functionality using their fingers to manipulate the on-screen cursor and content.

The mouse (or your finger on the trackpad) moves the on-screen cursor around the computer screen. The mouse can perform the following functions within the Mac OS X environment:

1. *Pointing.* Use the mouse to point the cursor to an item, such as an icon or pull-down menu command.
2. *Clicking.* This is done by pressing the mouse or touchpad's button once. The process involves pressing and then quickly releasing the button. To access a pull-down menu from the Desktop's Menu bar, for example, you'd position the mouse over a pull-down menu command displayed on the top of the screen, and then click the mouse once. You'd then move the mouse over the pull-down menu's command you want to execute and click the mouse again.
3. *Double-Clicking.* Certain functions, such as launching a program from the Desktop, require the user to double-click the mouse on an icon, for example. This means quickly pressing and releasing the mouse button twice.

## ⏻ Mac Tip

At any given time, a Mac user can have multiple windows open. This can include Finder windows and application windows. Only one window, however, can be active at a time. Because windows get layered on top of each other, one of the easiest ways to quickly switch between windows, and see what windows are open, is to reveal the Expose screen. (Squeeze the two side buttons on the Mighty Mouse simultaneously). The keyboard shortcut to access this screen is to press the F9 key.

4. *Dragging*. Using the mouse, you can point to an item, such as an icon, scroll bar, or a window, and then hold down the mouse button while simultaneously moving the mouse. This will drag the icon or window, for example, across the screen to another location. When the icon or window is properly positioned, simply release the mouse button.

5. *Pressing the Mouse Button*. Instead of quickly clicking the mouse button, you'd press and hold it down. This process is used to drag items, for example.

6. *Scrolling*. When surfing the web, looking at a long text document, or navigating your way around various windows that contain scroll bars, the scroll ball on the mouse can be used to scroll up or down (and in some applications, left or right as well). Pressing down on the mouse's scroll button will activate the Dashboard (as a default option), but can be reprogrammed to handle other tasks by accessing System Preferences and then selecting Keyboard & Mouse. For more information about the Dashboard, see Chapter 4.

7. *Squeezing*. When the mouse's two side buttons are simultaneously squeezed, the default task is for the Expose screen to appear. However, this too can be quickly reprogrammed to handle other tasks by accessing System Preferences and then selecting Keyboard & Mouse.

## ⏻ Mac Tip

The multitouch touchpad built into the MacBook Pro and MacBook Air offers all of the basic functionality of the regular MacBook's touchpad (which replaces the mouse). Using your finger, you can move the cursor around on the screen, and then use the touchpad's button just as you would the mouse button. However, the multitouch pad also allows you to pinch, swipe, rotate, and enlarge on-screen items when using certain applications.

## Keyboard Shortcuts

In addition to using the mouse to click on icons and access pull-down menu options, for example, you can utilize many timesaving keyboard shortcuts to handle various tasks or execute specific commands. Throughout this chapter, some keyboard shortcuts are explained. For a complete listing, however, access System Preferences, and then select Keyboard & Mouse. Next, click on the Keyboard Short-cuts icon near the top of the window.

Many of the keyboard shortcuts utilized within the Mac OS X environment require pressing the Command key in conjunction with another key on the keyboard. The Command key is located to the left of the Space bar and has the Apple logo and the "⌘" symbol (or the word Command) on it. If you see the keyboard shortcut Command (⌘) + C, for example, this would require you to press the Command (⌘) and C keys simultaneously.

As a PC user, you're probably already accustomed to pressing the Control key plus another key to execute a keyboard shortcut. While the concept is the same, you'll need to remember on your Mac to use the Command key instead. The actual keyboard shortcut command may also be different. For example, Control+P on the PC would allow you to paste text after it has been copied to the clipboard. On your Mac, you'd use Command (⌘) + V to paste text in many applications.

⏻ **Mac Tip**

Keep in mind, certain Mac applications will have their own keyboard shortcuts available. For example, when using Microsoft Word, Command (⌘) + B creates bold text and Command (⌘) + I creates italic text.

## The Mac OS X Desktop

The Desktop is a central work space that you can customize to meet your needs and personal taste. When you turn on your Mac for the first time, only one icon will appear in the main Desktop area. This icon represents your computer's internal Hard Drive. This Hard Drive contains all of the programs and what-ever data is already installed on your computer. When you install additional software, create new files, or transfer files from your old PC, all of this information will ultimately be placed in folders/directories within the computer's Hard Drive. As you begin using your computer, you can add all sorts of additional icons to your Desktop to give yourself quick access to files, programs, pictures, and many other types of data.

An icon placed on your Desktop can be associated with an application and serve as a shortcut for launching that application. It can also represent a file folder (which contains multiple files), or it can represent a specific file, such as a Word document (.doc file), digital image, audio file, PowerPoint presentation file, a single PDF file, or video file. For individual files placed on your desktop (which is equivalent to a Windows shortcut), the Mac OS X operating system will automatically create a thumbnail image representing that file, so you can graphically see what that file is without actually opening it.

## ⏻ Mac Tip

The icons you place on your Desktop are entirely up to you. You can maintain a neat and organized desktop, or you can clutter it up with hundreds of individual icons. You can also choose your Desktop wallpaper (the image that's always displayed on your Desktop) and determine the positioning of the Dock. If you create a messy and cluttered Desktop with dozens or hundreds of icons, you can clean it up by automatically rearranging the icons and placing them in a more organized way. This can be done by selecting the View pull-down menu from the Menu bar, and then choosing the Clean Up option. You can rearrange the icons by file name (alphabetically), by date modified, date created, size, kind, or label by selecting the Keep Arranged By command also found under the View pull-down menu. Icons on your desktop can be deleted by dragging them to the Trash. They can also be moved or copied into different folders using the Finder and your mouse.

## Menu Bar

The OS X Desktop has several distant areas. In the upper-right corner of the screen is the Apple logo (found on the Menu bar). Clicking the mouse on this logo, regardless of what programs are running, will allow you to access a pull-down menu with a handful of system-oriented functions, including:

- *About This Mac.* Quickly view details about the Mac system, including the Mac OS X version number and your system's information (including its configuration and unique serial number).
- *Software Update.* Manually check to determine if any new Mac OS X updates have been released by Apple. You can set the update feature to check for and install necessary updates automatically (which is recommended). To use this feature, the computer must be connected to the internet.
- *Mac OS X Software.* This menu option serves as a quick link to the Apple website's software download site, from which you can learn about, purchase (if applicable), and download thousands of applications for your computer.
- *System Preferences.* Access the System Preferences window to custom-config-ure your Mac. See Chapter 2 for more details about some of the options avail-able to you. From the System Preferences window, you can cus-tomize the look of your Desktop, change the screen saver, add and con-figure new hardware to be used with your computer (such as a scanner or printer), create user accounts, and han-dle a variety of other system mainte-nance tasks.

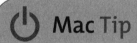

## Mac Tip

When using Windows XP or Windows Vista, a separate menu bar can appear at the top of every window. When using Mac OS X, the single Menu bar at the top of the Desktop always displays all applicable pull-down menu options for the active pro-gram. If you're running mul-tiple applications simultan-eously, when you switch between applications, the options available to you on the Menu bar will change accordingly.

- *Dock*. Adjust the appearance and position of the Dock using this pull-down menu option.
- *Location*. From this menu option, you can quickly adjust your computer's Network Preferences (used for connecting to the internet)
- *Recent Items*. Quickly access any of the last few programs you've run on your computer, or directly access any of the most recent document or data files you've used.
- *Sleep*. Put your computer into "sleep mode."
- *Restart*. Reboot your computer using this command.
- *Shut Down*. Always use this command to properly shut down and turn off your computer.
- *Log Out [Username]*. Use this menu option to log out the computer's current user so another user can log into the computer and access their own system preferences, files, and data.

Located next to the Apple logo, along the Menu bar, on the upper-left corner of the Desktop are the pull-down menu options directly related to the active application currently running on your computer. These options will be determined by what program you're running. If you're running Microsoft Word, for example, the menu option displayed next to the Apple logo will be

## ⏻ Mac Tip

You've probably noticed by now that your Mac's mouse only has one button. Unlike a PC, there is no right-click option. Depending on the application you're running on your Mac, pressing the Control button on the keyboard simultaneously with the mouse button serves the same purpose as the right mouse button on your PC. Another option is to give up your Apple Mighty Mouse and plug a two-button mouse into your Mac. You can attach a two-button mouse via the USB port.

Word. This gives you access to Word's applicable menus plus indicates that Microsoft Word is the current active application running on your Mac.

Moving across the top of the Desktop screen to the upper-right corner, you'll find a variety of system-related icons (several of which can be changed by the user). For example, you'll find an icon that'll allow you to adjust your Mobile Me settings and preferences for syncing data from your computer with your Mobile Me account. There's also an icon that by clicking on it will allow you to enter the Time Machine application and set your preferences for this backup software.

By clicking on the Bluetooth icon, you can turn the wireless Bluetooth technology built into your Mac on or off, plus adjust the system's Bluetooth preferences. Located near the Bluetooth icon (in the upper-right corner of the Desktop) at is the AirPort icon, which represents the wireless internet capabilities built into your Mac. When AirPort is turned on, the computer will be able to connect to a Wi-Fi hotspot giving you access to the web. You can also adjust your network preferences by clicking the mouse on this icon.

Adjusting the volume of your computer's speakers can be done by clicking on the Speaker icon located in the upper-right corner of the Desktop. You can also increase or decrease the volume by pressing the appropriate (labeled) keys on your Mac's keyboard.

If you're using a MacBook, MacBook Pro, or MacBook Air, the Power icon will also be displayed in the upper-right corner of the Desktop. This icon will tell you how much battery life you have remaining and whether the computer is currently charging. You can adjust the computer's Energy Saver Preferences by clicking the mouse on this icon.

The Day and Time are displayed on your Desktop in the upper-right corner. By clicking the Mouse on the magnifying glass icon (referred to as the Spotlight), you can quickly find anything that's stored on your computer, whether it's a file, a photograph, a contact's phone number, a web page you've recently visited, or an application. As soon as you begin typing what you're looking for, a listing of related files will appear on the screen.

Within the main Desktop area, you'll see your selected Desktop image (sometimes referred to as wallpaper) displayed. Over this image (your Desktop work space), you can place any number of icons representing programs or files.

Double-clicking the mouse on an icon placed on your Desktop will cause the relevant application to launch. (If it's a folder you click on, the contents of the folder will be revealed in a Finder window.) If, however, you place a Microsoft Word document (a .doc or .docx file) on your Desktop, when you double-click on that icon, Word and the file you selected will automatically load.

The one icon that's always present on your Desktop is the Hard Disk icon, which represents the Hard Drive built into your computer. If you have an external hard drive connected to your computer, another computer networked to your Mac, or a thumb drive, for example, inserted into the computer's USB port, icons representing these external drives will also appear on your Desktop automatically.

### The Finder

Double-clicking the mouse on the Hard Disk icon that's located on your Desktop will open the Finder window. This gives you access to the main folders in which your various applications, files, and data are stored. Within the

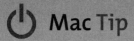 **Mac Tip**

Anytime a window opens on your Mac, there will be three colored dots in the upper-left corner of that window (in Windows, similar icons are found in the upper-right corner). The red dot closes the active window. The yellow dot minimizes the active window (and places it on your Dock so you know it's still running). The green dot zooms the active window. The Windows equivalent of these icons include the "–" icon to minimize a window, the "+" to maximize a window, and the "X" icon to close a window. When running Mac OS X, however, if you click on the red dot to close a window, that application continues to run in the background until you actually quit it.

Finder window, you'll see the Applications, Boot, Library, Hard Disk, System, User Guides and Information, and Users folder. Double-clicking on the Hard Disk icon is just like accessing the My Computer icon in Windows on your old PC.

As a former PC user, you're probably familiar with Windows' Start icon. The Finder icon on the Mac works very much the same way for locating and launching applications. When the Finder window opens (Figure 3.2), you'll see a sidebar menu on the left side of the window that allows you to quickly access specific folders on your Hard Disk, such as Desktop, Applications, Documents, Pictures, Music, and Movies (or any other folders you create). Whatever folder you click on using this sidebar, the contents of that folder (icons or text labels representing the files within it) will be displayed in the Finder window to the right of the sidebar.

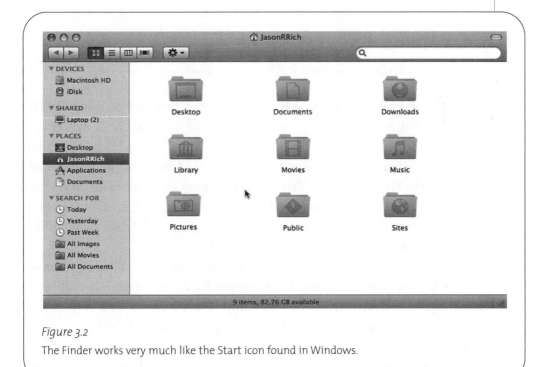

*Figure 3.2*
The Finder works very much like the Start icon found in Windows.

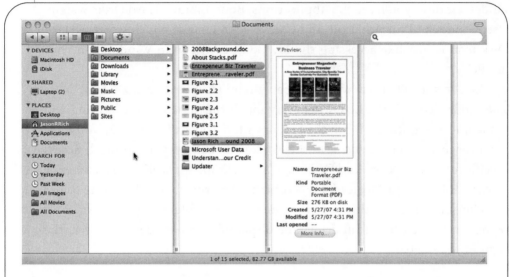

*Figure 3.3*

Using the Columns View within the Finder window, you easily see folders and the contents of subfolders, and thumbnails or graphical representations of actual files stored within these folders or subfolders.

The Finder window works a lot like Windows Explorer on your old PC. Below the red, yellow, and green dots used for closing, minimizing, and zooming windows when running Mac OS X, there are left (back) and right (forward) arrow icons used for navigating between folders displayed in the main portion of the Finder window. To the right of these arrow icons are four icons that allow you to control how you'll view folders, subfolders, and files in the main Finder window. The Icon View (shown in Figure 3.2) shows graphical icons representing files, folders, or applications.

The List View (located to the right of the Icon View icon) allows you to see a text-based list of files, folders, and applications, along with related information about each (Date Modified, Size, Kind). The Columns View (Figure 3.3) icon allows you to see the hierarchy of file folders and subfolders using a combination of text-based file names and small graphical icons.

The Cover Flow View icon (which is unique to Apple) allows you to quickly scroll through colorful graphic representations and thumbnail views of your

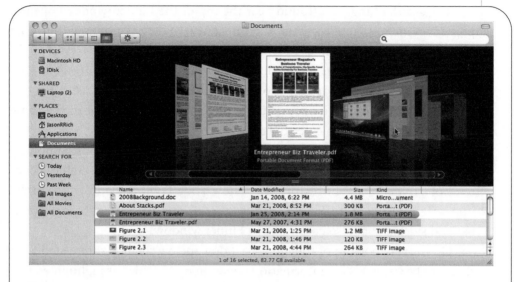

*Figure 3.4*
Using graphical thumbnails and icons, you can preview files within your directories using the Cover Flow View within Finder. To open a file, simply double-click on the text-based file name or the thumbnail/icon representing it.

files, folders, and applications. This view (see Figure 3.4) is similar to the graphical interface used by Apple iTunes.

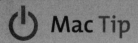 **Mac Tip**

To quit or exit an application running under Mac OS X, access the active application's pull-down menu at the top of the screen (located next to the Apple logo on the Menu bar) and select the Quit [Application Name] command. The equivalent keyboard shortcut is Command (⌘) + Q. You can tell an application is running on your Mac, even if the application has no open windows on your Desktop, because a small bluish dot will appear under the icon representing that program on your Dock.

The gear-looking icon (found near the top of the Finder window) opens a pull-down menu that allows you to create a new folder or subfolder, burn the contents of an existing folder to CD or DVD, open a file with its default application, open a file with an application you select, or move a file or folder to the trash. From this menu, you can also change a file or folder name using the Get Info option, duplicate a file, copy a file, or color-code a file so that its file name is always highlighted in a color of your choice.

On the upper-right side of the Finder window is the Search Box. Simply by typing a keyword, file name, or search phrase, you can quickly search the contents of a folder or an entire drive. The Show/Hide Toolbar icon, located in the upper-right corner of the Finder window, allows you to display or hide the toolbar and sidebar that also comprise the Finder window.

On the very bottom of the Finder window (below the horizontal scroll bar that may be visible) is file information about an open folder or highlighted file. For a folder, the number of files within it will be displayed, as well as the amount of memory available on the drive where the file is stored.

## The Size of Windows on the Desktop

Depending on the size of the Finder window (or any window displayed on the Desktop), vertical and horizontal scroll bars may appear. Using the mouse, you can slide these scroll bars up or down, or left and right, to view the entire contents of a window.

To increase or decrease the physical size of almost any window within Mac OS X, click and hold the mouse on the Drag To icon, found in the lower-right corner of the active window. You can move this icon up, down, left, right, or diagonally. The Drag To icon looks like three small diagonal lines in the corner of the window.

To move a window around on the Desktop without changing its size, click and hold the mouse on the upper or lower frame of the window and drag the mouse (and the window) to the desired location. The window size will remain the same, unless your mouse is held on the Drag To icon. If you want to increase the size of the window to take up the entire screen, move the upper-left corner of the active window to the upper-left corner of the Desktop screen (just below the Menu bar), and then place the mouse on the Drag To icon, and pull the lower-right corner of the window down toward the lower-right corner of the Desktop (in a diagonal direction).

## Using the Dock

At the very bottom of the Desktop is the Dock, which contains icons represent-ing software applications installed (and potentially running) on your com-puter. As was discussed in Chapter 2, you can easily drag any application icon from the Applications folder (found in your Hard Disk) to the Dock to cus-tomize it and provide you with quick access to frequently-used programs. And you can delete icons by dragging them from your Dock into the Trash.

Other application icons that by default are found on your Dock include applications bundled with the Mac OS X operating system, such as Dashboard (for controlling Widgets, which are explained in Chapter 4), Safari (Apple's web browser software), iTunes (for downloading, watching, or listening to various multimedia content, including videos, TV shows, movies, and audio files), iChat (used for sending and receiving IMs), Address Book (a contact manage-ment application), iCal (a scheduling and calendar application), Preview (for viewing PDF files and graphic images), Mail (for accessing e-mail), and Time Machine (a data backup application).

On the right side of the Dock, you'll find a Documents icon. This icon allows you to access any recent data files you've used on the computer. The Downloads icon opens the Downloads folder, which is where newly downloaded software or files are automati-cally stored (unless you stipulate otherwise).

Finally, in the lower-right corner of the Desktop is the Trash icon (it looks like a trash can). This is where files, applications, or folders that you'd like to delete from your computer are placed. Once files are placed in

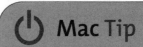

**Mac Tip**

In addition to accessing items and files using your mouse to click on related icons, the Mac OS X operating system also allows you to use keyboard shortcuts to handle a wide range of navigation and other tasks.

the Trash, they will remain there until you use the Empty Trash command found under the Finder pull-down menu (along the Menu bar) at the top of the Desktop. The keyboard shortcut for deleting a file or folder (placing it in the trash) is to highlight it within Finder and then press Command (⌘) + Delete.

Once you become familiar with navigating your way around the Desktop and accessing programs and files using Finder, using your Mac becomes second nature. The next section of this chapter describes some of the key differences between Mac OS X and Windows XP or Windows Vista in terms of how you navigate around your system.

# Switching from Windows

As a Windows user, you became accustomed to doing certain things on your PC. This section focuses on how to perform some of these same tasks on your Mac, because there are differences.

## When a Program Freezes

While the Mac OS X operating system is much more stable than Windows XP or Windows Vista and seldom, if ever, crashes, there will be times when individual programs either crash, freeze, or hang. Should this happen, instead of pressing Control + Alt + Delete, as you would on your old PC to reboot your entire computer, press the Command (⌘) + Options + Esc keys simultaneously on your Mac's keyboard to shut down a single unresponsive program.

When the Force Quit Applications window appears, highlight the unresponsive program and click on the Force Quit icon in the lower-right corner of this window. When you do this, any unsaved data related to that program is lost. (An alternative to pressing Command (⌘) + Options + Esc is to click the mouse on the Apple icon located in the upper-left corner of the screen and then select the Force Quit command.)

If you need to reboot your entire computer, which seldom is necessary, simply hold down the power button on your computer for about five seconds or until the computer turns off. Press the power button again to turn the computer back on and reboot. Unfortunately, any unsaved data will be lost.

## Ejecting a Disc

With the exception of the MacBook Air, all of the Mac computers have a built-in optical drive. However, upon taking a closer look at these drives, there is no "eject" button to remove CDs or DVDs when you're done with them. When using the Mac OS X operating system, the Eject feature is software driven. In the upper-right corner of your keyboard is the Eject button. Simply hold this button down to remove a disc from the computer's optical drive.

If you have another type of drive connected to your computer via a USB or Firewire cable, such as an external hard disk, thumb drive, or memory card reader (with a memory card inserted), these will all appear as separate drives on your Desktop in the form of separate icons.

In Figure 3.5, in addition to the Mac's internal Hard Drive (named Macintosh HD on this computer), there's a thumb drive (named Pen Drive), and an external 160GB hard drive (called Simpletech) connected to the computer via the USB ports, and there's a blank CD inserted into the computer's optical drive. Each of these is displayed as a separate icon on the Desktop. The contents of each drive can be accessed using the Finder or by double-clicking the mouse on the Desktop icon representing any of the drives.

While you could simply remove any of the drives connected to your Mac via a USB or Firewire port by pulling it out, it's necessary to first eject the drive to ensure the preservation of your data. To do this, use the mouse to drag the icon on your Desktop that represents the drive to the Trash (located in the lower-right corner of the Desktop). When the icon for the drive you're ejecting appears over the Trash icon, the Trash icon will morph into an Eject icon. The icon for the drive will then disappear off of your Desktop, indicating it's safe to remove it. (An iPod connected to your computer will show as a drive on your Desktop. The icon will look like an iPod. Your iPod must also be ejected before disconnecting it from your Mac.)

An alternative way to eject a drive is to highlight it on the Desktop using the mouse and then either access the File pull-down menu from the Menu bar at the very top of the screen and select the Eject [Drive Name] command, or press Command (⌘) + E when the icon representing the drive is highlighted on the Desktop. Once you eject the drive, it's safe to remove that drive from the USB or Firewire port.

*Figure 3.5*
Each active drive that's connected to your computer will show up on your Desktop and can be
accessed by double-clicking on the icon to open the Finder window. In this case, there's the Mac's
internal Hard Drive (Macintosh HD) displayed in the upper-right corner of the Desktop. Below it
is an icon for a USB thumb drive. Below the thumb drive is an icon for an external 160GB hard
disk that's connected to the computer, and below that is a CD-shaped icon indicating there's a
blank CD inserted into the computer's optical drive.

Failing to properly eject a drive when using the Mac OS X operating system
will cause a "Device Removal" warning window to appear on the screen. This window will remind you that all drives connected to the Mac must first be ejected
before being removed to prevent possible data loss. This includes when you connect a memory card reader to your Mac (which has a memory card inserted).

## Copying and Pasting Text

Anytime you want to copy and paste text using your Mac, whether it's within a text
document, when writing e-mails, or when using virtually any other application,

highlight the text using the mouse and then press Command (⌘) + C to copy the text into the scrapbook. When you're ready to paste the text, place the cursor in the desired location (using the mouse or the arrow keys on the keyboard) and then press Command (⌘) + V. This is just one of many keyboard shortcuts you can learn to make yourself more productive when using your Mac.

Instead of using the Command (⌘) + C and Command (⌘) + V keyboard shortcuts, you can highlight the text or data to be copied and then access the Edit pull-down menu from the Menu Bar and select Copy, and then when appropriate, select Paste.

## Renaming Files and Folders

There are several easy ways to rename files or folders when using the Mac OS X operating system. First, you can open the Finder, highlight the icon representing the file or folder

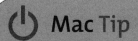

**Mac Tip**

When you copied text on your old PC running Windows, that data was temporarily stored in a virtual "clipboard." On your Mac, this same temporary storage space used when you take advantage of the Cut, Paste, and Copy commands is referred to as the "scrapbook." The scrapbook, however, allows you to store multiple scraps at once as you copy and paste text or data, for example.

(or the file name/folder name, depending on which Finder view you're using) and then click the mouse of the file or folder's name (as opposed to the icon for that file or folder). You can then type whatever file name you wish.

Another way to rename a file is to highlight it when in the Finder, select the File pull-down menu from the Menu bar, and then choose Get Info. (The keyboard shortcut is Command (⌘) + I.) This will open another window containing details about the file. About halfway down on this Get Info window is the Name & Extension field. You can type the new file name here (see Figure 3.6).

## Copying and Moving Files

Keeping all of your applications, data, and files organized on your computer should be a priority. When you first start using your new Mac, you'll discover

*Figure 3.6*
You can rename a file using the Get Info command found under the File pull-down menu on the
Menu bar. When this window (shown on the left side of the screen) appears, enter the new
screen name in the Name & Extension field.

that a series of folders, including Desktop, Applications, Documents,
Downloads, Music, Movies, and Pictures, has already been set up for you. Based
on your needs, however, you can create as many additional folders as you'd like.
Within a folder, you can also create an unlimited number of subfolders.

At any time, you can copy or move files between folders with ease. To do
this, follow these steps:

1. Using the Finder, open the folder containing the file or subfolder you
   want to copy or move.
2. Using the mouse, select the specific file or folder you want to move or
   copy. You can select multiple files or folders within the window.

3. To copy the selected (highlighted) file(s) or folder(s), from the Edit pull-down menu on the Menu bar, select Copy. The keyboard shortcut for this is to press Command (⌘) + C. To Move a file, which deletes it from one location and transfers it to another, first select the (highlighted) file(s) or folder(s). From the Edit pull-down menu on the Menu bar, select Cut. The keyboard shortcut for this is to press Command (⌘) + X.

4. Again using the finder, open the folder where you want to Copy or Move the selected file(s) or folder(s) to. When this window is open and active, access the Edit pull-down menu from the Menu bar. To Copy or Move the file(s) or folder(s) to this new location, select Paste. The keyboard shortcut for this is Command (⌘) + V.

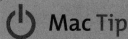 **Mac Tip**

To copy files between folders or subfolders, you can also use the drag-and-drop method. Use the Finder to open the original folder where the file(s) are that you want to copy. Next, open the destination folder where you want to copy the files to. Highlight the files or subfolders and then use the mouse to drag the selected (highlighted) files from one window to the other.

## Switching Between Applications

You already know that the Mac OS X operating system allows you to simultaneously run multiple applications on your computer. However, while several applications might be running, only one window can be active at any given time. The active window is the one you are currently working in. Switching between windows (applications) is as easy as moving the mouse and clicking on a different window.

Another way to switch between applications, if one or more of the application windows have been minimized, is to click the mouse on the application's icon found on the Dock. You can also use the Expose screen to quickly switch between windows.

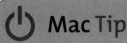

## Mac Tip

To hide an application, which will keep it running but remove the window from the Desktop and so eliminate clutter, press Command (⌘) + H when the application window is active. On the Dock, you'll see that the application is still active. To re-open the application window, click on the appropriate program icon on the Dock.

A slightly more advanced option for switching between applications that's available exclusively on the Mac is to use Spaces, a function built into the Mac OS X operating system. Spaces can be found in the Applications folder on your computer. To enable and customize this application, access System Preferences and select Expose and Spaces.

## Uninstalling Software and Applications

Unlike in Windows XP or Windows Vista on your old PC, there is no "uninstall" application within the Mac OS X environment. To delete an application that's installed on your computer, find the application within the Applications folder and simply drag its icon

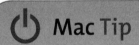

## Mac Tip

To instantly switch between open applications, regardless of whether the windows are open or not, press and hold down Command (⌘) + Tab. A window will pop up showing the icons for all open applications. Keep holding the Command (⌘) button to keep this window visible. Press the Tab key repeatedly to highlight each program icon one at a time. When you release the Command (⌘) button, the icon that's highlighted will be the one that re-opens on the Desktop as the active application. (The remaining applications will continue running in the background.)

to the Trash (on the Dock). When you empty the trash, the application will be permanently deleted from your computer.

## Mac OS X Is Powerful and Robust

The latest version of the Mac OS X operating system is extremely powerful and has thousands of features built into it. Over time, you'll probably want to learn more about these various features in order to get the most out of your computer. This chapter provides the core information you'll need to become acclimated to the Mac OS X operating system, especially if you're already proficient using Windows XP or Windows Vista.

Additional tutorials for the Mac OS X operating system can be found under the Support section of the Apple.com website (apple.com/support/leopard/). There are also dozens of how-to computer books that offer detailed information about using Mac OS X Leopard at any bookstore. The free workshops offered at all Apple Stores also provide an excellent, interactive introduction.

One really nice feature of Mac OS X is that every type of file depicted on your Desktop or within Finder uses a different type of graphical icon for easy identification. The thumbnails used to depict individual data files help you instantly see the contents of the file, whether it's a photo, Word document, Excel spreadsheet, PowerPoint presentation, music file, video file, or PDF file. Folders (containing multiple files) and application icons also have unique looks. Between using the Finder and becoming familiar with the look of different icons, learning to navigate your way around your new computer should come easily.

## Transferring Your PC-Based Data to Your New Mac

Now that you've set up your new Mac and have a basic understanding of the Mac OS X operating system, the next chapter will help you copy all of your important data from your old PC to your Mac. It will also help you sync data from your smartphone or wireless PDA (iPhone, BlackBerry, Treo, etc.), and help you set up your existing e-mail account(s) on your Mac.

# Personalizing Your Mac Experience

I'T'S TRUE, YOUR MAC IS JUST A MACHINE. IT'S NOT A MAGIC BOX, NOR IS IT A LIVING THING with intelligence. It has no personality of its own, and it can't "think" without being given a very precise set of instructions in the form of a program.

If used correctly, your new Mac is a high-tech electronic device that's a powerful tool, capable of assisting you in being more productive and better organized as you strive to meet the responsibilities of your job and excel in your career. Just as a construction worker relies on a hammer and nails, and a plumber or electrician has a specialized toolbox, the average businessperson or entrepreneur requires a computer as an essential and indispensable tool.

A Mac is also a machine that can be used as the ultimate entertainment system for listening to your favorite music, watching your favorite movies and TV shows, playing exciting games, exploring the web, and communicating with friends, family, co-workers, clients, and total strangers through online chats, Instant Messaging (IM), and even videoconferencing (via the web).

When you first purchase a new Mac, it's like being a painter facing a blank canvas. You have the ability to personalize and customize your Mac in a variety of ways, allowing you to work better and your computer to work better for you. For example, you can customize the look of your Desktop by choosing your wallpaper image. You can reorganize the Dock so it gives you easy access to the applications you use the most. You can also access the Preferences section of almost any application to fine-tune the user interface and personalize how you'll interact with each program. Most importantly, you have the ability to add software and peripherals to your computer in order to expand its capabilities and transform it into the perfect tool for whatever it is you want or need it to do. This chapter focuses on just some of the many ways you can personalize and customize your Mac and your overall computing experience.

## Choosing the Right Software

Any computer, whether it's a desktop or notebook model, is only as powerful and functional as the software installed on it. Sure, the operating system, in this case Mac OS X Leopard, gives a computer core functionality, but to work more efficiently, you'll need to add software.

As you'll discover from this book and once you start shopping for software, you have a variety of different choices for almost every type of application available, whether it's word processing, e-mail management, accounting, photo editing and archiving, website design, database management, contact management, or scheduling. Just taking a look at word processors, this book offers details about

Microsoft Word 2008, Apple iWork's Pages '08, and OpenOffice.org Productivity Suite's Writer.

Before you start filling up your computer's hard drive with a bunch of applications and perhaps spending hundreds or even thousands of dollars on commercial software, it's essential that you first evaluate what you want to be able to do with your computer. Consider carefully what applications you want or need, and how you'll be using those applications.

Some of the common uses a businessperson or entrepreneur has for a computer include:

- Bookkeeping and accounting
- Contact management
- Creating and giving presentations
- Creating and managing a blog, podcast, or webcast
- Database management
- E-mail
- Graphic design and photo editing
- Managing personal finances and investments
- Organizing and storing vast amounts of information
- Project management
- Real-time communications via instant messages, online chats, or video-conferencing
- Spreadsheets and number crunching
- Surfing the web
- Time management/scheduling
- Tracking expenses
- Website design and management
- Word processing, page layout, and desktop publishing

Once you determine what types of applications you want for your computer, you can begin researching your options in regard to specific programs, based on price, functionality, usability, compatibility with what your office or co-workers already use, and other criteria you deem important.

In addition to considering what software you'll need, focus on how the software will be used. What do you want the end result to be? Knowing what's needed helps you choose the best software for the task. Once you know what software you're looking for, you can visit a software retailer or an Apple Store, or use the web to purchase and download the necessary applications.

Chapter 8 focuses on the Microsoft Office 2008 suite of applications. Chapter 9 focuses on iWork '08 and additional applications developed by Apple that a businessperson or entrepreneur might find useful. In Chapter 10, you'll read about many other applications from third-party software developers that are currently available for your Mac. You'll also discover ways to save money by seeking out freeware, shareware, or open source software, as opposed to commercially available software that typically comes with a hefty price tag.

Just because thousands of different software applications and options are available for your Mac, you do not need to clutter up your computer's hard drive by installing dozens of different applications. Determine specifically what applications you'll need to utilize, and focus on acquiring and installing those first.

Once you've become accustomed to using all of the core applications you need in order to do your everyday work and handle your personal computing, then you can begin to find new and exciting ways of using your Mac to handle additional applications. You're better off, however, learning to use one or two applications at a time. Otherwise, the experience of becoming a Mac user and being exposed to many new programs at once could become a daunting and confusing task, especially if you don't consider yourself to be too computer savvy to begin with.

As you're learning to use new software, initially focus on how to use the features, commands, and functions that you'll need the most in your everyday work. For example, if you only need to do basic word processing,

## Mac Tip

By carefully defining your computing needs in advance, you can avoid purchasing and/or installing multiple software packages that serve similar purposes. For example, for spreadsheets, you won't need both Microsoft Excel and iWork's Numbers. If you plan to edit photographs, Adobe's PhotoShop CS3 or Apple's Aperture 2 will do the trick. You probably won't need to invest in both of these popular applications.

there's no need to learn about all of the page layout and desktop publishing features built into Microsoft Word, iWork's Pages, or OpenOffice.org's Writer. Later, as you become more familiar with the word processor you are using, you can expand your knowledge and tap into the program's additional features, which you may ultimately find very useful.

To avoid becoming overwhelmed with new applications and the new computing environment that your Mac offers, pace yourself and focus on what you need to know right away in order to make your transition as smooth and hassle-free as possible.

Another consideration when it comes to software is the growing number of online-based applications. Instead of installing and running specialized software on your computer, online-based applications are sited on the web and require only a web browser, such as Safari, to use. As this book was being written, companies like Microsoft and Google had begun offering online-based applications that could be an alternative to traditional software. One benefit to

 **Mac Tip**

Using the KISS philosophy (Keep It Simple Stupid) typically works best when choosing software. Don't invest in software that's too complex or that offers too much functionality for your needs. For example, if you want to maintain a basic database of your contacts, you can use the Address Book application that comes with your Mac. If, however, you need more control over your contacts database, you could use Microsoft Entourage or FileMaker's Bento application to manage that same contact database, but because these other programs have many more features built into them, they'll probably take you longer to learn. Often, finding the most basic and straightforward application to handle a specific task is easier than attempting to learn the most feature-packed, state-of-the-art software application that's on the market.

using these applications is that there are absolutely no compatibility issues between PCs and Macs.

To learn about online applications available from Google, such as Docs (a word processor), Calendar (a scheduling and time management application), and Picasa (a photo editing and sharing application), visit google.com/intl/en /options/. They are currently offered free of charge.

## Dashboard Widgets: Providing Easy Access to Tools and Information

In addition to the software you install onto your Mac to give it even greater functionality and make it a more powerful tool to handle your personal and work-related computing needs, the Mac OS X operating system includes an application called Dashboard, which allows you to load and use Widgets on your Desktop. These are mini-applications, available for free.

When you first load Dashboard (by pressing the F12 key, clicking on the Dashboard icon that's located next to the Finder on the Dock, or by pressing the Scroll Ball in the center of your Apple Mighty Mouse), you'll notice a handful of default Widget applications are already loaded and running on your Mac.

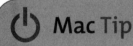 **Mac Tip**

Once the Dashboard appears, you can make it disappear from the Desktop by pressing F12, the Dashboard icon on the Dock, or the Scroll Ball button on the Apple Mighty Mouse.

Once Dashboard is active and Widgets appear on your Desktop, click on the Open button (the plus sign surrounded by a circle icon that appears to the left of the Finder icon near the Dock) to move these Widgets around and pick and choose additional Widgets already installed on your computer to add to your Dashboard. This is done using the Widget bar, which will appear below the Dock. Using the mouse, you can drag and drop Widgets from the Widget bar to your Desktop.

Pre-installed Widgets that come with the Mac OS X operating system include:

- *Address Book.* Quickly access the Address Book application to find someone's contact information.
- *Business.* Serves as a digital Yellow Pages for finding businesses within a specific city.
- *Calculator.* A simple calculator is displayed on the screen. Use the numeric keypad or the number keys on your keyboard to use the calculator.
- *Dictionary.* Look up the definition of words.
- *ESPN.* View sports-related news, scores, stories, and information from ESPN.
- *Flight Tracker.* Quickly track a flight based on the airline name, flight number, and date.
- *Google.* Enter a search phrase to quickly see Google links and listings.

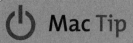 **Mac Tip**

Many Widgets require the computer to have an active internet connection in order to access data from the web, such as news headlines, weather or traffic reports, stock quotes, or other current information.

 **Mac Tip**

From the Apple.com website (apple.com/downloads/dashboard/) you can pick from thousands of additional Widgets, all of which are free of charge. To access this website from the Dashboard, click the Open button when the Dashboard is running. Next, click on the Manage Widgets icon that appears. On the bottom of the Manage Widget window, click on the icon that says More Widgets. Browse through the available Widgets. Download and install the additional Widgets you desire. Once the new Widget is installed, it will appear in the Manage Widgets window and on your Widget bar. Using the mouse, position the new Widget on the Dashboard by dragging it into position.

- *iCal.* View your appointments and other information from the main iCal application.
- *iTunes.* Access certain features of iTunes when this Widget is running.
- *Movies.* Enter your zip code and see what movies are playing locally, as well as their respective show times.
- *People.* This Widget serves as a 4-1-1 directory (White Pages) for looking up people in the phone book based on their name, city, state, and/or zip code.
- *Ski Report.* Enter the name of a ski resort and obtain an up-to-the-minute ski condition report.
- *Stickies.* Why spend money on Post-It® Notes when you have a never-ending pad of digital yellow sticky notes right on your Desktop. Keep track of notes, lists, memos, and reminders.
- *Stocks.* Access stock quotes and a performance graph for any stock symbol you enter (shown in Figure 4.1).
- *Tile Game.* A simple puzzle game to help you pass the time.
- *Translation.* Enter a word or phrase, select a language, and have your text instantly translated.
- *Unit Converter.* Convert from one unit to another quickly.

*Figure 4.1*
The Stock Widget is popular with Mac users who manage their own investment portfolios.

*Figure 4.2*
The Weather Widget offers a six-day weather forecast for any city you enter.

- *Weather.* See a multiday weather forecast for almost any city in the world (shown in Figure 4.2).
- *World Clock.* View a detailed world clock.

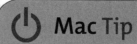

**Mac Tip**

When searching for additional Widgets to install, check the Business, News, Search, and Travel categories for Widgets of particular interest to business users.

Some Widgets need to be customized the first time they're used. To do this, click on the Info (i) button usually found in the lower-right corner of the Widget. It allows you to enter personalized information, such as your zip code, home city, or the details pertaining to that particular Widget.

To remove a Widget from your Dashboard, open the Dashboard and click on the Open icon. You'll notice that each Widget now has a X icon located in the upper-left corner. Click on this X icon for each Widget you want to delete. Deleted Widgets will return to the Widget bar, but will no longer appear when you open the Dashboard. To erase a Widget, drag it, using the mouse, from the Widget bar to the Trash.

# Adding Peripherals and Accessories

Using the USB and/or Firewire ports built into your Mac, or your computer's ability to utilize Bluetooth wireless technology, connecting peripherals to your computer is simple—and you don't have to worry about drivers, as you did when using a Windows-based PC. By visiting any Apple Store, computer retailer, consumer electronics store, or even an office supply superstore, you can purchase a wide range of Mac-compatible peripherals and accessories.

Some of the more common peripherals Mac owners connect to their desktop or notebook computers include:

- *Additional monitor(s).* Whether you're using a Mac Pro, Mac Mini, MacBook, or MacBook Pro, connecting a large monitor to your computer might be useful for applications such as video editing or those requiring multiple windows to be open on the Desktop simultaneously.

Any USB monitor can be connected to your Mac, but Apple's 20-inch, 23-inch, or 30-inch Cinema displays are top choices when it comes to high-resolution, flat-panel displays that truly showcase the graphics capabilities of Macs.

- *Cell phone or PDA.* By connecting your cell phone or PDA, such as an iPhone, to your Mac, you can synchronize your Address Book and iCal data, for example. Optional software is available for many smartphones and PDAs, enabling these devices to transfer data back and forth using a USB cable or Bluetooth. While an iPhone will use the iTunes application to accomplish this, other devices such as Palm OS-based PDAs can utilize the iSync software (built into the Mac) along with the HotSync application that came with a Palm OS-based smartphone or Treo PDA. For more information about synchronizing data with a Palm OS device and your Mac, visit apple.com/isync.

  Using a software application called PocketMac for BlackBerry (created by PocketMac, 866-762-5622, pocketmac.net/products.html), your contacts, calendars, tasks, and notes can be synchronized between a Mac and a BlackBerry using a USB cable to connect the two. For information about software for synchronizing data with other smartphones and PDAs, check the Productivity Tools category of the Apple website's Download section (apple.com/downloads/macosx/productivity_tools/).

- *Digital camera.* Most digital cameras allow users to connect a USB cable directly from the camera to the Mac to quickly transfer digital images into applications such as iPhoto. An alternative is to attach an external memory card reader to your Mac, and then insert your digital camera's memory card into the reader. Whichever method you use, the camera or memory card/reader will appear on your Mac as a separate drive, allowing you to copy and paste, drag and drop, or import images with ease.

- *Digital voice recorder.* Sometimes, when you're on the go or in the process of brainstorming, writing down ideas or typing them out isn't feasible. Then, many business professionals opt to use a digital voice recorder. These devices can connect to your Mac via a USB cable, allowing the recorded audio files to be copied to your Mac to be archived, edited, or listened to using an audio player such as iTunes.

● *External hard disk drive.* Connecting an external hard drive to your Mac gives you more data storage capacity and allows you to utilize the Time Machine program to maintain an up-to-date backup of your computer's primary hard drive. More information about external hard drives can be found in Chapter 11.

● *Graphics (pen) tablet.* If you'll be creating or editing graphics or photos on your Mac and don't want to use the keyboard and mouse to interact with programs like PhotoShop CS3 or CS4, you can attach a graphics tablet or pen tablet to your Mac using the computer's USB port. Companies like Wacom (wacom.com/intuos/index.cfm) offer a wide range of graphics tablets, ranging in price from under $100 to over $1,000, depending on their size and capabilities. Instead of moving the on-screen cursor around with a mouse, graphics tablets often use digital pens, which are much more precise.

● *Headphones.* Listen to music and audio in full stereo sound when you connect headphones to your Mac. If you're traveling with your MacBook, for example, and plan to watch a movie or TV show episode on an airplane, consider investing in noise-cancelling headphones from a company like Bose (bose.com). They eliminate outside noises and allow you to truly enjoy the audio from your computer. Good-quality noise-cancelling headphones are $100 to $400, depending on the style.

● *iPod.* Your Mac is designed to work seamlessly with your Apple iPod, iPod Touch, or iPhone to synchronize data, manage your music and video library, and allow you to download new content from iTunes. Use iTunes to create customized audio play lists, for example, on your Mac, and transfer the music to your iPod. When an iPod, iPod Touch, or iPhone is connected to your Mac via the USB port, you can recharge the battery-powered unit.

● *Keyboard and mouse (wireless).* While Mac desktop computers come with an Apple keyboard and Mighty Mouse, you'll notice that these two peripherals connect to your Mac via a USB cable. Apple also offers a wireless version of its keyboard and mouse, which creates less clutter on your desktop. When sitting at your desk and using a laptop, you can connect a full-size keyboard and mouse to make interacting with your computer more comfortable.

- *LCD projector.* Many businesspeople use their computers to create presentations for clients, customers, and co-workers. By connecting an LCD projector to your Mac, you can display whatever appears on your Mac's screen onto a giant screen, allowing an audience to follow along during your presentation. Programs like Microsoft PowerPoint and iWork Keynote '08 allow visually stunning presentations to be created for this purpose.

- *Microphone.* If you plan to record your own podcast or singing performances, or use your Mac to communicate online using voice-over-IP web-based videoconferencing (via Skype or iChat), you might want to use a better-quality microphone than the one built into your Mac. Using a special USB adapter, any professional-quality microphone can be connected to your computer. There are also high-quality USB microphones available.

- *Printer.* Creating hardcopies of any documents, data, or files you create on your Mac is, of course, done by connecting a printer. When it comes to choosing a printer, high-quality (fast) laser printers, full-color ink jet printers, thermal printers, and photo-quality printers are among your options. Printers start in price well under $100, but can be much more expensive, based on print speed, resolution, and the paper sizes that can be accommodated. Before investing in a printer, think about what you'll actually be printing. If you need high-quality black-and-white printing, a laser printer will be appropriate. For a more general purpose printer, capable of printing in black and white or full color, an ink jet printer might be more appropriate. If you need to print high-quality photographs from your printer, invest in a quality photo printer. There are also specialty printers on the market from companies like Dymo (dymo.com) that are designed to print mailing labels and/or U.S. mail postage stamps. Before purchasing a printer, investigate how much it'll cost to replenish or replace the toner or ink jet cartridges, and how long each will last. While the printer itself might have a low price tag, the ink or toner, which need to be replaced on an ongoing basis, might be rather expensive, depending on the make and model of the printer.

- *Scanner.* This device allows you to scan paper-based documents into your computer to create digital files that are exact replicas of the printed page. These files can be saved in a PDF format and edited, archived, or distributed electronically based on your needs. Scanners can also be used to import printed photographs or artwork into the computer, in order to create digital images. Scanners come in a wide range of sizes and can scan at various resolutions and speeds. The higher the resolution, the better. Companies such as Epson, Canon, and HP offer all-in-one printer, scanner, and fax units. There are also portable scanners on the market designed for scanning business cards (and importing data directly into Address Book) as well as receipts (so you can more easily keep track of expenses and import that data into a finance program such as Quicken).

- *Speakers.* While your Mac has two built-in stereo speakers, if you consider yourself an audiophile or require better-quality speakers to handle various applications that involve stereo or surround sound audio, external speakers can easily be connected to your Mac.

- *Thumb drive.* These tiny data storage devices connect to your Mac via a USB port and allow you to back up or copy files, programs, folders, or data. They provide a quick backup solution or allow you to easily transfer information from one computer to another. A thumb drive is small enough to fit in your pocket or purse, or connect to a keychain, yet it can store up to several gigabytes of data. More information about thumb drives can be found in Chapter 11.

- *USB hub.* Depending on the Mac system you own, it'll be equipped with from one to five USB ports. By connecting a USB hub to one of these ports, you can add extra USB ports to your Mac, allowing you to connect additional devices simultaneously. A single USB hub is an external device that will typically add four, five, or six additional USB ports to your computer.

- *Video recorder.* If you enjoy filming home movies or your work involves shooting corporate videos or seminars, connecting your digital video camera to your Mac allows you to transfer your movies quickly and edit them using a variety of applications. For transferring video footage, connecting the camera to the Mac's Firewire port is your best and fastest option.

- *Voice-Over-IP telephone.* Instead of using traditional telephone lines to make calls, using a service like Skype, you can make and receive telephone calls over the internet. While your Mac's built-in speakers and microphone allow your Mac to transform itself into a speaker phone, you can also connect a Voice-Over-IP telephone or Skype phone to your computer, offering you a more traditional telephone handset and dial pad for making or receiving calls. Especially if you travel overseas or spend a lot of time working out of hotel rooms, adding a Skype phone to your MacBook is a great way to stay in touch. Chapter 10 offers more information about the Skype Voice-Over-IP service.

## Easy Internet Access for Mac Notebook Computers

Apple iPhone, Palm Treo, and BlackBerry users enjoy easy access to the internet from virtually anywhere using their handheld wireless device. This is extremely appealing to business travelers who know the importance of staying connected and require the ability to access their e-mail and the web whenever and wherever they happen to be.

The drawback to accessing the web using a cell phone or wireless personal digital assistant (PDA) is the small screen, limited keyboard, and dramatically scaled-down web surfing capabilities these tiny devices offer. Without adding any additional software or equipment to their computer, MacBook, MacBook Pro, and MacBook Air users, however, can access the internet from wireless (Wi-Fi) hotspots or from hotel rooms.

This solution also has its drawbacks. While most airports and hotels offer high-speed internet access, it comes at a cost. Airports, internet cafés, bookstores, and

# Easy Internet Access for
# Mac Notebook Computers, *continued*

coffee shops (including Starbucks) throughout the country often charge a daily fee of $6.95 to $9.95 to connect to the web via a wireless hotspot. Hotels typically charge $9.95 to $19.95 per night to access the internet from a guestroom. For a business traveler constantly on the go, these charges add up quickly.

For budget-conscious web surfers, it is possible to find free, public Wi-Fi hotspots and utilize them during your travels. The Jiwire.com website, for example, offers a listing of more than 150,000 free Wi-Fi hotspots worldwide. The Wifi411.com website also lists public Wi-Fi hotspots that offer free and paid access in cities across America.

The CyberCafes website (cybercafes.com) provides an online directory listing thousands of internet cafés worldwide that allow users to access the web using supplied desktop computers for a low hourly fee, usually between $5 to $10 per hour. Most public libraries and Apple Stores across America also offer free internet access to the public. Using this solution, there's no need to travel with your own computer.

There is another alternative. For $39.95 to $79.95 per month, Mac notebook users can subscribe to one of the wireless broadband services offered by Sprint PCS, T-Mobile, AT&T, or Verizon. By connecting an inexpensive wireless modem to a computer (via the USB port), true wireless, high-speed (broadband) access is available from almost anywhere, especially in major cities. No phone lines or extra cables are required, and you're not limited to Wi-Fi coverage areas.

When choosing which wireless broadband internet service provider to sign up for, don't just compare the price of the monthly service. It's also necessary to evaluate the service coverage map and connection speeds offered by each

## Easy Internet Access for Mac Notebook Computers, *continued*

provider. Also, look at the duration of the required service agreement, the cost of the wireless modem, and whether or not unlimited internet access is granted through the service plan.

For someone who stays in a hotel three to four nights per month or needs internet access while on the go, wireless broadband internet is an extremely convenient business tool for enhancing productivity and staying connected. For those not on a corporate expense account, utilizing free Wi-Fi- hotspots, internet cafés, and web access through public libraries continues to be a low-cost option for surfing the web while on the go.

Depending on what peripherals and accessories you connect to your computer, the capabilities of your Mac will expand. While many peripherals are considered plug-and-play, meaning they'll work immediately upon connecting the peripheral device to your Mac, some will require that you install special software-based drivers before using the peripheral. Follow the setup directions that come with whatever peripheral you'll be connecting to your Mac to ensure that it functions properly right out of the box.

## Transferring Essential Data and Files to Your Mac

Once you've installed software onto your Mac, the next step involves importing your data from your old PC or Mac into your new Mac. For example, if you typically used Microsoft Word on your old computer, you'll probably want to import all of your Word documents (from your PC's My Documents folder) to your new Mac. You'll also want to import your web browser bookmarks, contact database, and schedule information, and set it up so your smartphone or PDA will synchronize information with your new Mac.

The various processes for transferring data between your old computer and your new Mac vary, based on what type of data you're transferring and whether that data is coming from a PC running Windows or another Mac. Either way, the process for transferring your data is the focus of Chapter 5.

# Transferring Your Data to a New Mac

AFTER SETTING UP YOUR NEW MAC, AS EXPLAINED IN CHAPTER 2, YOU'LL PROBA-bly want to begin installing additional software applications onto the computer. This process is explained in Chapter 4, and a sampling of Mac applications is described in Chapters 7, 8, 9, and 10. Once your software is installed, your computer is pretty much ready to start using.

At this point, you'll probably want to import your data and files from your old PC (or another Mac), giving you access to all of that information,

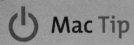

## Mac Tip

Before attempting to transfer files, folders, or data between your old computer and your new Mac, create a backup of your old computer's hard drive and all of your critical data and files. Also, if you already have important files stored on your new Mac, back those up as well. During the data transfer process, if you accidentally delete files or important data, or overwrite existing files, you'll have reliable backups available from which to restore those files or data. For more information on how to create backups on your Mac, see Chapter 11.

including your documents, databases, contacts, schedule information, and other files that are related to the applications you'll be using. Transferring or importing your data and files is the focus of this chapter.

## Transferring Files

Depending on your level of technical expertise, one way to transfer files between a PC and a Mac is to create a network within your home or office, and then link up both computers to that network so they can exchange files and share drives. This process is more complex than using the "drag-and-drop" or "cut-and-paste" methods described in the next section.

For the purposes of this book, transferring files refers to your program data, not the software applications themselves. Some of the files you can easily transfer from your PC to the Mac include:

- Text files and documents you've created using Microsoft Word or another word processor
- Documents and files saved in PDF format
- Spreadsheets you manage using Microsoft Excel
- Digital photos and graphic images
- Your library of music, audio, or video files
- Photoshop or PhotoShop Elements files

- Quicken files
- FileMaker Pro databases
- Contact and scheduling data from Outlook, Act!, or another contact management/scheduling application

Unless you'll actually be running Windows XP or Windows Vista on your Mac (a topic covered in Chapter 6), the actual PC programs (software applications) you've been running on your old computer cannot be transferred or used on your Mac. Instead, you'll need to use software created specifically for the Mac OS X operating system. There are, however, Mac versions of many popular applications that business users utilize on their PCs, even the applications found within Microsoft Office. While the programs or program versions may be different, in many cases, your data and files will be compatible and transferable between platforms.

## The Easiest Method: Let Someone Do the Data Transfer

If you buy your Mac from an Apple Store, you can bring your PC into the store and have a certified Apple Genius (a Mac specialist) transfer all of your files and data from your old PC to your Mac. In most situations, this is a free service and can be completed within one business day (providing an appointment is scheduled). To have an Apple Genius transfer your data, your PC must be running Microsoft Windows 98 or later (including Windows XP and Windows Vista), and the computer itself must have a working Ethernet port, Firewire port, internal zip drive, a 3.5-inch floppy drive, or a parallel port. You must bring your original Windows OS installation CDs, along with your computer's mouse and keyboard (if it's a desktop computer).

Anyone can take advantage of Apple's "Basic" file transfer service, which includes transferring files from a designated folder on your PC to your new Mac's Hard Drive, where you can then configure the files. If you're an Apple ProCare member, however, Apple offers a complete data transfer service. This means that all of your different file types will be transferred directly to appropriate folders on your new Mac.

For example, your Word documents will be placed in the Documents folder of your Mac (or in appropriate subfolders), while your digital photos will be

## ⏻ Mac Tip

To transfer just a few files between a PC and a Mac, consider using e-mail. Attach the appropriate file(s) to an e-mail message and send it to yourself from your PC. Next, retrieve the e-mail using your Mac, download the e-mail attachment onto your Mac, and then store the file in an appropriate folder. For a small number of large data files, you can use the iDisk feature of Mobile Me to upload the files from your PC and then download them to your Mac.

placed in the Photos folder (or in appropriate subfolder). At the same time, your web browser bookmarks from Internet Explorer will be imported into Safari (the Mac's default web browser), while e-mail messages and accounts will be set up on your behalf to work with the Mail application on your Mac.

If you've purchased your Mac from the Apple online store (apple.com) or from another authorized Apple reseller, you can still have your data transferred by an Apple Genius at any Apple Store; however, a fee of $50 to $150 will apply. To make an appointment with an Apple Genius at any Apple Store, visit apple.com/retail/geniusbar/.

### The Drag-and-Drop/Cut-and-Paste File Transfer Method

Using your PC and a USB external hard drive (or blank CDs), make a copy of all files, folders, and data you wish to transfer to your Mac. Whenever possible, keep the hierarchy of your folders intact, meaning that if you already have a My Documents folder that includes a handful of subfolders containing documents, keep the files in their existing subfolders. Once these files are copied to the external hard drive, disconnect the drive from your PC and plug it into your new Mac. You can now copy and paste or drag and drop the files and folders from the external hard drive to their new and appropriate locations on your Mac.

To do this, on your Mac use the Finder to open the external hard drive's folder(s) containing the data you want to transfer. Next, open a second window using Finder for the location on your Mac where you want the files to end up. There should now be two open folders on your Desktop: the external hard drive folder and the destination folder on your Mac's internal Hard Drive.

Using your mouse, highlight the file(s) and/or folder(s) you want to copy. Click on one file at a time in the Finder to highlight it. To highlight multiple files at once, hold down the Shift key as you highlight each file. Or, if you want to highlight all of the files and subfolders within a folder, use the Select All command available from the Edit pull-down menu on the Menu bar (located at the top of the Desktop). When the appropriate file(s) and/or folder(s) are highlighted (meaning they're selected), use the mouse to drag those files and folders to the destination folder window on your Mac's Desktop. This is the drag-and-drop method.

The alternative to dragging and dropping the files from one folder to another is to use the Copy command found under the Edit pull-down menu on the Menu bar once the appropriate files and folders are highlighted. Next, click the mouse on the window in which you want the files copied to and select the Paste command from the Edit pull-down window. The keyboard shortcuts for Cut and Paste are Command (⌘) + C and Command (⌘) + V, respectively.

Using this method, you can copy one file or folder at a time to your Mac or select groups of files and/or folders. Thus, if you have ten subfolders within your My Documents folder, you can highlight and copy that entire folder to the appropriate Documents folder on your Mac. All subfolders will be copied and their hierarchy will remain intact.

You'll notice that by default, your Mac already has a Documents, Downloads, Movies, Music, and Pictures folder. Within the Finder, you can create additional folders and subfolders to accommodate your various files for different applications. While your Word documents should be placed in the Documents folder (or in subfolders within your Documents folder), you might want to create a folder called Spreadsheets with additional subfolders in the folder to accommodate your Excel files. If you utilize PowerPoint, creating a separate PowerPoint folder for your presentations will help keep all of your files organized and easily accessible on your new Mac.

By default, Microsoft Word or iWork's Pages '08 will store the documents you create in your Mac's Documents folder. However, in all Mac applications, you can change the default location where files will be saved. To change this default file save location in Word, select Preferences from the Word pull-down menu when the program is running. From the Word Preferences window, click on the File Locations icon (under Personal Settings). In the File Location window that appears, you can set the default file saving location for all Word documents, clip art pictures, user templates, and other types of files associated with Word. When the File Locations window is active, either double-click on the file type (such as Documents or Clipart Pictures) or highlight your selection and click on the Modify icon. Using the Finder window that appears, select the location where you want the files to be saved and click on the Choose button. From the Choose a Folder window, you can click on the New Folder icon to create a new folder or subfolder while using Finder.

In PowerPoint, select Preferences under the PowerPoint pull-down menu. When the Preferences window appears, click on the Advanced icon. By clicking on the Select icon that appears next to the Default File Location option, you can create a special PowerPoint folder (and subfolders) and decide where your presentation files will be saved on your Mac.

To change the default location where Excel files will be stored, access the Excel pull-down menu and select Preferences. From the Preferences window, click on the General icon. Next, click on the Select icon next to the Preferred

## ⏻ Mac Tip

If you manually copy your files from a PC to your Mac, you'll want to place each type of file within the appropriate directory on your Mac to keep your files organized. For example, document and PDF files (from your PC's My Documents folder) should go in the Documents folder on your Mac. Files from your PC's My Music folder should be placed in the Music folder on your Mac. Photos and graphic files from your PC's My Pictures folder should be placed in the Pictures folder on your Mac. Of course, in each Mac folder, you can create an unlimited number of subfolders.

File Location option, and choose the folder or subfolder where all Excel files and data will be saved.

After setting up the default save locations for each program, you'll be using often, create the appropriate folders and subfolders you'll need. Then, you can copy your existing files from your PC's applications into the appropriate locations on your Mac.

## Importing Contacts and Schedule Data

Your Mac has a built-in Address Book application for managing your contacts as well as the iCal program for managing your schedule, time, and to-do lists. Instead of using these applications, however, you can opt to use Microsoft Entourage or another Mac application to handle these tasks. All of these applications, however, allow you to import data from another contact management or scheduling program (including PC programs like Microsoft Outlook or Sage Software's Act! Program).

To import your contact and schedule data from a PC application, you'll first need to export that data from your old computer in a format that your Mac will understand. If you'll be using Address Book on your Mac, this application can import data in the vCards format, LDIF format, text file format, or as an Address Book Archive (if you're importing the data from another Mac).

Using your existing contact management software on your PC, use the Export Data feature and select a Mac-compatible format. Save this file on a blank CD or DVD, or an external hard drive that can be connected to your Mac. You can also e-mail this file from your PC to your Mac.

When you're ready to import your contact data, select the Import Data command from the File pull-down menu in Address Book on the Mac. Next, select the file format the PC data was saved in, and follow the on-screen prompts. Additional methods of importing Address Book data are covered in Chapter 7.

If you'll be using iCal on your Mac to handle your schedule, time management, and to-do lists, you can also import existing data from other time management programs, including PC applications like Outlook or Outlook Express. Without using additional software, iCal can import data already in the iCal format, as well as in the vCal format or Entourage data format.

Once you have exported your data from the PC scheduling program you are using, you can import that file by starting iCal and selecting Import from the File pull-down menu. Select the appropriate file format the PC data was saved in, as well as the file's location. Next, click on the Import icon and follow the on-screen prompts.

## Using O2M Software to Transfer Outlook Data to Your Mac

On your PC, if you've been using Outlook, one of the easiest ways to transfer all of your Outlook data (contacts, schedules, to-do lists, notes, e-mails, etc.) is to use a third-party software application called O2M (Outlook to Mac) developed by a company called Little Machines (littlemachines.com).

O2M is a Windows-based program (to be run on your PC) that offers an easy and quick way to transfer all of your Outlook data to be used with the appropriate application on your Mac. Simply load this application, select the Outlook folders you want to export, choose the filtering options you want to use, and click Start. The software will then export your Outlook data so it can easily be imported into Mail, Address Book, and iCal. Or, if you'll be using Microsoft Entourage (which is bundled with Microsoft Office 2008), O2M will place all of your Outlook data appropriately within this application, including all of your e-mails and e-mail attachments. From the Little Machine's website, O2M can be purchased and downloaded for $10.

O2M is compatible with Microsoft Outlook 97, 98, 2000, 2002, 2003, and 2007, as well as with the latest versions of Mail, Address Book, iCal, and Entourage on your Mac. On your Mac, data from Outlook can also be imported into other third-party applications because data can be exported from Outlook in industry-standard formats, such as vCard.

## Transferring Photos

Transferring digital photos and images from a PC to your Mac is extremely easy. Once your photos are copied to an external hard drive on your PC (or onto blank CDs), you can use the drag-and-drop or copy-and-paste method to move them into your Mac's Pictures folder (or appropriate sub-folders).

An even easier method, however, is to use the iPhoto application, which will automatically find new photo images stored on an external hard drive (or on CDs inserted into the Mac's optical drive) and then walk you through the process of importing them, while at the same time, creating separate Events (the iPhoto equivalent to subfolders) to organize your photos, graphics, and digital images on your Mac.

## Transferring Windows Programs to a Mac

Actual programs installed on your PC will not operate on your Mac while it's running the Mac OS X operating system. Thus, you cannot transfer actual programs or software between your PC and a Mac.

As you'll discover in Chapter 6, however, you can use special software to install and run Microsoft Windows XP or Windows Vista on your Mac. Using this process, you can then install and run Windows applications on your Mac (when it's running Windows). To do this, however, you'll need the original program discs for each Windows application you'd like to install on your Mac. Or, you'll need to download the applications and install them again while your Mac is running Windows.

## Using Migration Assistant

Migration Assistant is a utility built into the Mac OS X operating system. Using Finder, select the Applications window. Next, double-click on the Utilities window found in the Applications window. You'll find Migration Assistant in the Utilities folder on your Mac.

Use Migration Assistant to transfer both programs and data from one Mac to another, without having to re-install any software or drivers. This application only works from Mac to Mac, and will copy all applications, files, user accounts, network and computer settings, folders, and data between two Macs that are connected using a Firewire cable.

Migration Assistant must be running on both Macs. The software itself will walk you step by step through the file and data transfer process. Before proceeding, however, be sure to create a backup of both Macs using the Time Machine software (see Chapter 11).

## PC to Mac: The iTornado Data Transfer Solution

Whether you want to transfer files and data between a PC and a Mac or two different Macs, there's a fast and easy way to do this using the iTornado, third-party software/accessory package from Data Drive Thru (214-459-8359/the tornado.com). The $79.95 package includes a special USB cable and software that directly connects a PC to a Mac (or two Macs together) and allows data to be transferred with ease, using a drag-and-drop user interface and a step-by-step process that the software guides you through.

For people who don't consider themselves to be very computer savvy but who need to transfer data and files between a PC and a Mac safely and securely, iTornado is the best solution (aside from having a certified Apple Genius from an Apple Store do the data transfer). To use iTornado, simply connect the four-foot USB cable from your PC to your Mac. Special software automatically loads on both computers, and within seconds, you'll see a split screen showing the file hierarchy of both computers. Using a two-step method, select which files and folders you want to copy from your PC and then the appropriate destination(s) on your Mac. Once the files and their destinations have been selected, click the mouse on the Continue icon, and your files will be transferred between computers.

 **Mac Tip**

If you need help transferring your data using iTornado, visit the company's website and watch the video tutorials that walk you through the process. Point your web browser to datadrive thru.com/training-videos/.

Using iTornado, you can also copy files from a Mac back to a PC, so if other people in your office still use PCs, you can easily transfer files back and fourth between your computer and theirs.

One of the best things about iTornado is that it's designed for nontechnically-oriented people. It provides a true seamless data transfer solution. According to the company, "When connected to the USB ports of two computers, iTornado immediately initiates a peer-to-peer network via its patented No Software To Load (NSTL) technology, which auto-loads and auto-runs the software and drivers needed to move the data bi-directionally from one computer to another, via a user-friendly split-screen display that within seconds appears on the monitor of both machines showing the contents of each machine. From this interface, files can be dragged and dropped from one machine to another at speeds up to 25MB per second."

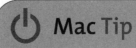

**Mac Tip**

Be sure to purchase the iTornado product, not DataDrive Tornado product (which only supports data and file transfer between two PCs).

## Transferring Files and Data Between a PC and Mac Using Move2Mac

Move2Mac from Detto Technologies (866-338-8663/detto.com/mac-file-trans fer.html) is similar to iTornado. It's a $49.95 software/USB cable bundle that also includes everything needed to transfer files between a PC and a Mac.

In addition to copying your data files from your PC applications to your Mac, Move2Mac also copies your Internet Explorer favorites and bookmarks to Safari. In fact, the software and cable combo is designed to migrate documents, folders, spreadsheets, photos, music, files, Internet Explorer Favorites, Internet Explorer Home Page, graphics, databases, address books, and backgrounds from a PC to your Mac.

Using Move2Mac, other PC programs you can export files and data from (and import them to similar application programs on your Mac) include Act!, Microsoft Project, Outlook (or Outlook Express), Microsoft Office, Microsoft Money, and Quicken. To transfer Outlook e-mail to a Mac, you'll want to use the O2M software described earlier in this chapter.

According to the company, when a PC and Mac are connected via the supplied USB cable and the Move2Mac software is used, it'll take approximately 15 minutes to transfer 500MB of files or data. If you're using a Parallel port (on your PC) to USB port (on your Mac) connection, the process will take a bit longer.

As you'd expect, when files and folders are transferred between machines, Move2Mac preserves the folder structure. For example, the Windows folder My

## ⏻ Mac Tip

The USB cable that comes bundled with the Move2Mac package must be used exclusively to transfer data between a Mac and PC using the supplied software. It is not a standard USB cable that can connect your Mac to a printer, for example. The Move2Mac application can only be used to transfer files and data from a PC to a Mac, not vice versa (like iTornado). The single user license for this software only allows for data to be transferred from one specific PC to an unlimited number of Macs, not from an unlimited number of PCs to an unlimited number of Macs.

Documents, its contents, and its subfolders will be moved to the Mac and placed in the appropriate Documents folder.

Move2Mac is used exclusively for transferring files and data between a Mac and PC. It does not move applications or convert PC files to Mac format. Most applications, however, have a PC version and a Mac version, so no file conversion is required. In cases when file conversion is required, this is typically something that can be done using the data import feature of a particular program.

## Setting Up Your E-Mail Account(s)

Some file transfer applications automatically take your data from Microsoft Outlook, for example, and import it into Mail or Entourage on your Mac. This means you do not have to configure your e-mail account settings on your Mac, whether you're using Mail, Entourage, or another e-mail application.

If, however, you won't be transferring existing e-mail data from your PC (or from another Mac), the first time you run Mail or Entourage, you'll need to configure your existing e-mail account(s). This process takes just a few minutes and is a straightforward process, assuming you have the correct configuration information, which is supplied by your e-mail service provider.

## Configuring Your E-Mail Account(s) in Mail

The first time you run Mail on your Mac, you'll be instructed to configure your existing POP e-mail account. You can add an unlimited number of e-mail accounts, such as work e-mail and personal e-mail.

From the Mail pull-down menu (when the Mail program is running), select Preferences. When the Preferences window opens (see Figures 5.1 and 5.2), click on the Accounts icon at the top of the window (look for the blue-and-white @ symbol). To add a new account, click on the plus sign (+) in the

*Figure 5.1*

As you create a new account using Mail, you'll need to fill in the appropriate information when the Incoming Mail Server window appears.

lower-right corner of the Accounts window. A new Add Account window will appear that contains three fields:

1. *Full name.* Enter your full name in this field.
2. *E-mail address.* Type your full (existing) e-mail address in this field.
3. *Password.* Enter your e-mail account's password.

*Figure 5.2*

Be sure to choose the correct type of e-mail account when setting one up. Your choices are POP, IMAP, or Exchange. Your e-mail service provider will give you the appropriate information needed to properly configure your pre-existing e-mail account.

Once you've filled in these three fields, click on the Continue icon in the lower-right corner of the Add Account window. The Incoming Mail Server window will now appear. This window contains the following five fields you must fill in:

1. *Account type.* Select POP, IMAP, or Exchange, depending on what type of e-mail account you'll be setting up. Your e-mail account provider will provide this information. For personal e-mail addresses, you will probably be setting up a POP account. If you're configuring a business/company e-mail address supplied by your employer (through its network), you'll need to configure either an IMAP or Exchange account.

2. *Description.* Type a simple description of this e-mail account, such as "Personal E-mail," "Work E-mail," "Yahoo! Mail," or "Hot Mail."

3. *Incoming mail service.* This is information that will be supplied by your e-mail service provider. It will be in the following format, but must be customized for your specific e-mail service provider (mail.example.com).

4. *User name.* Type your e-mail account's exact username here.

5. *Password.* Type your existing e-mail account's password here. Dots will appear instead of what you actually type.

If you have any questions about what to enter in any of these fields, simply click on the question mark icon in the lower-left corner of the Incoming Mail Server window. When all five fields have been properly filled in, click on the Continue icon in the lower-right corner of the Incoming Mail Server window. Upon clicking Continue, the message "Checking connection to e-mail server" is displayed.

To complete the next step in the e-mail account configuration process (which only needs to be done once for each account), the Incoming Mail Security window appears. Unless your e-mail service provider instructs you otherwise, leave the default options as is and click on the Continue icon in the lower-right corner of the Incoming Mail Security window.

Next, you'll need to enter information pertaining to your existing e-mail account's outgoing mail server. The Outgoing Mail Server window will appear. Once again, you'll use information provided by your e-mail service provider to fill in each field correctly. In the Description field, enter a brief description of your e-mail account. Within the Outgoing Mail Server field, however, you must enter the information provided by your e-mail service provider in the following format: "smtp.example.com." The outgoing server is used to send the e-mails you create to their appropriate destinations. In most cases, you can leave the Use Authentication option and related User Name and Password fields empty, unless instructed to do otherwise by your e-mail account provider.

When the appropriate fields within the Outgoing Mail Server window have been properly filled in, click on the Continue icon in the lower-right corner of this window. The Outgoing Mail Security window now appears. Unless instructed otherwise by your e-mail account provider, leave the defaults as is, and simply click on the Continue icon in the lower-right corner of this window.

An Account Summary window will now appear. Review that all of the information you've entered is correct and then click on the Create icon in the lower-right corner of the window. If you notice a typo, click on the Go Back icon to the appropriate window and adjust your entries.

Your existing e-mail account is now configured and ready to be used with Mail. You will be returned to the Accounts window of the Mail application. You can customize the program by clicking on the Mailbox Behaviors or Advanced tabs located near the top of this window. Or, you can click on any of the command icons at the top of the Accounts window to adjust various features of the Mail application. To close this window, click on the red dot in the upper-left corner of the window.

You'll need to repeat this process for each of your e-mail accounts. If you'll be using Microsoft Entourage to manage your e-mail (or another third-party e-mail application), you will have to complete a similar process for each existing e-mail account in order to configure it for that e-mail application.

# Setting Up iChat and Your Instant Messaging Account(s)

Windows Live Messenger (get.live.com/messenger), AOL Instant Messenger (aim.com), Yahoo! Messenger (messenger.yahoo.com), and Google Talk (google.com/talk) offer free, service-specific downloads for their various online instant messaging (IM) services. These services allow for real-time communication using text, voice, and/or web-based videoconferences. The Mac OS X operating system comes bundled with iChat, which is compatible with several of the popular instant messaging services.

If you haven't already done so, you'll need to set up a free account with one or more of these services by visiting their respective websites. Then, you can configure iChat to work with the services you've selected and incorporate your personalized account information (your username and password).

Once you've set up a Mobile Me, AIM, Google Talk, or Jabber account, launch iChat. From the iChat pull-down menu, select Preferences. When the Preferences window appears, click on the Accounts icon. To create a new account, click on the + icon in the lower-left corner of the window (see Figure

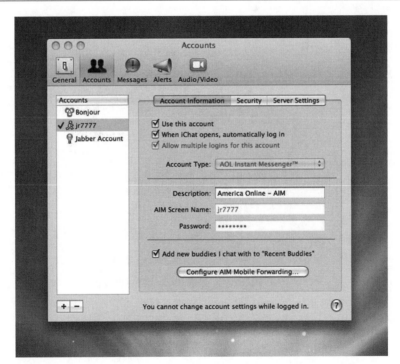

*Figure 5.3*
Before you can use iChat, you must set up a free account with one of the supported instant messaging services and then configure the iChat software accordingly by entering your username and password.

5.3). There will be three fields in the Account Setup window (see Figure 5.4) that appears, including:

1. *Account type*. Select from Mobile Me, AIM, Jabber, or Google Talk.
2. *Account/user name*. Enter the username you've registered with the specific IM service.
3. *Password*. Enter the password you selected when registering your IM account.

When you've entered the appropriate information in these three fields, click on the Done icon in the lower-right corner of the Account Setup window.

*Figure 5.4*
Membership to the Mobile Me service can be purchased online or at any Apple retailer. *Photo courtesy of Apple.*

You can now log onto your preferred instant messenger service and communicate with the people in your friends or buddy list. In addition to sending and receiving real-time text messages or videoconferences (using your Mac's built-in iSight camera, microphone, and speakers), you can also send and receive files directly with someone on your friends/buddy list.

## Syncing Your Apple iPhone, iPod Touch, or iPod

For connecting your Mac with an iPhone, iPod Touch, or iPod, you'll need to use the iTunes application, which in addition to being a syncing program is designed to manage your music (audio) and video files on your Mac and to connect you directly to the iTunes online store so you can purchase and download music, TV show episodes, and movies, and rent movies. Your iPhone, iPod Touch, or iPod came with a USB cable and/or docking station for connecting the unit to your Mac.

In addition to syncing your video and music files, iTunes allows you to sync your iCal and Address Book data with your iPhone, iPod Touch, or iPod, as well as photos archived using iPhoto. By the time you read this book, if you're using an iPhone or iPod Touch, you'll also be able to use iTunes to download hundreds of specialized applications that can be transferred and used on your iPhone or iPod Touch.

Additional information about iTunes can be found in Chapter 10 or by visiting apple.com/itunes/.

## Syncing Your BlackBerry or Smartphone (PDA) with Your Mac

As a BlackBerry or smartphone (PDA) user, chances are you'll want to sync your Address Book and iCal data with your PDA device. Using the iSync application, which comes bundled with Mac OS X Leopard, you can connect your phone or PDA device to the Mac via a USB cable (or Bluetooth) and determine what information will be shared.

**Mac Tip**

Aside from the third-party syncing software available from Mark/Space, there are other programs available for connecting specific types of PDAs and smartphones to the Mac for syncing purposes. To find these applications, visit the Downloads section of the Apple website and search the Productivity Tools category (apple.com /downloads/macosx /productivity_tools/).

The iSync application can be found in your Mac's Applications folder. When your smartphone or PDA device is connected to your Mac, the software will walk you through the syncing process. Depending on what type of smartphone or PDA you're connecting, it may be necessary to download and use additional syncing software. For example, if you're using a Palm OS-based PDA or smartphone, iSync will need to be used in conjunction with Palm's HotSync software. Additional software will also be needed for syncing your Mac with a Pocket PC device. To view an updated list of smartphones and PDAs that are compatible with iSync, visit apple.com/macosx/features/isync/.

Mark/Space offers specialized syncing software for BlackBerry, iPhone, Palm OS, Sony PSP, Symbian, and Windows Mobile devices. Priced at $39.95, and available for purchase and downloading from the company's website (markspace.com), the Missing Link for BlackBerry, for example, allows you to sync contact data from Address Book, scheduling data from iCal, photos from iPhoto, and notes created using the Mark/Space Notebook application on your Mac. Using this software, you can also synchronize iTunes play lists and unprotected music files. Using this third-party software makes the syncing process easier because much of the configuration settings are automatically set for you.

When setting up iSync or most syncing applications for the first time, you'll need to determine if you want to merge the data between your Mac and device, or if you want the Mac data or PDA/smartphone data to overwrite the other. Be sure to create backups before doing this because it's easy to accidentally overwrite and delete important data.

# Run Windows XP or Windows Vista on Your Mac

Before you start learning about the different software applications created specifically for Macs, the next chapter offers information for new Mac users who are interested in running the Window XP or Windows Vista operating system on their Mac (in addition to or instead of Mac OS X) so they can run Windows-based programs and applications.

One reason why this might be necessary is if you've opted to give up your PC and use a Mac, but your office or place of employment still predominantly operates using specialized, vertical market or proprietary software created for and exclusively available on Windows.

The ability to run Windows applications on your Mac gives you the best of both computing worlds. You can run your Windows-based applications when it's absolutely necessary, or you can enjoy the convenience and functionality of programs designed specifically for the Mac OS X operating system.

# Running Windows Programs on a Mac

F OR THE MAJORITY OF PEOPLE WHO SWITCH TO A MAC, MOST (IF NOT ALL) OF THE applications they ran on their PC are also available for the Mac, or there's a comparable program that will import their PC data files. But for some, necessary applications require Windows.

If you've made the decision to switch from a PC to a Mac, the primary reason you want to run Windows XP or Windows Vista on your new machine is probably that you need to use proprietary software that only

## Mac Tip

The Boot Camp program comes pre-installed on all Macs running Mac OS X Leopard. You'll find this application in the Utilities folder (a subfolder of the Applications folder on your Mac).

runs on a PC. (You may also be experiencing separation anxiety from your PC. After a few more weeks using your Mac, that anxiety should disappear forever.)

There are still certain types of applications (albeit a shrinking list) that still run exclusively under the Windows operating system. If you absolutely require access to Windows and Windows applications at work, you can still transfer to Mac, but you'll want to install both the Windows and Mac OS X operating systems on your machine. This will allow you to have full access to your Windows-only application(s), yet benefit from being able do the rest of your computing in the Mac OS X environment.

If you opt to run Windows XP or Windows Vista on your Mac, there are several ways to do this. You will, however, need to use a special program, such as Boot Camp, Parallels Desktop, or VMware Fusion on your Mac (while still running Mac OS X), in order to install and run the Windows operating system. Installing Windows also requires that you have original Microsoft Windows XP

## Mac Tip

To install Windows XP or Windows Vista onto a Mac, you must have an original full-install Windows disc. (Service Pack 2 is required if you're installing Windows XP.) A Windows XP or Windows Vista upgrade disc will not work. Much to the disappointment of many Windows users, Microsoft has opted to discontinue the Windows XP operating system in favor of Windows Vista. Thus, if you have not already purchased the Windows XP operating system at retail, you'll probably be forced to install Windows Vista (so good luck with that).

or Windows Vista installation CDs. Once Windows is running on your Mac, you'll then need to install each Windows-based application on the Mac while it's running under the Windows operating system. Your original Mac OS X Leopard disc may also be required.

Thanks to the Intel microchips inside your Mac, you should notice little or no speed reduction when running Windows. All Windows applications should run as if they are running on a Windows-based PC.

# Installing Windows XP or Windows Vista on Your Mac

Whether you use Boot Camp (a software application bundled with Mac OS X Leopard), Desktop Parallels from Parallels Software International (425-282-6400/parallels.com), or another third-party software application designed to allow you to install and run Windows XP or Windows Vista on your Mac, the software you utilize for this purpose will leave all of your Mac programs and data in place that are currently saved on your Mac's primary Hard Drive. A new and separate partition, however, will be created on your Mac's primary Hard Drive. This separate area of the Hard Drive will be used exclusively for Windows and your Windows applications.

There is a big difference between Boot Camp and VMware Fusion or Parallels Desktop. Using either of these commercially available programs, both Mac and PC applications can run simultaneously, so you can switch back and forth without rebooting your computer. This is not possible using Boot Camp (the application bundled with the Mac OS X operating system).

In essence by installing Windows, you'll be giving your Mac a split personality. From

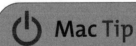

## Mac Tip

The Parallels Desktop software ($79.99) is available from the Parallels website (parallels.com), or it can be purchased wherever Mac software is sold, including all Apple Stores. A free demo version of the software is available for download from the Parallels website or the Downloads section of Apple.com.

## Mac Tip

Another third-party software application that is very similar to Parallels Desktop in terms of its functionality is VMware Fusion (877-486-9273 /vmware.com/products/fusion). Using an intuitive Mac-native interface, VMware Fusion provides a seamless way to run Windows applications on a Mac. Using Expose (a feature built into the Mac OS X operating system), you can instantly switch between Mac and PC applications running at the same time. VMware Fusion is $79.99, and can be purchased and downloaded from the company's website. A retail version of the software is also available wherever Mac software is sold.

the same hard drive, you will be able to run Windows and/or the Mac OS X operating system, along with programs/applications designed exclusively for each one.

A benefit to running Windows on your Mac is that you don't have to worry about downloading and installing dozens of different Windows drivers to make your Windows applications work with your printer(s) and other peripherals. All of your Mac's settings will be utilized.

## Mac Tip

In addition to meeting the hard disk space requirements, your Mac must have at least 2GB of RAM installed to run efficiently.

Once Boot Camp and the Windows operating system are installed, when you first turn on your Mac, you can decide which operating system should boot up. Hold down the Option key when you power up and choose either Mac OS X or Windows. If you choose Windows, you will be able to run all of your Windows-based applications. If you choose Mac OS X, you'll be able to run all of your Mac applications.

One benefit to the Parallels Desktop and VMware Fusion software is that you can switch between running Windows XP or Windows Vista and the Mac OS X operating system without having to reboot your computer. Windows programs can be run on your Mac Desktop, and you can use the Mac's Expose feature to switch between applications. These software applications also allow you to open Windows files with Mac applications. You can also drag-and-drop files and folders between the Mac OS X and Windows environments.

Before installing and running Boot Camp, Parallels Desktop, or VMware Fusion and then the Windows operating system, be sure to make a backup of your entire Mac Hard Drive using Time Machine.

The steps for installing the Windows operating system and Windows applications onto your Mac are as follows:

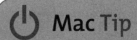

**Mac Tip**

To run Windows and Windows applications on your Mac, you must have plenty of available hard disk space to install the Windows operating system and your Windows applications, as well as the Boot Camp, Parallels Desktop, or VMware Fusion software. At least 10GB to 15GB of additional hard disk space is also needed for your applications to run properly.

1. Back up your Mac's Hard Drive.
2. If you're using a MacBook, MacBook Pro, or MacBook Air, be sure the computer is plugged in and not running on battery power.
3. Install and run either the Boot Camp software (bundled with the Mac OS X operating system), the Parallels Desktop software, the VMware Fusion software, or another third-party software application that allows you to install Windows on your Mac. Figures 6.1 and 6.2 show screens from the easy installation procedure involved with loading Parallels Desktop and the Windows operating system onto your Mac.
4. Once Boot Camp (or an equivalent program) is installed and running, follow the on-screen prompts offered by that software to install a 32-bit version of Windows XP (with Service Pack 2) or Windows Vista.

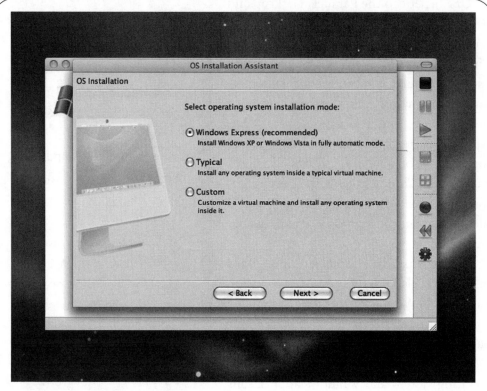

*Figure 6.1*
When running Parallels Desktop, the software will walk you through the process of installing
either Windows XP or Windows Vista on your Mac. Simply follow the on-screen prompts.

5. Install the necessary drivers, based on what's recommended by Boot Camp or the software you're using after Windows is installed.

6. When your Mac is running under the Windows operating system, install your individual Windows applications using the original installation CDs, just as you would on a PC.

7. For detailed directions on how to install Windows XP or Vista using Boot Camp, download and print the free Boot Camp Installation & Setup Guide from the Apple website (manuals.info.apple.com/en/Boot_ Camp_Install-Setup.pdf).

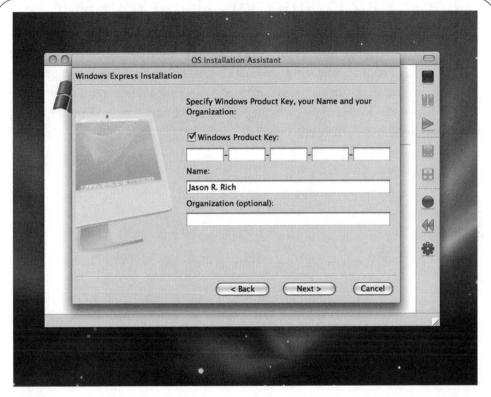

*Figure 6.2*
Just as you would when installing Windows XP or Windows Vista on a PC, you'll need to enter the
Windows Product Key that's provided by Microsoft. The full-install version of either Windows XP
or Windows Vista is required.

## ⏻ Mac Tip

If you'll be using Parallels Desktop to install and run Windows, install this software on your Mac and then follow the on-screen prompts for installing
Windows once the Parallels Desktop software is running.

## Boost Your Productivity Using Your Mac

Whether you opt to configure your Mac to also run Windows applications, chances are that the majority of programs you do run on your Mac will use the Mac OS X Leopard operating system. The next chapter focuses on some of the applications built into the Mac OS X operating system that will help you improve your productivity by managing your schedule, maintaining a database of contacts, and surfing the web.

# CHAPTER 7

# Address Book, iCal, and Surfing the Web

YOU ALREADY KNOW THAT THE MAC OS X OPERATING SYSTEMS IS CHOCK FULL OF programs designed to create a comprehensive, intuitive, and effi-cient computing experience for Mac users. This chapter focuses on Address Book, iCal, and Safari, programs that come bundled with all Macs and that give users the power to efficiently manage their contacts, handle their scheduling, and surf the web.

## ⏻ Mac Tip

Depending on your needs, there are multiple software alternatives to Address Book, iCal, and Safari applications that offer improved or varied functionality. For example, Microsoft Office's Entourage 2008 (see Chapter 8) is a powerful scheduling, time management, and e-mail program. Filemaker's Bento (see Chapter 10) can be used to effectively manage a detailed contact database and address book. When it comes to surfing the web, Mozilla's Foxfire (foxfire.com) is a free web browser alternative that's popular with Mac users. It typically offers better access to certain websites that Safari isn't completely compatible with.

# An Introduction to Address Book

Located on your Dock is a program icon for Address Book, the Mac OS X's solution to managing your personal and business contacts. It's an electronic address book application that works seamlessly with other Mac applications, such as Mail and iChat, so critical information about the people you know and work with is always available at your fingertips.

Address Book is a digital alternative to an old-fashioned Rolodex, capable of managing a vast database of information relating to friends, family, co-workers, customers, and clients. Each contact is stored as a unique Address Book Card entry, and can contain the following details:

- Contact's Photo
- First Name
- Last Name
- Job Title
- Company
- Work Phone
- Mobile Phone
- Home Phone

- Work E-mail
- Home E-mail
- Friend/Assistant/Spouse Name
- AIM/Jabber/MSN/ICQ/Yahoo! User Name
- Work Address
- Home Address
- Notes

## Finding Your Way Around Address Book

Like all Mac programs, Address Book's functions and commands can be accessed from the Menu Bar located across the top of the Desktop. From left to right, you'll find the following pull-down menu options:

- *Apple.* This is the same pull-down menu that's available regardless of what application you're running. Options include: About This Mac, Software Update, Mac OS X Software, System Preferences, Dock, Location, Recent Items, Force Quit, Sleep, Restart, Shut Down, and Log Out [user-name].
- *Address Book.* From this pull-down menu, you can access the About Address Book screen (which displays your software's version number and copyright information), adjust the program's Preferences, Hide the address book window, Hide other windows on your Desktop, Show All windows on your Desktop, or Quit the Address Book application. The keyboard shortcut to Quit Address Book is Command (⌘) + Q.
- *File.* From this pull-down menu, you can select New Card (to create a new contact card), New Group (to create a new group of contacts), Close a Group, Import or Export Address Book data, Subscribe to an Address Book (if you're a member of Mobile Me), Send Updates from your Address Book to your subscribers (if you're a member of Mobile Me), and Print your address book data.
- *Edit.* In addition to the typical commands you'd find under the Edit pull-down menu of any program (such as Undo, Redo, Cut, Copy, Paste, Delete, and Select All), you can also Rename a Group, Edit a Card, and Edit a Distribution List from this pull-down menu in Address Book.

- *View*. Choose the on-screen view you'll use with Address Book. Your choices include Card and Columns, Card Only, and Directories.
- *Card*. The commands under this pull-down menu allow you to select which Cards in your database you wish to view, look for duplicate Cards, and add fields to the default format of your Cards.
- *Window*. Minimize the Address Book program window, increase the size of the window (Zoom) when it's active, or bring all related Address Book windows to the front of the Desktop using the commands under this pull-down menu.
- *Help*. Access the Help sections of Address Book.

## Understanding the Program Window

When viewing the Card and Columns View in Address Book, the program window is divided into three sections (see Figure 7.1). On the left is a listing of Groups. Using Address Book, you can create many different groups of names, so you can separate your personal contacts from your business contacts. From the File pull-down menu, select the New Group command to create any number of Groups to accommodate your needs.

To the right of the Groups list is the Names list. This is a listing of all names within your Groups database. If you select All under Groups, a comprehensive list of all of your contacts, in all of your Groups will be displayed.

On the right side of the Address Book program window, when utilizing the Card and Columns View (Figure 7.1), you'll see the detailed Card information for the active Card. In the upper-right corner of the program window, you'll see the familiar Searchlight field. Here, you can type any search criteria, such as

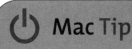 **Mac Tip**

One nice feature of Address Book is that the contact information you enter is automatically saved. There's no need to manually save your data each time you add a new entry or before you exit the program. It is a good idea, however, to periodically back up your Address Book data (a topic covered later in this chapter, as well as in Chapter 11).

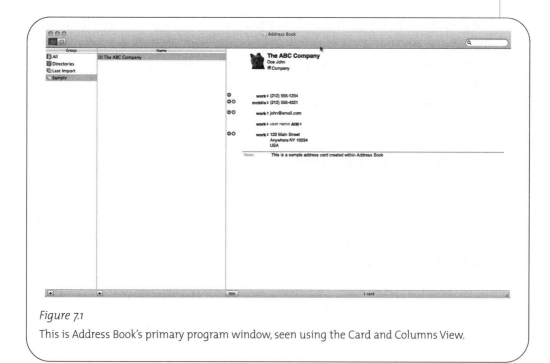

*Figure 7.1*

This is Address Book's primary program window, seen using the Card and Columns View.

a name, company name, phone number, city, state, zip, or anything you can remember about a contact in order to quickly locate that entry.

Along the bottom of the Address Book program window, you'll find a plus-sign icon (+) below the Group and Name columns. Clicking on the icon below the Group column, you can quickly create a new Group. By clicking the plus-sign icon (+) below the Name icon, you can quickly add a new Contact entry by creating a new Card within your Address Book database. (This same task can be accomplished by selecting the New Card command found under the File pull-down menu or by using the Command (⌘) + N keyboard shortcut.)

Found under the Card area of Address Book program screen, to the right of the two plus-sign icons, is an icon labeled Edit. Clicking on this icon allows you to edit the Card entry that's displayed in the Card section above. For example, you'd use this Edit command if you wanted to add or modify a phone number, e-mail address, or note that's related to the entry.

In the upper-left corner of the Address Book program window, you'll find the familiar red, yellow, and green dots for closing, minimizing, and zooming the program window itself. Just below these three icons (found on all windows that appear on your Desktop) is a screen view icon. This allows you to switch between the Card and Columns View and the less cluttered Card Only view that Address Book offers. In the lower-right corner of the program window is the familiar icon for resizing the window using the mouse.

## Adding and Editing Contacts

When you first start using Address Book, you can import your contact data from another application that you used on your old computer (such as Outlook or Act!), or you can re-enter each contact manually. When Address Book is running, there are three ways to add a new contact (i.e., create a new Card within your Address Book database):

1. Select the New Card command found under the File pull-down menu.
2. Use the Command (⌘) + N keyboard shortcut.
3. Click on the plus-sign icon displayed under the Name column within the Address Book program window.

Upon selecting the New Card command, a blank card will appear on the right-most pane of the program window when using the Card and Columns View (see Figure 7.2). Now, you can manually enter the new contact's details, starting with her last name. The Card field that's highlighted in light-blue is

## ⏻ Mac Tip

From the Address Book pull-down menu, you can select Preferences and then determine how your database will be sorted. You can select by Last Name or First Name. This determines the order your entries will be displayed in the Name column (when using the Card and Columns View) or when you print out a directory of contacts.

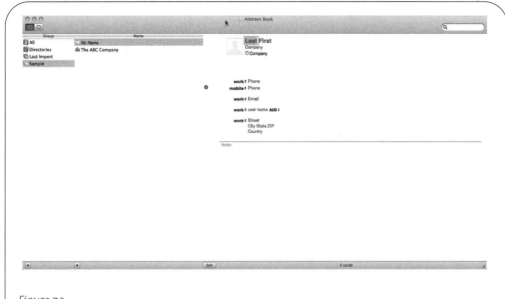

*Figure 7.2*
Upon adding a New Card to your Address Book database, you can manually type in a new contact's details, including her name, address(es), phone number(s), e-mail addresses, and so on.

the one where you can type in new information. Use the Tab or Return/Enter key to move to the next field.

Below the new contact's Last and First Name, you can enter her Company Name. There's also a box that you can check using the mouse that allows you to determine if this particular Card will be filed and sorted based on the Company Name or the contact's name. If a checkmark is placed next to the Company, the Card will be filed in the database based on the Company Name.

After entering the Last Name, First Name, and Company Name on the Card you're creating, you have the option of importing a photo of the contact to be displayed in the photo square next to the contact's name. Click the mouse on the empty photo box to pull up the photo import screen (Figure 7.3).

When the photo import screen is visible, you can click on the camera icon, found in the lower region of the window, to activate the Mac's iSight camera to instantly take a photo. An alternative is to click the mouse on the Choose icon

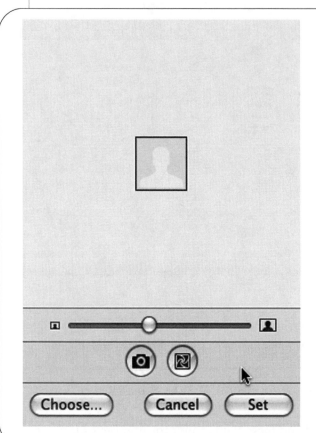

*Figure 7.3*
As you create a new Card in your Address Book contact database, you can add the person's photo by clicking the mouse on the empty photo box located next to the name. This photo import screen will appear.

and import a photo that's already saved on your computer's Hard Drive. When the photo appears in the photo import screen, you can crop it using the image magnification/reduction slide bar found just below the image itself. Use the mouse to move the slide bar left or right to increase or decrease the image size and crop it accordingly. When the photo appears exactly as you'd like it to in your Address Book database, click the mouse on the Set icon in the lower-right corner of the photo import screen.

Use the Tab key or the mouse to position the on-screen cursor over the next blank Card data field you'll like to fill in, and then start filling in the phone number(s), e-mail address(es), addresses, and notes related to that contact.

As you fill in a Card, you can leave any field blank if it does not apply. By clicking on the small green plus icon or red minus icon, you can add additional fields or remove unneeded data fields from the Card while in Edit mode. You can also add additional fields on a Card by selecting the Add Field command found under the Card pull-down menu. This allows you to select from more than 15 field types, such as Job Title, Department, Maiden Name, URL, Birthday, or Instant Messaging Username.

Once you've added all of the contact's details into his Address Book Card, simply click the mouse on either the Group or any Name within the Names column to automatically save the data and continue using the program. Or, you can choose the Select New Card command or execute another command within the program.

At any time, you can go back and edit a Card by displaying the Card you want to edit and then clicking the mouse on the Edit icon that appears at the bottom of the program window.

## Accessing Your Contacts Using Spotlight

One you've compiled your Address Book database, either by importing contacts from another address book or contact management program or by manually entering each contact's information, you can search and access the information in your Address Book database very easily when the Address Book program is running. You can find and view entries in your Address Book easily:

1. From the Card and Columns View, scroll up or down the Name column, highlight the entry you wish to view, and click on the entry with your mouse.

2. Use the Spotlight field in the upper-right corner of the Address Book program window and type in any keyword or search phrase related to the entry you're looking for: first name, last name, company name, city, state, or any piece of information (or partial piece of information) found in your Address Book database. For example, in the Spotlight field, if you type "John," every entry containing the word *John*, anywhere within the entry, will be listed in the Name column. You can then choose which specific entry you want to view in detail.

**Mac Tip**

To import contact data from a Palm OS PDA or wireless device, such as a Treo, first download the free iSync Palm Conduit software (apple.com /isync). You can then sync your Palm OS device with Address Book using iSync on your Mac and HotSync on your Palm device.

## Importing Your Contact Data

If you've created and maintained a contact database using a PC–based program (or even another Mac program), you can easily import all of your contact data into Address Book, without having to manually re-enter dozens, hundreds, or even thousands of names, addresses, and phone numbers.

All address book and contact management programs, such as Microsoft Outlook or Act!, for example, allow you to export your contact database using one of several widely recognized formats. Address Book has the ability to important data that's been saved by another program in a vCards, LDIF, tab-delimited, or comma-separated values (CSV) format.

From whatever program your contact database is currently in, select the database Export option and choose one of the previously mentioned formats. Save the file onto a CD or thumb drive, or e-mail yourself the exported data file. Next, open the Address Book program on your Mac and select the Import command from the File pull-down menu. Select the format your address book data (your exported file) has been saved in (vCards, LDIF, Text File, or Address Book Archive), and follow the on-screen prompts to import your data. This process also works for importing contact information from smartphones and wireless PDA devices (aside from the iPhone or iTouch, which can be synchronized using iTunes).

Depending on the size of your contact database, exporting your current database from your old address book or contact management program and then importing the data into Address Book should take between 10 and 30 minutes.

## Synchronizing Your Contacts with Other Computers and Users

The ability of your Mac to exchange files with other Macs makes sharing and synchronizing your Address Book data with other people (or yourself if you have a Mac desktop and MacBook notebook computer) easy. Address Book is fully compatible with the Mobile Me online service (see Chapter 9 for details about this optional service offered by Apple).

Using your Mobile Me account, not only can you automatically back up your Address Book data to a remote location on the web, you can easily and automatically synchronize your Address Book data with other Macs. This means that your Address Book's entries will always remain identical on each of your Mac computers. So, if you add or edit an entry on one computer, those changes will automatically become part of your Address Book file on each computer you have synchronized together.

To synchronize multiple Address Book databases on different Macs, you must first subscribe to the Mobile Me service. Next, from the Address Book pull-down menu, select Preferences. When the Preferences window appears, click on the General icon and add a checkmark next to the Synchronize My Contacts With Other Computers Using Mobile Me option.

## ⏻ Mac Tip

By subscribing to other Address Books (an option found under the File pull-down menu), your Address Book database can synchronize with the Address Book databases of other Mac users (assuming you're given permission to do this). If there's another .Mac member with whom you'd like to synchronize your Address Book data, you'll need to know that other subscriber's .Mac e-mail address. Using this option, the other user can make it so you can either just view his Address Book contacts, or adjust the settings so you can edit, add, or delete Cards from his database as well as your own. To set up Address Book sharing, choose the Preferences option from the Address Book pull-down menu. Select the Share Your Address Book check box. Click the Add (+) button and then select the .Mac accounts you'd like to share your data with. You can then send an e-mail invitation to that other .Mac user.

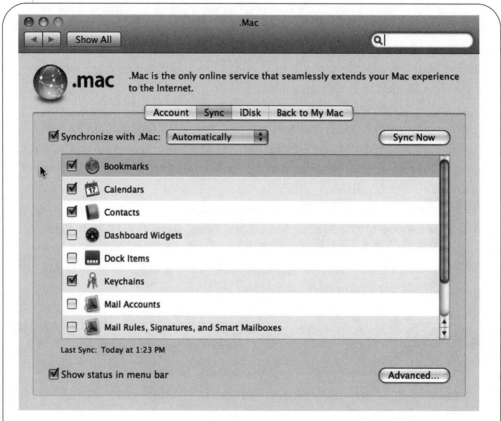

*Figure 7.4*

From this .Mac Preferences window, click on the Sync icon to set your Mac so it will sync the data you want with your other Macs. The new Mobile Me service, which replaced the .Mac service, may look a bit different, but the service should offer similar functionality.

Continue by clicking the mouse on the Mobile Me icon found below where you just placed the checkmark next to the Synchronize My Contacts With Other Computers Using Mobile Me option. Doing this will open the Mobile Me preferences window. When this window appears, click on the Sync icon near the top of the window (located next to Account, as seen in Figure 7.4).

In the main portion of the Mobile Me window, once the Sync option is selected, use the mouse to place a checkmark next to Contacts. This instructs your Mac to synchronize your Address Book data with other Macs. You must

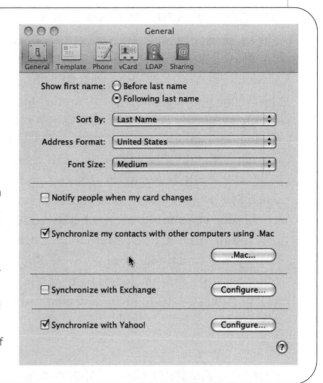

*Figure 7.5*

From the Address Book pull-down menu, select Preferences, and then General. From this window, you can instruct Address Book to automatically synchronize with other Macs using the Mobile Me service, with Microsoft Exchange, or with Yahoo!. If you have additional questions about how this is done, click on the purple question mark icon that appears in the lower-right corner of this window.

do this on each of your Macs that will be logging into your Mobile Me account in order to synchronize data.

In addition to synchronizing your Address Book data with other Macs, you can also automatically synchronize your data with any computer running Microsoft Exchange, Yahoo!, or Microsoft Entourage 2008. To synchronize with Microsoft Exchange, access the Address Book's Preferences option, then select General. Next, add a checkmark to the Synchronize with Exchange option. To the right of this option will be a Configure icon. Click on this icon and enter in your Exchange Username, Password, and Outlook Web Access Server information.

To synchronize with Yahoo! Address Book, place a checkmark next to the Synchronize with Yahoo! option (shown in Figure 7.5). Next, click on the Configure icon, located next to this option and enter your Yahoo! ID and Password, after agreeing to the permission request for your Mac to access your Yahoo! account.

## Backing Up Address Book Data

The easiest way to back up (make a copy of) your Address Book database for safe-keeping is to utilize the Time Machine application built into the Mac OS X operating system. You can also automatically back up your Address Book data using the Mobile Me online service. Yet another method is to do a manual backup.

Open Address Book, select the Export command found under the File pull-down menu, and then choose Address Book Archive. Select and enter a backup file name for the file you're about to create. The default file name will be Address Book, followed by the date. You must also select the destination where you'd like the backup file to be saved to.

Ideally, you should select an external location for your backup file, such as a thumb drive, CD, or external hard drive. Click the Save icon to create a backup file containing your Address Book data. If you are not using any other backup solution (such as any of the options described within Chapter 11), be sure to perform manual backups of your Address Book data on a regular basis.

## Printing Address Book Information

The information stored in your Address Book can be used to create address labels, printed phone lists, print envelopes, and to create printed, pocket-size address books.

To print mailing labels, envelopes, lists, or a pocket address book, start the Address Book program and select the Print command that's found under the File pull-down menu. The condensed Print window will appear. To the extreme right of the Printer field (within the Print window) will be a down arrow icon. Click on this icon to expand the Print window (shown in Figure 7.6).

From the expanded Print window, select the output printer from the Printer field menu in the upper-right corner of the window. Next, choose the Style printout you want to create. Your options from the Style field's menu include Mailing Labels, Envelopes, Lists, and Pocket Address Book. Choose the Paper Size and Orientation.

If you select Mail Labels from the Style field, you will be given options to choose the Layout of the label (including specific Avery or Dymo label formats),

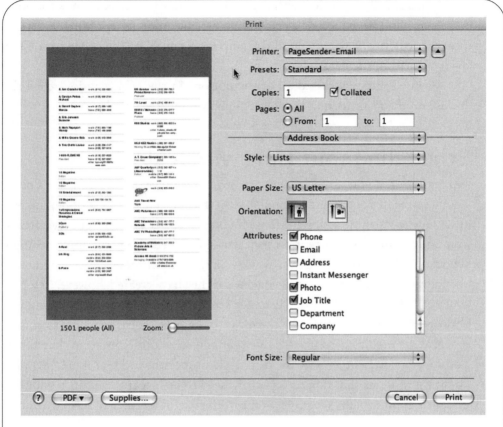

*Figure 7.6*

From the Address Book Print window, you can print out customized mailing labels, envelopes, lists, or address books for individual contacts, entire Groups, or your entire Address Book database.

plus you can choose the content of each label and choose for each Contact whether you want to print the Home, Work, or Other address.

If you select Envelopes from the Style field, you'll be given additional options within the Print window to adjust the Layout, Label, and Orientation of what will be printed from your Address Book database onto each envelope. On the left side of the Print window is a preview of what will be printed.

If you select the Lists or Pocket Address Book option from the Style field, you can choose the paper size, page orientation, and what information from each contact will be printed within your list. From the Attributes box found in the Print window, you can select Phone, E-Mail, Address, Instant Messenger, Photo, Job Title, Department, and Company from all of the other data fields available within the database.

When you have adjusted all of the options in the Print window, click the mouse on the Print icon in the lower-right corner to proceed.

## Scheduling Your Time with iCal

No matter what you do for a living, chances are you've discovered there's never enough time in the day to accomplish everything you need to get done, successfully juggle your professional life with your personal life, and give everything you do the amount of attention it deserves. Unfortunately, the folks at Apple who design Macs and create the software for these machines have not yet discovered a way of adding hours to the day. What they have created, however, is a program called iCal, which can be used for scheduling your time and helping you stay organized so you can make the most of the time that is available to you.

iCal is a highly customizable calendar and scheduling program that allows you to view your itinerary by the day, week, or month, and maintain a detailed to-do list of items that don't necessarily need to be incorporated into your calendar or appointment schedule. Some of the useful features of iCal include:

- The ability to set an unlimited number of alarms.
- The ability to share your calendar with co-workers.
- The ability to sync your calendar data with other Macs (as well as your iPhone, iTouch, or iPod).
- The ability to import other people's calendars or event calendars into your own schedule.
- The ability to view your schedule by the day, week, or month—either on the computer screen or via printouts.
- The ability to link contacts within your Address Book to appointments or scheduled items included in your calendar.
- The ability to maintain separate Calendar Groups, so you can keep separate calendars for work, personal time, vacation time, your children's

school schedule, etc., and then merge all of the information into a central database so you don't accidentally double-book your time. Each Calendar Group is displayed in a different color on the screen, so you can visually see how your time is allocated.

* The ability to keep track of recurring events, such as birthdays, anniversaries, holidays, or regularly scheduled daily, weekly, monthly, or annual appointments.

Like many of the programs that come bundled with the Mac, iCal is designed for ease of use and to be highly intuitive. You can also utilize only the features and functionality within the program that you actually want or need.

## Finding Your Way Around iCal

Like all Mac OS X programs, iCal can be launched in several ways. You can click on the iCal program icon (the icon that looks like a calendar) that appears on your Dock. You can also access your Applications folder and double-click on the iCal icon in that folder. Once the iCal program is running, the Menu Bar location at the top of your Desktop will change and offer the following program-related menus:

* *Apple.* This is the same pull-down menu that's available regardless of what application you're running. Options include About This Mac, Software Update, Mac OS X Software, System Preferences, Dock, Location, Recent Items, Force Quit, Sleep, Restart, Shut Down, and Log Out [Username].

* *iCal.* Options available from this pull-down menu include About iCal (an information screen appears that lists the program version number and copyright information), Preferences (set the program's preferences, such as the hours in your workday and whether you want to synchronize your calendars using Mobile Me). From the iCal menu, you can also select Quit iCal to exit the program. The keyboard shortcut to exit the program is Command (⌘) + Q.

* *File.* Add a New Event, New To Do Item, New Calendar, or New Calendar Group using the commands found under this menu. You can also Get

Info (change file names), Import, Export, Close, Back Up iCal, Resort iCal, and Print calendar information.

- *Edit.* The commands available under the Edit pull-down menu are similar to those found in many other Mac applications, such as Pages '08. Commands include Undo, Redo, Cut, Copy, Paste, Delete, Select All, Duplicate, Edit Event, Find, Show Spelling and Grammar, and Special Characters. The Edit Event command is unique to iCal and is used to edit, for example, appointments or meetings that are already part of your calendar.

- *Calendar.* You can Subscribe to other calendars (via the internet), Publish or Unpublish your own iCal calendars to the web (using Mobile Me), Refresh one or all of your calendars and update their synchronization with the web, change your location, and Find Shared Calendars that you can subscribe to from the web.

- *View.* Select how you'll view the information displayed within your iCal program window. Choose a Day, Week, or Month display. You can also move to the next or previous day, week, or month (depending on the view selected), Go To a specific date, and determine what information elements will be displayed within the iCal program window (such as Mini Calendars).

- *Window.* From this pull-down menu, you can select Minimize (to remove the iCal window from your Desktop), Zoom (change the program window size), access your Address Book contacts using the Address Panel, open Address Book (using the Address Book command), and access your Availability Panel. You can also bring all windows associated with iCal to the front of the Desktop using the Bring All to Front command.

- *Help.* Access the Search field, access the iCal Help feature, or obtain a list of keyboard shortcuts available using this program.

## The iCal Program Window

The main iCal program window has several different and unique sections. At the top of the window will be the familiar red, yellow, and green dots. Below these dots is the Today icon. Clicking on this icon immediately shows your calendar or schedule of appointments for the current day.

Along the top of the iCal program window, in the center, are five icons. The left-most icon allows you to scroll backwards, between days, weeks, or months (depending on the view you have selected). The right-most icon allows you to scroll forwards, between days, weeks, or months (depending on the view you have selected).

Clicking the mouse on the Day icon offers a detailed and close-up view of your entire schedule for a single day (Figure 7.7) in the main area of the iCal program window. Clicking the mouse on the Week icon displays your schedule and all appointments slated for that week (Figure 7.8). By clicking the mouse on the Month icon, you can view your entire month on the screen at once (Figure 7.9).

Along the left side of the program window is the list of Calendar Groups available to you. You can create one central calendar or create separate calendars for your work-related and personal time, for example. You can also maintain a

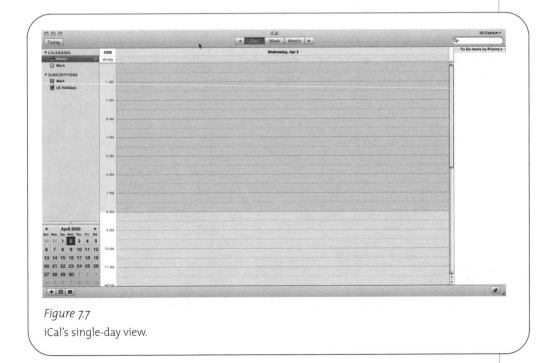

*Figure 7.7*
iCal's single-day view.

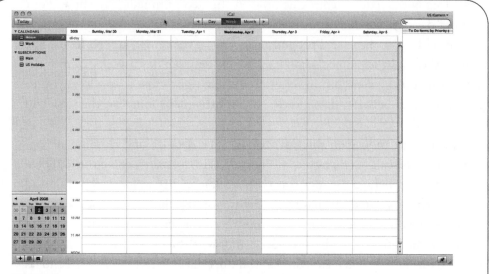

*Figure 7.8*
iCal's weekly view.

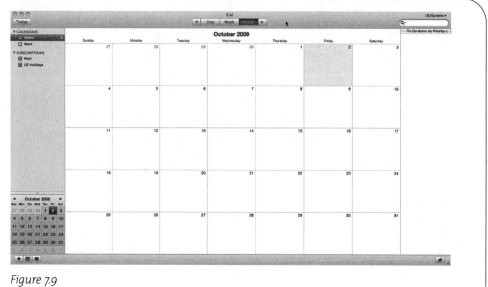

*Figure 7.9*
iCal's monthly view.

separate calendar to keep track of your children's' schedule or subscribe to public calendars that will automatically insert related events into your main calendar, such as holidays or when your favorite professional sports team plays.

In the lower-left portion of the iCal program window, you'll see a Mini Month calendar. This area of the program window can also be set to display notifications. By default, this area of the window displays a single Mini Month calendar. However, using the mouse, you can drag this portion of the window upward to reveal up to four Mini Month calendars.

In the lower-left corner of the iCal program window, you'll see three icons. The plus-sign icon (+) can be used for adding a new Calendar Group. Clicking the mouse on the small calendar-looking icon (located to the right of the plus-sign icon) will make the Mini Month display appear or disappear. The envelope-looking icon (located to the right of the plus-sign icon) will replace the Mini Month display with the Notifications display in the lower-left portion of the screen.

The center of the iCal program window displays the Day, Week, or Month view of your calendar. Below this calendar, you can opt to display your Search results information. On the right side of the main calendar view, you can opt to display your to-do list. Clicking the mouse on the thumbtack-looking icon in the lower-right corner of the iCal program window will cause your to-do list to appear or disappear from the display.

### JUMPING BETWEEN DAYS AND DATES

By clicking on the Today icon (found in the upper-left corner of the iCal program window), the current day's schedule will be displayed in either the Day, Week, or Month calendar view. To instantly switch between days or dates, select Go To Date option found under the View pull-down menu and type the

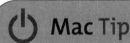

## Mac Tip

Find information within your calendar(s) fast using the Search feature found in the upper-right corner of the iCal program window. Simply type in a search word or phrase to highlight related appointments, calendar entries, scheduled events, and to-do items. A list of relevant items will be displayed at the bottom of the iCal program window.

date you're interested in viewing. An alternative for switching dates or days is to use the left or right arrow icons located near the top center of the iCal program window. You can also click on a date on the Mini Calendar (displayed in the lower-left corner of the iCal program window) to jump to an alternate date.

### ADDING/EDITING APPOINTMENTS

There are several ways to manually add a new appointment or event into your schedule. One method is to select the New Event option from the File pull-down menu. The equivalent keyboard shortcut is Command (⌘) + N. An alternative is to double-click the mouse on the time/day on the calendar displayed in the main program window where you want to add the new event. If you're using the Month view, double-click on the date (you can add the time of the event/appointment shortly). If you're looking at the Day view, you can double-click on the actual time of the new appointment/ event to be added. If you're looking at the Week view, you can select the time and day of the event by double-clicking the mouse on the appropriate area.

To add an event, first click on and highlight the appropriate Calendar Group on the left side of the iCal program window. The default Calendar Groups available are Home and Work. Next, move the mouse to the appropriate location on the main calendar display and double-click where you want to add the new event.

A colored box will appear that says New Event in conjunction with the time. Double-click on this box to reveal the New Event window (Figure 7.10). From this window, you can enter the following information that's related to the new event:

- *New Event Title/Name.* Enter a description of the event you're adding.
- *Location.* Enter the location of the event/meeting/appointment.

**Mac Tip**

One excellent feature of iCal is that in conjunction with any new event, you can drag and drop photos, video clips, or any kind of document(s) into it, so those attachments become associated with and attached to the specific event entry.

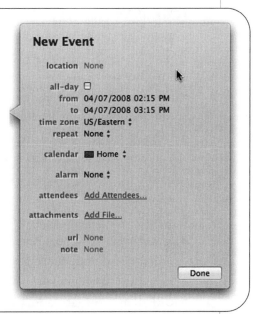

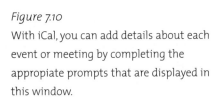

*Figure 7.10*
With iCal, you can add details about each event or meeting by completing the appropiate prompts that are displayed in this window.

● *All-Day*. Use the mouse to add a checkmark next to the All Day option if the appointment will last an entire day and you want to block out your time accordingly. You can define the length of your entire day by accessing the Preferences option found under the iCal pull-down menu.

● *Time From*. Enter the start date and time of the event.

● *Time To*. Enter the end date and time of the event.

● *Time Zone*. Choose the time zone for the event. The default selection will be the time zone you're in (or that the computer thinks you're in). If you know you'll be traveling, you can have iCal automatically adjust the event time based on time zone changes, or you can set iCal to keep the event time the same as your home time zone, regardless of what time zone you're in.

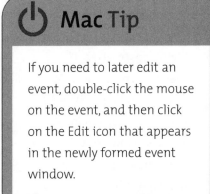

**Mac Tip**

If you need to later edit an event, double-click the mouse on the event, and then click on the Edit icon that appears in the newly formed event window.

- *Repeat.* You can set iCal to repeat the new event every day, every week, every month, or every year, or at any time interval you select from the Custom option found at the bottom of the pull-down menu associated with Repeat.
- *Calendar.* If you're managing multiple Calendar Groups using iCal, you can determine which Calendar Group(s) the new event will appear in.
- *Alarm.* Set a text-based and/or audible alarm to remind you of an event. You can set the alarm to ring or be displayed at a pre-determined time before the event, such as 15 minutes, 1 hour, or even a day or a week in advance.
- *Attendees.* Enter the names of the other people involved in the event.
- *Attachments.* If appropriate, link a specific file (such as a photograph, Word document, PowerPoint presentation, or spreadsheet file) to the new event listing in your calendar.
- *URL.* If appropriate, add a website URL link to the new event listing.
- *Note.* Add text-based notes about the new event.

When you're done entering the event information that's relevant, click on the Done icon in the lower-right corner of the New Event window. The newly created event will become part of your schedule.

## Mac Tip

If you're a movie buff, you can subscribe to the Movie New Release Calendar (apple.com /downloads/macosx /calendars /movienew releasecalendar.html) and/or the DVD Release Calendar (apple.com/downloads/macosx /calendars/dvdnewrelease calendar.html).

### SUBSCRIBING TO ADDITIONAL CALENDARS

By subscribing to other calendars, you can share calendar information with other Mac users who are members of the Mobile Me online service. There are also hundreds of public calendars that you can subscribe to that will add all types of information to your calendar, such as popular holidays or the dates when your favorite sports team plays.

To subscribe to an existing calendar, select the Subscribe icon found under the Calendar pull-down menu. When prompted,

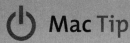 **Mac Tip**

If your co-workers use Microsoft Entourage to manage their schedules, you can sync your iCal schedule with theirs by importing Entourage calendar data. To do this, open iCal and select the Import option from the File pull-down menu. Click the Import Entourage Data option, followed by the Import icon.

enter the Calendar URL for the calendar you wish to subscribe to and click on the Subscribe icon.

To view a directory of shared calendars available to the public (all of which can be accessed free of charge), select the Find Shared Calendars command from the Calendar pull-down menu. Your computer must be connected to the internet, so that iCal can forward you to the Apple website's iCal Calendar page (apple.com/downloads/macosx/calendars/). At the time this book was being written, there were 143 different calendars a Mac user could subscribe to. The most popular calendar was the U.S. Holidays Calendar (apple.com /downloads/macosx/calendars/usholidaycalendar.html).

### SHARING YOUR CALENDAR WITH OTHERS

Using the Publish command found under the Calendar pull-down menu, you can make your Calendar available to other Mac users (or automatically synchronize your iCal data with your other Macs), but only if you're an active member of the Mobile Me online service.

Once your iCal data is published on Mobile Me, you will receive a special URL, which other Macs (also using iCal and Mobile Me) can subscribe to. To learn more about this feature, visit apple.com/ical. To use this feature, you must first select

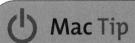 **Mac Tip**

Using iTunes, your iCal and Address Book data can automatically be synchronized with your iPhone, iPod Touch, or iPod. See Chapter 5 for more information about data transfer between your Mac and other Apple devices.

---

**Mac Tip**

If you're sharing your calendar and trying to coordinate meetings with several people, iCal offers an Auto Pick feature that helps to select appointment/meeting dates and times that are convenient for everyone. This can be done with a single click of the mouse. This feature only works if your iCal calendar data is shared through a CalDAV server. You can also give an assistant or co-worker full control over your calendar while you're away from the office.

---

Preferences from the iCal pull-down menu, and then select General. At the bottom of the General window, add a checkmark next to the "Synchronize my calendars with other computers using Mobile Me" option.

### Printing Your Schedule

From the File pull-down menu, select the Print option to print hard copies of your calendar. From the Print window, you can determine the calendar view to be printed (Day, Week, Month, or List), Paper Size, Time Range, Calendar Groups to print, and also choose additional options (like the ability to print All-Day Events, Timed Events, Mini Months, and/or Calendar keys). A preview of your selections will be displayed on the left side of the Print window. When you're ready to print, click on the Continue icon.

### Backing Up Your iCal Data

It's definitely a good idea to back up your iCal data often using the Time Machine application, the Mobile Me service, or one of the other methods described in Chapter 11. You can also instantly back up your iCal data to a separate file, CD, or an external disk drive by selecting the Back Up iCal option from the File pull-down menu. Upon selecting this command, choose a Save As file name (the default is iCal + the current date), and then choose the destination where the file will be saved.

# Web Surfing with Safari

In today's business world, being connected and staying connected, by phone, fax, and the internet, has become absolutely essential. When it comes to surfing the internet, Mac users can rely on Apple's own Safari 3.1 (or later) web browser, which comes bundled with all Mac computers. While other web browsers, like Mozilla Foxfire, are available for free from other developers, the majority of Mac users continue to rely on Safari for their web surfing needs.

For former PC users already used to surfing the web using Microsoft Explorer, you'll find that Safari offers much of the same functionality and compatibility. One benefit, however, is that as a Mac user, you need not worry about downloading viruses or spyware. Apple also boasts that Safari is the fastest-performing web browser on the market, which means it takes less time to load web pages.

Safari provides a clutter-free web browsing experience in terms of the user interface, plus all of the features you'd want or need to get the most out the of internet. As you'd expect, Safari is compatible with widely used browser plug-ins, such as Flash, QuickTime, Java, Windows Media, and Adobe Acrobat Reader.

Keeping track of your favorite websites is also simple using Safari. You can save bookmarks under a pull-down Bookmarks menu or along the Bookmark bar (located just under the browser's Toolbar found at the top of the program window. Adding Bookmarks as you surf takes just two mouse clicks. It's possible to later organize your Bookmarks by clicking on the Show All Bookmarks icon (found on the right side of the Bookmark bar).

While Bookmarks offer one way to determine where you're going online and where you'll surf to next, Safari also keeps track of your surfing history, so it's easy to return to sites where you've already been. If you want to quickly switch between multiple web pages, Safari offers tabbed browsing. Oh, and those annoying pop-up windows that often drive web surfers crazy can be eliminated simply by activating Safari's Pop-Up Window Blocker (an option found under the Safari pull-down menu).

Using the Forms AutoFill feature of Safari, you don't need to constantly retype information when completing online forms. Safari remembers field entries, pulls data from Address Book, and then automatically places appropriate text when an online form appears on the screen. The Find command is also useful for quickly scanning a web page and looking for all occurrences of a specific word or search phrase.

Like Microsoft Explorer, which you probably used on your old PC, Safari is fully compatible with RSS feeds and allows users to keep their browser-related cookies, history, and caches private, while also offering the latest data encryption security.

As you begin using your new Mac, you'll discover the Safari program icon on your Dock ready to use if your computer is connected to the internet. At any time, you can customize Safari to meet your surfing habits by modifying the command icons displayed on the Toolbar. To do this, access the Customize Toolbar command found under the View pull-down menu.

While Safari is designed to work seamlessly with Apple's Mighty Mouse (with its built-in Scroll Ball) as well as with the touchpad built into all MacBooks, you can speed up your surfing with keyboard shortcuts used in conjunction with the mouse.

## The On-Screen Anatomy of Safari

Like all Mac programs, commands available to you when using Safari can be accessed in several ways, including from the Menu bar located along the top of the Desktop. When you load Safari, your Menu bar will offer the following pull-down menu options:

- *Apple*. This is the same pull-down menu that's available regardless of what application you're running. Options include: About This Mac, Software Update, Mac OS X Software, System Preferences, Dock, Location, Recent Items, Force Quit, Sleep, Restart, Shut Down, and Log Out [username].

- *Safari*. The commands under this pull-down menu offer the following options:

- *About Safari*. See the version number of the software you're using as well as copyright information.
- *Report Bugs to Apple*. When connected to the web, you can send Apple information about any bug you encounter in the Safari program. This isn't a feature you'll use often, if ever.
- *Preferences*. The options offered in the Preferences window allow you to customize your web surfing. For example, you can set the default font and font size, as well as your homepage.
- *Block Pop-Up Windows*. When this feature is active, a checkmark will appear next to it on the pull-down menu. While surfing, you will not be bothered by lots of annoying pop-up windows appearing on your Desktop.
- *Private Browsing*. This features gives you added security and anonymity when surfing the web because Safari will not record any of your surfing-related information. If, for example, you're planning your vacation online from your office computer, this feature might come in handy.
- *Reset Safari*. This feature allows you to delete information relating to your surfing, such as your history, cache, downloads window, cookies, Google searches, and AutoFill text entries.
- *Empty Cache*. Use this command to delete files related to websites you've visited that are being stored on your computer's Hard Drive.
- *Services*. Launch other applications while running Safari.
- *Hide Safari*. Close your current Safari program window(s) without quitting the program.
- *Hide Others*. Close any windows not related to Safari that are currently open on your Desktop. Use this command to unclutter your desktop without closing applications you're currently running.
- *Show All*. Any windows that have been hidden reappear when you use this command.
- *Quit Safari*. Close and exit the Safari program.

- *File*. The commands available under this pull-down menu include:
  - *New Window*. Open additional browser windows so you can surf to several web pages simultaneously.

- *New Tab*. Use the Safari tab feature to quickly switch between multiple open browser windows (another method of visiting multiple web pages simultaneously).
- *Open File*. Open a web page file or another compatible file that has been saved on your computer's Hard Drive, for example.
- *Open Location*. Access websites you've previously visited that are listed in your History folder.
- *Close Window*. Close a current Safari browser window.
- *Close Tab*. Close a current Safari browser window that's been assigned to a Tab.
- *Save As*. Save the contents of a web page you're currently visiting to your computer's Hard Disk or another storage medium, such as a thumb drive.
- *Mail Contents of This Page*. E-mail the contents of the web page you're currently viewing to anyone via your Mac's Mail program.
- *Mail Link to This Page*. Instead of e-mailing the contents of a web page you're viewing, you can share information about a website by e-mailing someone its link. This command opens the Mail program and creates an e-mail message with the web page link already embedded in it.
- *Open in Dashboard*. If there's a section of a website you'd like access to from your Dashboard, you can clip it and save it to your Dashboard using this command.
- *Import Bookmarks*. This command allows you to import your bookmarks from another web browser.
- *Export Bookmarks*. Save a file containing your current Safari bookmarks, which you can then load into another Mac running Safari or share with someone else.
- *Print*. Use this command to Print the web page you're currently visiting.

 *Edit*. With the exception of the AutoFill Form option available under this pull-down menu, the commands available are similar to those you find under the Edit pull-down menu of many other Mac applications. These commands include Undo, Redo, Cut, Copy, Paste, Delete, Select All, Find, and Spelling and Grammar. If you select the AutoFill command when you need to complete an on-screen form, Safari will pull pertinent information, such as your name, address, and phone number from your Address Book Card as well as from data stored from web forms you've filled out in the past.

* *View.* Use the commands available from this pull-down menu to customize the look of your Safari browser window. Using the Hide command for many of the features, you can unclutter your web browser screen, allowing more space to view actual website content. Options include:
  - *Show/Hide Bookmarks Bar.* Make the Bookmarks bar (which is normally found under the Toolbar) appear or disappear from the screen.
  - *Show/Hide Status Bar.* Causes the Status bar to appear or disappear from the screen.
  - *Show/Hide Tab Bar.* Causes the Tab bar to appear or disappear from the screen.
  - *Show/Hide Toolbar.* Causes the Toolbar to appear or disappear from the screen.
  - *Customize Toolbar.* Select which command icons you want displayed on your Toolbar as well as the order they appear in.
  - *Stop.* Causes a web page that's currently loading to stop.
  - *Reload Page.* Causes the current web page to update itself.
  - *Make Text Bigger.* Increase the size of the on-screen text on your browser window.
  - *Make Text Normal Size.* Return the text displayed in your browser window to its normal/default size. You can set this default size from the Safari Preferences window that's found under the Safari pull-down menu.
  - *Make Text Smaller.* Decrease the size of the on-screen text on your browser window.
  - *View Source.* When you use this command, a new window will open that displays the HTML programming used to create the web page you're currently viewing.
  - *Text Encoding.* Allows foreign language text to be displayed in the browser.

* *History.* The commands under this pull-down menu allow you to quickly revisit websites you've visited in the recent past. Use the Show All History

command to display a list of every website you've been to within a predefined period. The Clear History command deletes the History that's stored by Safari.

- *Bookmark*. The commands under this pull-down menu are used for customizing your bookmarks and accessing the bookmarks you have saved. Options include:
  - *Show All Bookmarks*. Opens the bookmarks management window, from which you can delete and rearrange bookmarks, categorize them into groups, and adjust the order in which they appear.
  - *Add Bookmark*. Click on the plus-sign icon (+) on the Toolbar or press Command (⌘) + D to add a bookmark for the web page you're currently visiting.
  - *Add Bookmark for These Tabs*. Create bookmarks for web pages opened using the Tab feature of Safari.
  - *Add Bookmark Folder*. You can sort your bookmarks into groups and store them in an unlimited number of folders in order to better organize them. For example, you can create bookmark folders called Work, Clients, Vacation, Travel, Personal, Investments, Research, etc., and then store related bookmarks in the appropriate folder.
  - *Bookmarks Bar*. Access the bookmarks stored on your Bookmarks bar. You can open these sites individually, or open several at once using Tabs.
  - *Open In Tabs*. Open all of your bookmarked web pages in separate Tabs using Safari.

- *Window*. In addition to Minimizing or Zooming the Safari program window, from this pull-down menu you can access commands for switching between Tabs, opening your Downloads window (to see files you've downloaded from the web), and opening the Activity window (to see how web pages you're visiting load into the browser and to examine various elements of those pages). You can access the Bring All to Front command, which reopens any hidden windows relating to Safari.

- *Help*. This pull-down menu reveals the Search feature, which allows you to access the Help information available for Safari. If you have a question about how a command or feature works, for example, you'll find information here by typing a relevant keyword or search phrase. You can also visit the Safari section of Apple's website (apple.com/safari/) for more information about this browser's features and how to use them.

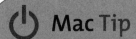

## Mac Tip

The command icons located along the Toolbar (found below the Menu bar) as well as keyboard shortcuts can also be used to access features and commands available within Safari.

The size of the main Safari program window can be adjusted manually using the mouse and dragging the Window Resizing symbol that's found in the lower-right corner of the window. To resize the window, click on the resizing symbol, hold down the mouse button, and drag the window's lower-right corner up, down, left, right, or diagonally. Using the red, yellow, and green dots located in the upper-left corner of the program window, you can close, minimize, or zoom the window with a single mouse click.

Safari's Toolbar contains icon-based commands that you can customize. Upon selecting the Customize Toolbar command, you can drag any of the following command icons onto your Toolbar and choose their positioning. Thus, you can place these command icons (used mainly for navigating the web) in the same order as comparable icons appeared when you used Explorer on your old PC.

Available command icons that can be placed on your Toolbar include:

- *Back and Forward Arrows*. Use these commands to navigate to web pages you've already visited during your current surfing session.
- *Home*. Return to your homepage.
- *AutoFill*. Complete the on-screen form fields with information from Address Book and other data you've already entered when completing similar forms.
- *Text Size (Bigger and Smaller)*. Increase or decrease the text size on the screen within the browser window.
- *Stop/Reload*. Stop a web page from loading, or reload the current page.
- *Open in Dashboard*. Access a portion of a website from your Dashboard, as opposed to from Safari directly.

* *Add Bookmark.* Save a bookmark for the web page you're currently visiting.
* *Print.* Print the web page you're currently visiting.
* *Report Bug.* If you discover a problem using Safari, use this command to send a report to Apple. (You will not receive a reply using this method.)
* *Address Field.* Manually enter the website URL you wish to visit. For example, you could enter websitename.com, www.websitename.com, or http://www.websitename.com.
* *Google Search Field.* Instead of opening Google in your main web browser window, you can perform a Google search by entering a search phrase or keyword in this field and then see relevant links displayed on your main browser page.

The Bookmarks bar is located below your Toolbar in Safari (unless you choose to hide it by selecting the Hide Bookmarks bar command from the View pull-down menu). Here you can place links to your favorite websites. Below this

## ⏻ Mac Tip

When you start using Safari for the first time, one of the first things you'll want to do is set your homepage. This is the website that will appear each time you start using Safari. Many web surfers set a popular internet search engine, such as Yahoo! (yahoo.com) or Google (google.com) as to their homepage, but you can have it be your company's website, the Apple.com website, or any other website you choose. To set your homepage, access the Safari pull-down menu and choose Preferences. Click the mouse on the General icon that appears in the Preferences window. In the homepage field, type the complete URL for your desired homepage (i.e., yahoo.com or google.com). If the web browser is currently at your desired homepage, you can simply click on the Set to Current Page icon found below the homepage field in the General Preferences window.

is the Tabs bar. It can also be hidden from view to simplify the appearance of your browser window.

On the extremely left edge of the Safari program window (and potentially running along the bottom of the window) are your scroll bars. At the very bottom of the program window is the Status bar. When web pages are loading, the status of the process is displayed in the lower-left corner of the screen.

The main portion of the Safari program window, below the Toolbar, Bookmarks bar, and Tabs bar and above the Status bar, is where the web pages you visit will be displayed. Use the mouse to click on hyperlinks and other elements found in the web pages you visit. In addition to the mouse's Scroll Ball, you can use the scroll bars along the side and bottom of the program window or the keyboard's arrow keys to move up and down pages.

If you're already familiar with Microsoft Explorer, FireFox, or another web browser, learning to use Safari will be a straightforward and intuitive experience. In fact, when you're transferring your PC data to your new Mac, you can also transfer all of your existing bookmarks. (Details on how to do this are in Chapter 5.) One fast way to do this is to export your Bookmarks using Explorer and save them into a file. Next, use Safari's Import Bookmarks command (found under the File pull-down menu) to load your Bookmarks into the web browser software. For users of multiple Macs, you can automatically keep all of your bookmarks synced between computers using the Mobile Me online service.

## Ensuring Your Web Surfing Privacy

If you don't want others to be able to determine what you've been doing online or what websites you've visited, each time you're done surfing (before quitting Safari), select the

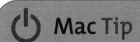

## Mac Tip

Because new security issues are constantly arising, it's an excellent strategy to periodically ensure you're using the latest version of the Safari web browser software. To manually check if any new updates have been released by Apple, click on the Software Update command found under the Apple pull-down menu.

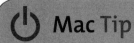

## Mac Tip

As a time-saver, Safari does not require you to type "http://" before a website URL (i.e., type only website name.com) when you are entering it in manually.

Empty Cache command from the Safari pull-down menu. Next, under the History pull-down menu, click on the Clear History command.

Another, more extensive privacy option is to select the Reset Safari command found under the Safari pull-down menu. When the Reset Safari window appears, be sure the Clear History, Empty the Cache, Clear the Download Window, Remove All Cookies, Clear Google Searches, and Close All Safari Windows options have a checkmark placed next to them, and then click the Reset icon.

Still another method for keeping your web surfing habits and history private is to activate the Private Browsing feature of Safari. To do this, click on the Private Browsing command found under the Safari pull-down menu. Upon activating this feature, web pages you visit will not be added to your history, all items you download will be deleted from your Downloads window, any information you type will not be saved using the AutoFill option (including usernames and passwords), and any searches you perform will not be saved.

## Surfing the Web

When you're ready to start surfing the web, simply type the website you wish to visit into the Address bar (located on the Toolbar) and press Return/Enter. Or you can click on any active link within your homepage or choose a website from your Bookmarks pull-down menu or the Bookmark bar.

If you're looking for something on the web, you can use the Google Search field to type a search word or phrase and press the Enter/Return key. Search results and links to related websites will be displayed. You can visit any of the websites listed as a result of your search by clicking on the appropriate hyperlinks. However, should you want to return to the initial listing of search results, click on the SnapBack icon that's located on the right side of the Google Search field. (It's a small, orange icon with an arrow displayed within it.)

At any time, you can increase or decrease the size of the text that appears on your browser screen by selecting the Make Text Bigger or Make Text Smaller commands found under the View pull-down menu. You can also opt to return the displayed text to normal size by selecting the Make Text Normal Size command. The keyboard shortcut commands for these functions are: Command (⌘) + (+ key), Command (⌘) + (- key) and Command (⌘) + 0, respectively. If you're using the MacBook Air or a MacBook Pro, you can also use your fingers on the touchpad to increase or decrease text size by spreading your thumb and index finger apart, in a diagonal direction while maintaining contact with the touchpad to increase text size, and by reversing your finger motions to decrease text size.

To open multiple browser windows simultaneously, without using the tabs function, simply select the New Window command found under the File pull-down menu or press Command (⌘) + N. To open a new tab so you can easily switch between browser windows without having to minimize and zoom them, use the New Tab command that's found under the File pull-down menu, or press Command (⌘) + T.

If you find a website you want to share with friends, co-workers, clients, or colleagues, select either the Mail Contents of This Page or Mail Link to This Page command, found under the File pull-down menu. This will open Mail (or the mail client software you have set as your default for sending mail), and an e-mail containing the related link and content will be created. Simply type the recipient's name and click Send.

To close a browser window, without quitting the Safari program, click on the red dot in the upper-left corner of the window, select the Close Window command from the File pull-down menu, or press Command (⌘) + W. To quit Safari, select the Quit Safari command found under the Safari pull-down menu, or press Command (⌘) + Q.

# Microsoft Office 2008
# for Mac

N 1984, MICROSOFT INTRODUCED WORD 1.0 FOR THE MAC, WHICH QUICKLY BECAME
the most popular word processing application in the world and was
later adapted for the Windows platform. Today, the most popular suite
of business software available for the Mac OS X or Windows operating
systems is Microsoft Office 2008. It includes Word, Excel, PowerPoint, and
Entourage, all widely utilized programs in corporate America. This 2008
Mac edition of Office has been totally redesigned by a team of over 200
full-time programmers and Mac software designers. The result is a suite

of applications that are easier to use and universally compatible across the Mac and PC platforms.

Microsoft Office 2008 is also more graphically oriented than past versions, allowing a wide range of images and graphic elements to be incorporated into documents and files. Each application is also bundled with dozens (in some cases hundreds) of templates, making it very simple to create professional-looking results with the various applications without having to worry about formatting, layout, color schemes, or other design elements.

If you'll be using your new Mac for word processing, page layout, spreadsheets, creating and making presentations, keeping track of contacts, managing your time and schedule, managing e-mail, and/or utilizing online chat services (such as AIM, AOL, or MSN), Office 2008 offers the software solutions you need.

According to Craig Eisler, general manager of Microsoft Corporation's Macintosh Business Unit, "We developed Office 2008 for Mac as a comprehensive productivity suite that also helps people simplify their work. To complement the deep set of new and improved features, we redesigned the interface so that it is truly easier to use. Even Office beginners can create great looking documents very quickly. And, at the core, we focused on delivering reliable compatibility so that users can confidently share documents across platforms."

Microsoft reports that Office 2008 for Mac is the most compatible software suite on the market, allowing data to be seamlessly moved between applica-

## ⏻ Mac Tip

Specifically for business users, Microsoft has created the Mactopia website (microsoft.com/mac) that showcases the features of Microsoft Office 2008 and offers tutorials for using each included application within a work environment. The site also offers troubleshooting information, training courses, and user-rated help articles.

tions and platforms. For example, spreadsheet or chart data created with Excel can easily be imported into a PowerPoint presentation or a report being created with Word.

## *Three Editions of Office to Choose From*

Available wherever Mac software is sold, including Apple Stores and the Apple.com website, Microsoft Office 2008 for Mac is available in three different configurations: the Microsoft Office 2008 for Mac Standard Edition ($399.95), Microsoft Office 2008 for Mac Home & Student Edition ($149.95), and Microsoft Office 2008 for Mac Special Media Edition ($499.95). If you're upgrading from an older version of Office, the upgrade prices for the 2008 edition are $239.95 for the Standard Edition and $299.95 for the Special Media Edition. No discounted upgrade is available for the Home & Student edition.

All three versions of Office 2008 for Mac support the Open XML file format, which virtually guarantees the compatibility of all Office files, data, and documents between the Mac and Windows platforms. It's important that the Mac and PC users, however, are both using the latest version of Office in order to experience true cross-platform compatibility. Otherwise, you'll need to manually save your Office files in formats compatible with older versions of the software.

Microsoft Office 2008 Standard Edition includes Microsoft Word 2008, Microsoft Excel 2008, Microsoft PowerPoint 2008, and Microsoft Entourage 2008. This version features more than 100 new themes and templates, improved Windows Exchange Server support, and more than 70 Office-specific Automator Actions.

The Special Media Edition includes all of these programs combined with the Microsoft Expression Media digital assistant management system. This version is geared for users who require Microsoft Exchange Server support, and Automator tools, and who are looking for one product to meet their productivity and digital asset management needs.

The Home & Student Edition is a specially priced version of the software suite for users with basic productivity needs. This version does not include connectivity to Microsoft Exchange Server or Office-specific Automator Actions.

Even if you're an experienced Office user, the new 2008 edition features a totally redesigned Elements Gallery, which is the foundation for the software suite's new user interface. This graphically inspired interface offers easy access to the most commonly used tools and templates available in each Office application. To help you learn to utilize all of the new features, the Help feature built into the software suite has also been greatly improved.

The Office Toolbox is a separate window that appears in conjunction with each Office application. It is designed to give you easy access to many of the formatting features and other tools available within each program. This Toolbox remains constant as you switch between Office applications, so once you get used to using it, the commands will always be found in the same place, whether you're using Word, Excel, PowerPoint, or Entourage.

The ability to instantly create PDF files from any printable file, data, or document created using any Office application is also now available. Using the PDF format helps ensure that your documents will appear with the correct layout and fonts, on any computer or platform others are using—whether it's a PC, Mac, personal digital assistant, smartphone, or a website capable of displaying PDF files. The Save to PDF feature is available directly from Word, PowerPoint, and Excel by using the Save As command.

 **Mac Tip**

As you read this chapter, turn on your Mac, load each Office application, and follow along on your computer. This will help you get to know the layout of each application and where to find the various functions, features, and commands.

Using a built-in file converter, files created using the Windows (PC) versions of Office 2003, Office XP, Office 2000, or Office 97 can easily be loaded and used in Office 2008 for Mac. In addition, a greater emphasis has been placed on the page layout capabilities offered by the various programs, allowing users to create truly professional-looking documents without any graphic design skills.

Of course, all of the features you've come to rely on when using any Office application can still be found within Office 2008, but your ability to quickly find and use each feature is probably more intuitive.

# Word Processing: Microsoft Word 2008

As the world's most popular word processor, Word has evolved dramatically over the years. This latest edition (available for both Macs and PCs) offers all of the powerful word processing features users have come to expect from this application and a new user interface that makes accessing features and commands more intuitive. If you're already familiar with Word, you'll have no trouble adapting to this version on the Mac. What you will discover, however, is an arsenal of new or improved page layout tools you can use to transform your basic text documents into professional-looking, graphically-oriented desktop published documents (see Figure 8.1).

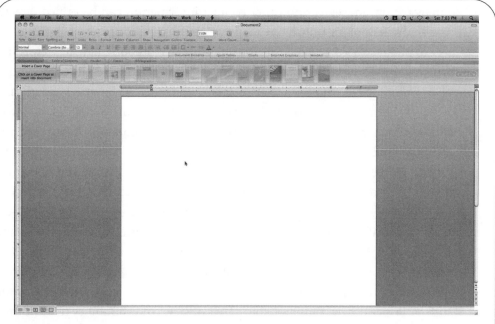

*Figure 8.1*

Shown here is the Microsoft Word program window. At the very top of the Desktop is the Menu bar. The Print Layout view of a blank document is shown here. The Elements Gallery displays thumbnail images of possible templates you can use with your document to handle formatting.

When you need to create a cover page, a table of contents, headers, footers, or a bibliography within your document, for example, you no longer have to navigate through a complex maze of pull-down menus, pop-up windows, and keyboard shortcuts. Instead, you can add these and other document elements to your documents with a few clicks of the mouse.

Of course, Word can still be used as a straightforward word processor, and your documents can still be saved in a wide range of different formats. However, using the templates, creating visually stunning and professional-looking reports, brochures, newsletters, invoices, resumes, and business letters has become much easier, as is incorporating photos, clip art, graphic images, and content from other Office applications into your documents.

Even the once complex Mail Merge feature of Word, used for sending personalized form letters, has been made much easier to use via the new Mail Merge Manager. Now addresses and other contact information can be pulled directly from Address Book or Entourage to create your list of document recipients.

For people who use Word for note taking, the Notebook Layout view transforms your on-screen work space, giving it the appearance of lined notebook paper from a three-ring binder. This view adds tabs, automatic headers, and displays the time and date on each page. These features make organizing information from a meeting, seminar, or brainstorming session more organized and readily accessible.

The Notebook Layout view also offers Word's exclusive Audio feature, allowing you to use your Mac's built-in microphone (and speakers) to record and play back voice memos or lectures that can be attached to notebook documents. Especially useful when participating in meetings or seminars, for example, select the Notebook Layout from the View pull-down menu in Word to access this handy feature. From the Toolbar, click the mouse on the Audio icon.

In addition to the Notebook Layout view, Word offers a Draft, Web Layout, Outline, Print Layout, and Publishing Layout view, and the ability to customize your work space by selecting background colors. If you want to add a chart to your document, this, too, is much easier using Word's Chart Manager. Simply click on the Charts icon, choose your chart format (Area, Bar, Bubble, Column, Doughnut, Line, Pie, Radar, Stock, Surface, or X Y Scatter), import or add the necessary numerical data using Excel, and place the newly created chart in your document using the mouse to size and position it. You can even change the color scheme and appearance of the chart with a few additional mouse clicks.

Along with the pull-down menus, and Toolbar and keyboard shortcuts available in Word, virtually all of the most used functions and commands are available through the Toolbox, which when displayed, offers a separate window that gives you easy and intuitive access to Word's Formatting Palette, Object Palette, Citations, Scrapbook, Reference Tools, Compatibility Report, and Project Palette. Similar functionality via the Toolbox is now offered in all of Office's applications.

## Navigating in Word 2008

Like any Mac application, Word has a main pull-down menu that appears across the top of your Desktop. The main options available from this menu include:

- *Apple*. This pull-down menu remains constant, regardless of what pro-gram(s) you're running on your Mac. See Chapter 3 for details.

- *Word*. Commands available from this pull-down menu include:
  - *About Word*. View your unique Product ID, see what version of Word you have installed, get technical support contact information by clicking on the Support icon, and view the program's copyright information.
  - *Online Registration*. Register your purchased copy of Word. This process needs to be completed just once.
  - *Preferences*. Personalize the features of Word. This includes choosing the default folder where your document files will be saved, selecting your default printer, and adding your personal information.
  - *Services*. Launch other applications while running Word.
  - *Hide Word*. This command makes the active Word program window disappear from the screen, but does not quit the program.
  - *Hide Others*. This command causes non-Word windows that are open on your Desktop to be hidden, thus making the Desktop appear less cluttered.
  - *Show All*. Displays all hidden windows.

- *Quit Word*. Exit the Word application. Be sure to save your active documents before quitting the program, or any work you've done since last using the Save command (or the auto backup feature) will be lost.

- *File*. This pull-down menu offers a variety of options and commands for opening, saving, printing, sending, and closing files. Options include:
  - *Project Gallery*. From the Project Gallery you can open a template, allowing Office to help you create a wide range of documents, such as calendars, brochures, lists, labels, fliers, newsletters, marketing materials, resumes, stationery, business reports, or presentations.
  - *New Blank Document*. Utilize Word's core word processing features to create a text document without using a template.
  - *Open*. Open an existing file from your Mac's hard drive or any other media (such as a CD, thumb drive, external hard drive, or a document file you've downloaded).
  - *Open Recent*. Display a list of Word files you've recently worked with and select which one to open from this list.
  - *Close*. This command closes the current Word file you're working with. If applicable, you'll be prompted to first save your work. This command closes the individual Word document that's active, but does not quit the Word application.
  - *Save*. Use this command to save your work using the existing file name. If no file name has been created, you'll be promoted to create one and choose where the document will be saved. (You can select a folder or subfolder. The default is to save all new documents in your Mac's Documents folder.)
  - *Save As*. This allows you to save a copy of a Word file that's already been saved using another file name or file format. It can also be saved in an alternate format.
  - *Save as Web Page*. Save the Word file you're working with as a web page, as opposed to as a standard Word (.docx or .doc) file.
  - *Web Page Preview*. This command opens the file you created in the Safari browser so you can see what it would look like if it were published to the web.

- *Page Setup*. From this window you can adjust your document's margins, paper size, orientation, and scale, and format the document for a specific printer.
- *Print Preview*. See an on-screen depiction of what your document will look like on the printed page.
- *Print*. This command allows you to send your current Word document to a printer that's connected to your Mac. From the Print window, you can choose which printer to send the document to (if more than one is connected to your computer) set the number of copies to be printed, and identify which pages within a multipage document you'd like to print. You'll see a preview of the file in the Print window and have the option of creating a PDF file of the document.
- *Send To*. You can send the document to another application, such as Mail (to e-mail it to someone else) or to PowerPoint (to be incorporated into a presentation).
- *Properties*. View details about the document you're currently working with. The Properties window is divided into five categories: General, Summary, Statistics, Contents, and Custom. The General section, for example, allows you to view information about when the document was first created and last modified. From the Summary section, you can enter details about the document's author. The Statistics section displays information about the word count, character count, as well as the number of lines, paragraphs, and pages within the document.

- *Edit*. As you're typing and creating a document, the commands available from this pull-down menu will be useful. Commands include Undo, Cut, Copy, Copy to Scrapbook, Paste, Paste from Scrapbook, Paste Special, Paste as Hyperlink, Clear, and Select All, which are common in many Mac applications. Additional commands found under this pull-down menu include:
  - *Find*. Locate a specific word or phrase within a document.
  - *Replace*. This allows you to find all mentions of a specific word or phrase in a document and replace it with something else.
  - *Go To*. Jump to any page or section in your document.

- *Links*. Add, modify, or delete hyperlinks in your document.
- *Object*. Add, modify, or delete an Object in your document.

 *View*. In Word, you can fully customize the menu bars and command icons that appear on the screen, the appearance of the Word program window, and how you view your documents. The following commands are offered under this pull-down menu:

- *Draft*. View your document in Draft mode.
- *Web Layout*. View your document in web Layout mode.
- *Outline*. View your document in Outline mode.
- *Print Layout*. View your document in Print Layout mode.
- *Notebook Layout*. View your document in Notebook Layout mode.
- *Publishing Layout*. View your document in Publishing Layout mode.
- *Toolbox*. Adjust which part of the Toolbox you have access to (Formatting Palette, Object Palette, Citations, Scrapbook, Reference Tools, Compatibility Report, or Project Palette.)
- *Elements Gallery*. From this you can quickly create Cover Pages, Tables, and Charts, or incorporate SmartArt Graphics or WordArt into your document.
- *Toolbars*. Choose which Toolbars will be displayed within the Word program window. Options include: Standard, Formatting, Contact, Reviewing, Tables and Borders, AutoText, Background, Database, Drawing, Forms, Movie, and Speech.
- *Customize Toolbars and Menus*. Decide how your Word program window will look and what Toolbars and command icons will be visible.
- *Navigation Pane*. When this feature is active, thumbnail views (or a document map) of each page within your active document will be displayed along the left side of the program window.
- *Ruler*. Adjust the ruler(s) displayed along the top and left side of your Word work space. Rulers help you visualize page margins, for example.
- *Header and Footer*. Add headers and footers to your document, and insert page numbers.
- *Footnotes*. This tool is used for creating footnotes in your document.
- *Markup*. View comments or tracked changes on the screen.

- *Reveal Formatting*. When this feature is active, you can place the cursor over a specific paragraph or area of your document to see a window that displays detailed information about the paragraph and font formatting.
- *Full Screen*. View your document in full-screen mode. This causes all of the Toolbars and menus to disappear from the screen, thus increasing the size of your work space. Press the Esc key to exit out of this mode.
- *Zoom*. Increase the size of the text that appears on the screen. This command does not impact the size of the text that will ultimately be printed or incorporated into your document. It simply makes small text easier to see on the screen or shrinks large text so more can be displayed on the screen. You can also adjust the display to show the full page width, the whole page, or multiple pages.

● *Insert*. Anything you might want to import or add to a Word document, whether it's a special symbol, graphic, photo, chart, page number, bookmark, or hyperlink, can be done using the commands offered under the Insert pull-down menu. These options include:

- *Break*. Add a page break, column break, or section break to your document.
- *Page Numbers*. Add and customize page numbers within your document.
- *Date and Time*. Insert the date and/or current time in your document.
- *Auto Text*. Choose blocks of pre-created text and insert it into your document. This can include a pre-written closing, header, footer, signature, or salutation, for example. This feature can save you time if many documents you create, such as business letters, have blocks of identical text incorporated in them.
- *Field*. Insert a specific type of content into your document, such as the time, date, a Mail Merge field, page number, or formula.
- *Symbol*. Insert a special symbol into your document that isn't one of the characters on your keyboard, such as a bullet, arrow, (™), (®), or checkmark.
- *Comment*. Insert a comment that will be incorporated within a document, but not actually be part of the document. Think of adding a comment as being just like attaching a yellow sticky note to a page.

- *Document Elements.* Insert a template for a cover page, table of contents, header, footer, or bibliography listing in your document.
- *Quick Tables.* Create and insert a table in your document. It can contain any number of rows and columns, and be fully customized in terms of its appearance.
- *Chart.* Create and insert any type of chart into your document.
- *SmartArt Graphic.* Insert a piece of SmartArt, a clip art collection that's built into the Office suite, in your document.
- *WordArt.* Create and insert WordArt, special visual effects, in your document.
- *Footnote.* Insert a footnote or endnote in your document.
- *Caption.* Insert a caption below a graphic or photo that you have already added to your document. The size and appearance of the caption can be fully customized.
- *Cross-Reference.* Make a notation in a document that cross-references other text, such as a bookmark, footnote, table, or figure.
- *Index and Tabs.* Add an index or adjust the tabs in the text of your document.
- *Watermark.* Add a watermark to the document you're currently creating.
- *Picture.* Import a photo or picture into your document. Once the photo is inserted, you can adjust its size, plus perform a variety of editing and cropping functions.
- *HTML Object.* Insert an HTML Object into your document.
- *Text Box.* Add a text box within a document. This is a separate, graphic box, of any size, that will contain text that's separate from the main body of your document.
- *Movie.* Insert a video or movie file into your document.
- *File.* Insert another Word file (or compatible type of file) into your document.
- *Object.* Insert an object, such as a graphic, into your document.
- *Bookmark.* Add a bookmark to any location in your document and name that bookmark so it can be cross-referenced.
- *Hyperlink.* Add a hyperlink to a website or specific web page in your document.

- *Format.* From this pull-down menu, you can adjust font and typestyle settings, and page formatting options, set columns or tabs, add borders or shading, create numbered or bulleted lists, or adjust the overall style of your document. These commands are also available in the Formatting Palette of the Toolbox.

- *Fonts.* This pull-down menu displays a list of all fonts stored on your Mac's Hard Drive (in your Fonts folder) that can be used in your Word documents. The list is in alphabetical order, or it can be viewed by Font Collection (similar fonts are grouped together).

- *Tools.* Word has a multitude of special tools built into the program that allow you to check your spelling and grammar, access a dictionary or thesaurus, hyphenate text within a document, display foreign language text, obtain a word count for the current document, and track changes made to a document, for example. You'll find the following commands and options under the Tools pull-down menu:
  - *Spelling and Grammar.* Check the spelling and grammar of your document.
  - *Thesaurus.* Can't find the perfect synonym or antonym? Look up a word in Word's built-in thesaurus.
  - *Hyphenation.* Add hyphenation to your text to make it easier to read on the screen or printed page.
  - *Dictionary.* Look up the definition or spelling of a word with Word's built-in dictionary.
  - *Language.* Insert text from a foreign language into a document.
  - *Word Count.* View information about the number of words, paragraphs, spaces, and pages in a document.
  - *AutoSummarize.* This handy feature scans an entire document and picks out keywords and phrases, allowing you to view a summary.
  - *AutoCorrect.* Adjust the rules Word uses when correcting your spelling, punctuation, and grammar.
  - *Track Changes.* Visually view changes made to an existing document. Changes are highlighted as you make them in another color. Later, you can accept the changes and incorporate them into the main document.

- *Merge Documents.* This command takes two Word documents and merges them into one, adjusting for changes in the content.
- *Protect Document.* This command ensures that a document cannot be altered when the Track Changes or Comments feature is used.
- *Flag for Follow-Up.* Add an alarm into a document that will go off at a predetermined date and time.
- *Mail Merge Manager.* Create customized and personalized form letters, e-mails, or other documents by inserting contact names, addresses, and phone numbers, for example, imported from Address Book or Entourage.
- *Envelopes.* Use this command to auto address envelopes using the recipient's address that's already incorporated into your Word document. Choose your envelope size. No time-consuming formatting is required.
- *Labels.* Create and print labels using Word.
- *Letter Wizard.* Use this tool to create professionally formatted and visually appealing business correspondence and other letters.
- *Address Book.* Pull information from Address Book and insert it into your document.
- *Macros.* Record and run Macros in Word for handling repetitive tasks.
- *Templates and Add-Ins.* Manage the templates and add-ins available to you in Word and the Office suite of applications.
- *Customize Keyboard.* Customize the keyboard shortcuts available to you within Word.

- *Table.* The tools needed to create, edit, and display a multicolumn (and multirow) text or numeric table in your document are offered from this pull-down menu. Once the table is created, commands in this pull-down menu allow you to sort and/or manipulate the data displayed.

- *Window.* The functions available under this menu allow you to zoom, minimize, and arrange the Word program window as well as other windows displayed on your Desktop. All of the current open documents are also displayed under this menu option, so you can quickly switch between open documents with a click of the mouse.

- *Help*. Learn how to use any of the features or commands in Word using the Search feature in the Help pull-down menu. You can also access the Mactopia website and check to see if any new program updates have been made available by Microsoft.

- *Automator Workflows*. Available only in certain versions of Word, this menu offers access to AppleScripts and Automator Workflows that can be used in Word. For example, you can:
  - Add password protection and a watermark to a document
  - Covert text to audio and send the file to an iPod
  - Convert the format of a specific Word document
  - Save the document as a PDF file
  - Save the current document in an older Word format

## Word's Program Window

All of the commands available from these main menu options and submenus are also available from the Toolbar, Toolbox, and/or by using keyword short-cuts. With the exception of the Toolbox, which appears as a separate window on your Desktop, the Word application itself runs in its own program window. At the upper-left corner of this window, you'll find the red, yellow, and green dots for closing, minimizing, and zooming the program window itself. In the lower-right corner of the window is the window-resizing symbol, which when used in conjunction with the mouse or trackpad allows you to resize the program window.

Running along the right side of the program window, and potentially along the bottom of the window, are scroll bars for navigating up and down (as well as left and right, if applicable) in the program window. This is done using a mouse, the mouse's Scroll Ball, the arrow keys on the keyboard, or your MacBook's trackpad.

Whenever a document is open in the Word program window, its file name and a graphic icon indicating which viewing mode you're using are displayed along the top center of the program window.

Below the file name, Word's Toolbar is displayed. This is a row of graphic command icons that change based on the View you select. The Toolbar can be customized by selecting the Customize Toolbars and Menus command that's found under the View pull-down menu. The main command icons found along the Toolbar include:

- *New*. Create a new document in Word.
- *Open*. Open an existing document.
- *Save*. Save your current work.
- *Print*. Send the current document to the printer.
- *Undo*. Remove or delete the last thing you just did within Word.
- *Redo*. Re-create whatever you just undid.
- *Format*. Apply specialized formatting to a section of your document without impacting the document as a whole.
- *Tables*. Create and edit a table in your document.
- *Columns*. Add multiple columns of text in your document.
- *Show*. See the otherwise invisible formatting symbols in your document, such as paragraph breaks.
- *Navigation*. Make the thumbnails or document map pertaining to your current document appear (or disappear) from the left side of the Word program window.
- *Gallery*. Make the Toolbar for adding cover pages, tables of contents, headers, footers, and bibliographies appear or be hidden from the Word program window.
- *Toolbox*. Display (or hide) Word's Toolbox, which appears as a separate window on your Desktop.
- *Zoom*. Adjust the size of the document as it appears in your on-screen work space.
- *Help*. Access the Help features built into Word. You can use the Search field to find what you're looking for by entering a keyword or search phrase.

Below the Toolbar in Word's program window is the Formatting Bar, which allows you to select fonts, typestyles, type sizes, text justification, numbered lists, bulleted lists, indents, highlights, and text color. All of these options can also be adjusted using the Toolbox, pull-down menus, and in many cases, keyboard shortcuts.

Below the Toolbar are five graphic tabs that allow you to quickly add Document Elements (Cover Pages, Table of Contents, Headers, Footers, Bibliographies), Quick Tables, Charts, SmartArt Graphics, or WordArt into your document with a few clicks of the mouse. When you click the mouse on any of these options, an additional graphic-based menu bar offering more options appears.

The majority of Word's program window consists of your document work space. This is where your document will appear. At any given time, you can open multiple Word program windows and switch between multiple documents. How your document appears in your work space is determined by the View you select from the View pull-down menu.

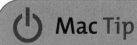

**Mac Tip**

It's important to understand that many of the pull-down menu commands are context sensitive. Thus, they may not appear if they're unavailable to you given what you're currently doing. In some cases, unavailable commands or menu options are displayed in a lighter gray color and won't be accessible.

Running along the top and left side of your work space are rulers, which change based on the size of the page and the margins you select. Any tabs and margins you add to your document can also be adjusted using the rulers.

In the lower-left corner of the Word program window are five icons that allow you to use the mouse to quickly switch views. Displayed from left to right, click the mouse on the icon that represents the Draft, Outline, Publishing Layout, Print Layout, or Notebook Layout view. To the right of these icons (also along the very bottom of the Word program window), information about the number of pages in your document, the number of words in your document, an icon representing the spelling and grammar checking status, and a track changes icon are displayed.

Now that you understand the basic layout of the Word program window and the options available from the Menu bar and the Word Toolbox, you can begin fully utilizing this powerful word processing application. But if at any time you have a questions about how to access or use a feature, go to the Help pull-down menu and type a keyword or phrase into the Search box to quickly

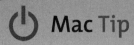

**Mac Tip**

To make your work space a bit larger in Word, or any Office application, you can opt to hide the Toolbar, Formatting bar, and Elements Gallery by clicking the mouse on the oval icon in the upper-right corner of the Word program window. You can also select the toolbars you'd like to view or hide by selecting the Toolbars option from the View pull-down menu.

find answers. If your computer is connected to the internet, you can also use the Visit the Product website command found under the Help menu (microsoft.com/mac/default.mspx) to access the Mactopia website. This site offers video and text-based tutorials, downloads, and other educational and tech support tools relating directly to Office 2008.

# Spreadsheets: Microsoft Excel 2008

If you deal more with numbers than words in your line of work, chances are you're already well-acquainted with Excel, the spreadsheet application that allows you to analyze, share, and manage your numerical data and easily create charts and graphs. Excel 2008 for the Mac offers all of the features and functionality of the PC version, and it also contains templates (accessible through the Elements Gallery) that feature pre-designed worksheets for managing inventories, invoices, budgets, payroll, and portfolios. So, instead of having to create the spreadsheet from scratch, you can load in a template that includes pre-formulated cells and then simply plug in your own numerical data.

The Ledger Sheets feature allows you to use Excel to handle a variety of common money-management tasks associated with personal finance and small-business finance. Pre-created ledgers bundled with Excel offer checkbook balancing functionality, account tracking, and inventory management, for example.

Thanks to Office 2008's OfficeArt graphics engine, Excel allows users to create complex and visually stunning 2D and 3D graphs and charts. These graphics can be printed individually, exported into Word documents and PowerPoint presentations, or transformed into PDF files, for example, to be shared with others.

To help users create and manage complex spreadsheets without having to learn too much about programming formulas, Excel offers Formula Builder (available from the Toolbox). It walks users through the steps needed to create formulas.

Like the PC version of Excel 2008, the Mac version allows users to create spreadsheets with up to 16,000 columns and 1 million rows, for a total of 17.18 billion cells. In addition to being fully compatible with other Office applications, Excel can also easily import data from a FileMaker Pro database.

## Navigating in Excel 2008

The user interface in Excel 2008 for Mac is very similar to other Office 2008 applications, including Word 2008. Users of the PC version will find all of the features and functionality they're already familiar with.

The main commands and the majority of the functionality available in Excel 2008 can be accessed from the pull-down menus located along the Menu bar at the top of the Desktop. Anything having to do with formatting, objects, or formulas, for example, can also be accessed from the Toolbox window, which is separate from the Excel program window.

In addition to the Excel program window and the Toolbox, Excel also uses a separate miniwindow for the Formula bar, which is where you can enter specific formulas to be attached to or utilized in a cell, row, or column of your workbook. By default, the Formula bar is located near the top of the Desktop, just below the Menu bar (and above the Excel program window).

The commands available from the Excel pull-down menus, found along the Menu bar at the top of the Desktop, include:

- *Apple*. This pull-down menu remains constant, regardless of what program(s) you're running on your Mac. See Chapter 3 for details.

- *Excel*. The commands and features available from this pull-down menu option include:

- *About Excel.* View your unique Product ID, see what version of Excel you have installed, get technical support contact information by clicking on the Support icon, and view the program's copyright information.
- *Online Registration.* Register your purchased copy of Excel. This process needs to be completed just once.
- *Preferences.* Personalize the features of Excel, including choosing the default folder where your spreadsheet data files will be saved, selecting your default printer, and adding your personal information. You can also set defaults for calculation procedures, error checking, and custom lists, for example.
- *Services.* Launch other applications while running Excel.
- *Hide Excel.* This command makes the active Excel program window disappear from the screen, but does not quit the application.
- *Hide Others.* This command causes non-Excel windows that are open on your Desktop to be hidden, thus making the Desktop appear less cluttered.
- *Show All.* Display all hidden windows.
- *Quit Excel.* Exit the Excel application. Be sure to save your active spreadsheet data before quitting the program, or any work you've done since last using the Save command (or the auto backup feature) will be lost.

- *File.* This pull-down menu offers a variety of options and commands for opening, saving, printing, sending, and closing spreadsheet data files. Options include:
  - *Project Gallery.* The Project Gallery window allows you to choose a template. Figure 8.2 shows a sample Excel template you can select from the Project gallery and then customize to fit your needs.
  - *New Workbook.* Start creating a new spreadsheet (referred to as a "workbook") without using a template.
  - *Open.* Use this command to open an existing workbook (spreadsheet) file.
  - *Open Recent.* This command displays a list of recently used workbook files and allows you to choose which one to open.

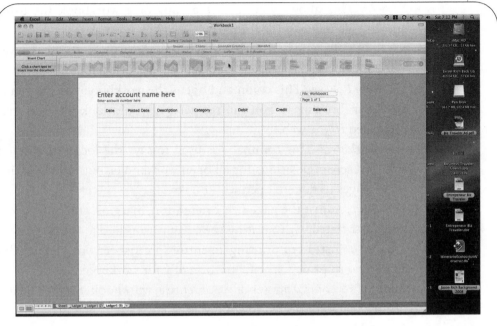

*Figure 8.2*
If you're already proficient using Microsoft Excel on a PC or you've been using other Office applications on your Mac, you'll find this Mac version of Excel familiar. Using the templates from the Project Gallery, you can load  pre-created spreadsheets and simply fill in the cells with your own numeric data.

- *Close*. Use this command to close your active workbook file. Be sure to save your work, however, before closing the file.
- *Save*. Use this command to save your work using the existing file name. If no file name has been created, you'll be prompted to create one and choose where the document will be saved. (You can select a folder or subfolder. The default is to save all newly created files to your Documents folder.) From the Save window, you can also determine in what format Excel will save the workbook file. The default is XML-based workbook format (.xlsx), which is compatible with Excel 2008 for Mac and Excel 2007 for Windows.

- *Save As.* This allows you to save a copy of a workbook file using another file name or file format.
- *Save as Web Page.* Save the workbook file you're working with as a web page, as opposed to as a standard Word (.xlsx or .xls) file.
- *Web Page Preview.* This command opens the workbook you created in the Safari browser so you can see what it would look like if it were published to the web.
- *Save Workspace.* This command is used to save the location, window size, and screen positions for all open workbooks, but not for saving the changes to data in open workbooks.
- *Page Setup.* Adjust the page size, orientation, margins, and other properties associated with printing the current workbook.
- *Print Area.* Instead of printing an entire spreadsheet, you can use this command to print a specific portion of your workbook.
- *Print.* This command sends your entire workbook to the default printer that's connected to your Mac.
- *Import.* Use this command to import numeric data from other applications. Compatible file formats include a CSV file, FileMaker Pro database, HTML file, or text file.
- *Send To.* This command allows you to e-mail your workbook to anyone in HTML format (to be viewed using Safari, for example) or as an e-mail attachment so it can be loaded into the recipient's Mac as an Excel workbook file.
- *Properties.* View details about the workbook you're currently working with. Just as in Word, the Properties window is divided into five categories: General, Summary, Statistics, Contents, and Custom.

- *Edit.* As you're creating or editing a workbook, the commands available from this pull-down menu are useful. They include: Undo, Cut, Copy, Copy to Scrapbook, Paste, Paste from Scrapbook, Paste Special, Paste as Hyperlink, Clear, and Select All, which are common in many Mac applications. Additional commands available from this pull-down menu, some of which are specific to Excel, include:
  - *Fill.* This feature allows Excel to auto-complete fields by predicting what you're typing, based on the first few characters. For example, if

you're intending to type "January," and you enter "Jan," Excel will fill in the rest in order to save you time.

- *Clear.* Use this command to erase specific types of content in your workbook, such as formats, contents, or comments.
- *Delete.* Use this command to delete cells, rows, or entire columns of your workbook.
- *Delete Sheet.* Delete a sheet within your workbook.
- *Move or Copy Sheet.* Copy a sheet from your workbook to another area of your workbook or to another workbook altogether.
- *Find.* Locate a specific word, number, or phrase within a workbook.
- *Replace.* This allows you to find all mentions of a specific word, number, or phrase in a workbook and replace it with something else.
- *Go To.* Jump to any page or section in your workbook.
- *Links.* Add, modify, or delete hyperlinks in your workbook.
- *Object.* Add, modify, or delete an object in your workbook.

- *View.* Many of the commands available from this pull-down menu are identical to those found in Word. The commands that are unique to Excel, however, include:
  - *Formula Bar.* Like the Toolbox, the Formula bar is part of the Excel application, but not contained in the main Excel program window. This menu option allows you to reposition the Formula bar anywhere on your Desktop while you're using Excel.
  - *Status Bar.* In Excel, the Status bar contains information about your workbook that's displayed at the very bottom of the Excel program window.
  - *Custom Views.* Use this command to fully customize your on-screen view of the workbook/spreadsheet you're working with.

- *Insert.* Anything you might want to import or add to your workbook, whether it's a graphic, photo, chart, or hyperlink, can be done from the commands offered under the Insert pull-down menu. While many of these commands are the same as those you'll find under Word's Insert pull-down menu, there are a few commands here that are unique to Excel, such as:

- *Cells*. Insert a cell into your active workbook.
- *Rows*. Insert a horizontal row into your active workbook.
- *Columns*. Insert a vertical column into your workbook.
- *Charts*. Create a chart from data within your workbook. You can choose from an area chart, bar chart, bubble chart, column-based chart, doughnut chart, line chart, pie chart, radar chart, stock chart, surface chart, or X Y (Scatter) chart. Upon choosing this option, the Elements Gallery icons will appear in the program window.
- *List*. Select the location where your list data is located or start with a blank list that will be inserted into your workbook. Selecting this option will activate Excel's List Wizard function (an automated, three-step process for creating lists).
- *Sheet*. Incorporate a Blank Sheet, Chart Sheet, or List Sheet into your workbook, or choose another type of sheet from the Project Gallery.
- *Function*. Excel has an assortment of built-in functions that can be incorporated into a workbook. This command allows you to choose one or more of these functions, which are divided into categories such as Database Functions, Date and Time Functions, Engineering Functions, Financial Functions, Information Functions, Logical Functions, Math and Trigonometry Functions, and Statistical Functions.
- *Name*. Excel allows you to create formulas and assign them names. Names can also be associated with cells or ranges of cells, for example. This command allows you to insert a named formula or cell into your workbook.

- *Format*. When it comes to formatting your workbook or elements of your workbook, you'll use these commands (which are also available from the Formatting Palette of the Toolbox):
  - *Cells*. Format a specific cell or range of cells. When selected, a Format Cells window appears, allowing you to assign a cell category and set the cell's alignment, font, border, patterns, and protection.
  - *Rows*. Using this command, you can set the height of a row, hide a row, and use the Autofit command to make a row fit on the page/screen.

- *Column.* Adjust the width of a column in your workbook. Set a standard width, or use the Autofit command to make the column fit on the page/screen.
- *Sheet.* Format a sheet in a workbook.
- *AutoFormat.* Using this command allows the formatting in your workbook to be done automatically based on preferences that are predetermined by you or the template you're using.
- *Conditional Formatting.* Adjust the formatting of cells, for example, based on the results of a formula. For example, if a result is positive, the number will be displayed in green. If the result is negative, the result will be displayed in red.
- *Style.* Apply formatting to images, pictures, charts, text boxes, and shapes used in your workbook. These same commands and options are available from the Formatting Palette of the Toolbox.

- *Tools.* As you work with spreadsheet data in your workbook, the following tools are available to you:
  - *Spelling.* Correct the spelling of any text in the workbook.
  - *Thesaurus.* Look up a word in Office's built-in thesaurus.
  - *Dictionary.* Look up a word in Office's built-in dictionary.
  - *Language.* Add text from a foreign language.
  - *AutoCorrect.* Adjust the rules Excel uses when correcting your spelling, punctuation, and grammar (related to text in your workbook).
  - *Error Checking.* Check for errors within your workbook.
  - *Share Workbook.* This feature allows multiple users to access an Excel workbook and make changes to the data.
  - *Track Changes.* When changes are made to an existing workbook, all changes, both additions and deletions, are displayed in a different color for easy identification. The alterations can later be approved and fully integrated into the workbook.
  - *Merge Workbooks.* Combine two or more workbook files.
  - *Protection.* Add password protection to a sheet and/or workbook.
  - *Flag for Follow-Up.* Add an alarm to the document that goes off at a predetermined date and time.

- *Goal Seek*. This function sets a calculated cell to a desired value by adjusting an entered value. Use this function to address what-if scenarios that involve a cause and effect, or to see how one data item in a formula impacts another.
- *Scenarios*. Using this function you can quickly substitute values in a number of cells and save that condition under a unique name. You can, thus, test a number of scenarios and demonstrate the impact of different events or possibilities.
- *Auditing*. This tool helps you pinpoint and correct errors or design flaws in spreadsheets.
- *Calculator*. Perform basic mathematical functions in your workbook.
- *Conditional Sum*. Conditional Summing allows a user to calculate a value as a sum of a collection of cells based on the evaluation of the cell value. For example, you could sum only those values that are above average.
- *Macros*. Record and run macros in Excel for handling repetitive tasks.
- *Add-Ins*. Manage the add-ins available to you in Excel.
- *Customize Keyboard*. Customize the keyboard shortcuts available to you in Excel.

- *Data*. The commands found within this pull-down menu—Sort, Filter, For, Subtotals, and Validation—allow you to manipulate the data in your workbook. The Get External Data option found under this menu allows you to import data from a text file, FileMaker Pro database, or FileMaker server. Using the PivotTable Report option, also found here, you can create an interactive table that combines and compares large amounts of data.

- *Window*. The functions available under this menu allow you to zoom, minimize, and arrange the Excel program window, as well as other windows displayed on your Desktop. All of the current open workbooks are listed under this menu option, so you can quickly switch between workbooks/spreadsheet files with a click of the mouse.

- *Help*. Learn how to use all of the features and commands available for Excel.

- *Automator Workflows*. Available only in certain versions of Excel, this menu offers access to AppleScripts and Automator Workflows that can be used in the program.

With the exception of the main pull-down menus found along the Menu bar and the Toolbox, everything that happens in Excel is done within the Excel program window. The layout of the program window is basically the same as that of Word; however, the uses of this application and the functions available within the main work space are totally different. The Toolbar, for example, found at the top of the Excel program window, is comprised of command icons, which from left to right include the following:

- *New*. Create a new workbook.
- *Open*. Open an existing workbook.
- *Save*. Save the current workbook.
- *Print*. Send the current workbook to a printer.
- *Import*. Import data from another application, such as FileMaker Pro.
- *Copy*. Highlight and copy information from your workbook. Once copied, the data can be placed in your Scrapbook, pasted to another location in your current (active) workbook, or copied to another workbook.
- *Paste*. Place the copied data in a specific location.
- *Format*. Apply a different customized formatting to a special area of your workbook.
- *Undo*. Erase or delete the last step(s) you've taken or the last things you've done while using Excel.
- *Redo*. Reapply whatever you used the Undo command to delete or remove.
- *AutoSum*. Perform mathematical calculations on cells, rows, and/or columns.
- *Sort A–Z*. Sort the content of cells alphabetically or in numerical order.
- *Sort Z–A*. Sort the content of cells in reverse alphabetical or numerical order.
- *Gallery*. Access the Elements Gallery to create specialized spreadsheets or charts, or to incorporate SmartArt Graphics or WordArt into your workbook.

- *Toolbox.* Make the Toolbox window appear or disappear from view while running Excel.
- *Zoom.* Increase or decrease the size of text (including numbers) displayed on your Mac's screen.
- *Help.* Access the extensive help features related to Excel to answer your questions and further explain the specific commands and features available.

Located below the Toolbar is the Elements Gallery, which offers command tabs that allow users to add pre-created Spreadsheets, Charts, SmartArt Graphics, and WordArt into any spreadsheet/workbook file. Navigating around the work space is done using the scroll bars along the right side of the window (to scroll up and down) and the bottom of the window (to scroll left or right). The Scroll Ball built into the Apple Mighty Mouse can also be used to navigate around the work space, and so can the arrow keys on the keyboard.

# Presentations: Microsoft PowerPoint 2008

When it comes to creating a graphic presentation, there's no more popular application than PowerPoint. Use this software to create a high-tech slide show that offers compelling visuals, flashy animations, and engaging layouts in order to impress your audience. This latest edition of PowerPoint makes full use of Office's SmartArt Graphics, allowing you to quickly transform boring text, bulleted lists, and numeric tables into impressive 2D and 3D charts and graphs accompanied by professional-looking and highly relevant graphics.

From the Object Palette in PowerPoint, it's easier than ever to incorporate shapes, clip art, symbols, and photos (including images imported, edited, and archived using iPhoto) into the slides for your presentation. For each slide, you can also incorporate a wide range of animations to make your messages burst off the screen and capture the attention of your audience. More transition animations can be used to switch from one slide to the next.

In addition to being able to share PowerPoint presentations with other Mac users and PowerPoint users on the PC, your presentations can be exported to an iPod. When you're ready to give your presentation, this version of PowerPoint gives you, the speaker or presenter, more control over your presentation than ever, including access to digital timer features.

With the goal of making professional-looking presentations fast and simple to create, PowerPoint offers a wide range of templates and design tools that allow you to easily maintain a color scheme or formatting style throughout your presentation, even if you know little or nothing about graphic design. From the Element Gallery, you'll discover dozens of themed templates, allowing you to simply drop your own text and graphics into each slide, without having to worry about the time-consuming task of formatting.

Additional templates can be downloaded from the Microsoft website for free or purchased from third-party companies. Each template has multiple slide formats, allowing you to choose the very best way to visually communicate each piece of information, fact, statistic, or figure you need to convey during your presentation. Pre-formatted title slides, bulleted list slides, chart slides, comparison slides, picture with caption slides, and other slide formats give you plenty of options and flexibility.

Just as with other applications in Office, the majority of PowerPoint's features are available using the program's main menu (located along the Menu bar at the top of your Desktop). Commands and features can also be accessed using the Toolbox, keyboard shortcuts, or from the toolbars that appear within the PowerPoint program window.

In addition to creating and displaying animated slide shows that can be presented on your Mac's screen (or by connecting your Mac to an LCD projector for a larger audience), this program is also ideal for creating web-based presentations, paper-based presentations, and animated presentations that are self-running and can be e-mailed to others.

Using PowerPoint, presentations are created one slide at a time. After choosing a theme or template to be used throughout the presentation (which ensures you'll use consistent fonts, typestyles, layouts, and color schemes), you'll need to select a slide format for each slide to be added to your presentation, and then incorporate your text and graphics accordingly.

With PowerPoint, you'll have access to several different viewing options when creating individual slides, when putting together your presentation, or when actually presenting your presentation to an audience. Beyond just jazzing up a presentation with graphics, adding sound effects and music is also possible.

As you'd expect, PowerPoint 2008 for Mac is an extremely powerful program with many potential uses. For anyone already familiar with PowerPoint on a PC or who has used older editions of the program on a Mac, learning to fully utilize this version will be a straightforward process, mainly because the user interface is similar to what you've already become accustomed to when using other Office 2008 applications.

## Navigating in PowerPoint 2008

The pull-down menu options in PowerPoint look very similar to those in other Office applications. Displayed along the top of the Desktop (outside of the program window) when PowerPoint is active, you'll see the following options:

- *Apple*. This pull-down menu remains constant, regardless of what program(s) you're running on your Mac. See Chapter 3 for details.

- *PowerPoint*. These commands are similar to those you find under a comparable pull-down menu when running another Office application. For example, you can access the program's version number, Product ID, and copyright information, access the PowerPoint Preferences window, or choose the Quit PowerPoint option, thus exiting the application.

- *File*. The commands offered from this pull-down menu are similar to those found in Word. From this menu, you can create a new presentation, open an existing presentation, close a presentation, save the presentation in any of several different file formats, print a presentation, send your presentation to others via e-mail, or adjust PowerPoint's Properties.

- *Edit*. Under this pull-down menu are the familiar commands and features that allow you to undo, redo, cut, copy, paste, clear, select all, find, and replace content in your slides. You can also copy content to Office's Scrapbook, duplicate a slide, or delete a slide within a presentation.

- *View*. This pull-down menu gives you access to the commands and features offered in the Toolbox, and allows you to determine whether or not the Gallery Toolbar or other toolbars will be displayed within the program window. You can also adjust the rulers and guides in the program window and adjust the zoom. Like all of Office's applications, PowerPoint offers multiple views. Each view, however, is useful for accomplishing a different task. The following are your main view options:

- *Normal*. Used to create individual slides (see Figure 8.3).
- *Slide Sorter*. View small thumbnails of all your slides in a presentation and use the mouse to rearrange them as needed (see Figure 8.4).
- *Notes Page*. View your slides on the screen with a special area for writing and adding speaker's notes (to be seen by the presenter, not the audience). This view is excellent for writing the script or rehearsing your presentation after the slides are completed.
- *Presenter Tools*. Use this view to rehearse your presentation and keep track of your time as you speak. A view of the current slide, a preview

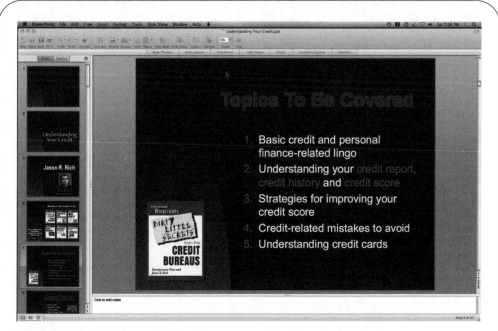

*Figure 8.3*
As you build your slide presentation by creating one slide at a time, the Normal View shows the slide you're currently creating, viewing, or editing, while the remaining slides are shown as thumbnails along the left side of the program window.

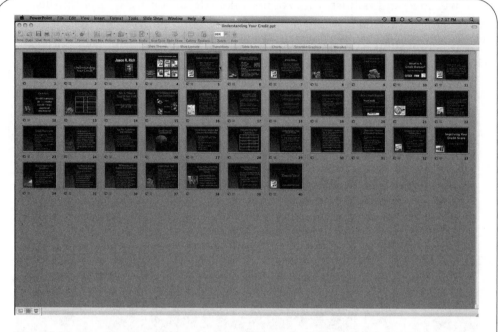

*Figure 8.4*
The Slide Sorter View allows you to see thumbnail images of each slide in your presentation at once. Using the mouse, you can move the order of the slides around. From this view, unwanted slides can also be deleted.

of the next slide, a window showing your speaker's notes, plus thumbnails of your entire presentation (along the left side of the screen) are displayed simultaneously.

- *Slide Show*. This view is used to present your slide show to an audience. This can be done using your Mac's screen or by connecting your Mac to a LCD projector or larger monitor.
- *Master*. View your presentation as it will appear when printed as handouts or when accompanied with your speaker's notes.

 Insert. The commands under this pull-down menu are used to create individual slides and to edit your slides within a presentation. Available commands and options include:

- *New Slide*. Create and add a new slide to your presentation. Figure 8.5 shows a sample blank Title Slide that you can fully customize to meet your presentation needs.
- *Duplicate Slide*. Copy an existing slide that's already in your presentation.
- *Slides From*. Add slides to your current presentation from another presentation or from a different slide layout.
- *Master Placeholders*. Determine if your slide(s) will display the time and date, a header, a footer, page number, or other content.
- *Slide Number*. Add numbers to your individual slides, just as you would add page numbers to a Word document.
- *Date and Time*. Insert the date and/or time into a slide.

*Figure 8.5*
When creating a PowerPoint presentation, you'll create one slide at a time. For each slide, you select its format. Then you stick to a template to ensure your entire presentation remains cohesive from a visual standpoint.

- *Symbol*. Insert a special symbol, such as (™), (®), or a special arrow or bullet, into a slide.
- *Comment*. Add a comment to a slide that can be viewed by you in PowerPoint but that won't be part of the presentation. This feature allows you to add a digital yellow sticky note to a slide.
- *Chart*. Add a 2D or 3D chart or graph to a slide. Charts and graphs can be created using Excel and imported into PowerPoint.
- *SmartArt Graphic*. Add a graphic from Office's SmartArt library to a slide.
- *WordArt*. Add WordArt to generate more visually compelling text or headlines to the slides in your presentation.
- *Text Box*. Add a text box to a slide and then add text to that box. It will be separate from other text on the slide.
- *Picture*. Import an existing picture or photo to a slide.
- *Clip Art*. Import pre-existing clip art to a slide.
- *Shape*. Import and then modify a graphic shape in a slide, such as a box, circle, arrow, or heart. There are dozens of shapes available for PowerPoint (and all other Office applications).
- *Table*. Add a table consisting of customizable columns and rows into a slide.
- *Movie*. Import a movie or video clip to a slide.
- *Sound and Music*. Music and sound effects can be added to individual slides or to your entire presentation. These audio effects can be added from a file stored on your Mac's hard drive, they can come from an audio track on a CD, or you can custom-record music or sound.
- *Object*. Insert an object, such as a Word document or Excel chart, into a slide.
- *Hyperlink*. Add a hyperlink to a slide.

 *Format*. As you're creating individual slides in your presentation, the commands found in this pull-down menu (as well as the Formatting Palette of the Toolbox) will be useful. Commands and options include:
- *Font*. Choose the font and typestyle for text that will appear on a slide.

- *Paragraph*. Adjust the paragraph formatting on a slide.
- *Bullets and Numbering*. Create a bulleted or numbered list on a slide, and customize the bullets and the appearance of this list.
- *Columns*. Divide text or content on a slide into multiple columns.
- *Alignment*. Adjust the alignment of content on a slide. Left, right, centered, or left and right justification are available.
- *Text Direction*. Instead of just having text appear horizontally on a slide, you can make it appear vertically or at an angle.
- *Change Case*. Adjust text to be displayed from uppercase to lowercase or vice versa.
- *Replace Fonts*. Change the font(s) used on a slide.
- *Slide Theme*. Change the theme used in a slide. A theme can be selected from the Gallery or from a downloaded file, for example.
- *Notes Color Scheme*. Adjust the color scheme used in your slides and notes.
- *Notes Background*. Adjust the background color used in your slides and notes.
- *Objects*. Edit and manipulate objects incorporated into your slides.

- *Tools*. Just as in Word, the commands found under this pull-down menu deal with spelling, the thesaurus, the dictionary, the foreign language text you can display, and the ability to review comments. A Flag for Follow-Up alarm can also be set from this menu.

- *Slide Show*. After your individual slides are created, the tools available under the Slide Show pull-down menu allow you to put together and show off your entire slide show presentation. Commands and features accessible from this pull-down menu include:
  - *View Slide Show*. View your entire slide show, complete with animations and sound (if applicable) from start to finish.
  - *View Presenter Tools*. Access the tools available to presenters in PowerPoint.
  - *Custom Shows*. Create a customized slide show presentation.
  - *Set Up Show*. From this window, you have a variety of options for customizing the slide show. For example, you can determine if the

## Mac Tip

As you view the commands available from each pull-down menu, you'll notice a keyboard shortcut for that command is also displayed. Instead of using the pull-down menu, you can execute a command or access a feature using the equivalent keyboard shortcut. For example, to quit PowerPoint, you can press Command (⌘) + Q. To access the Project Gallery and select a template, press Shift + Command (⌘) + P. To open an existing PowerPoint presentation, press Command (⌘) + O. To send a slide or a presentation to the printer, press Command (⌘) + P.

presentation will be given by a speaker (in full-screen mode), browsed by an individual (within a window), or browsed at a kiosk (in full-screen mode). You can also choose to loop the presentation, adjust which slides will be displayed, and determine how slides will be advanced (manually or using timings).

- *Rehearse Timings.* This screen displays your slides while you rehearse and displays a digital timer in the lower-right corner.
- *Record Narration.* If your presentation will be viewed by an individual or as part of a website or kiosk display, for example, you can use this feature to record your narration to accompany each slide. This can be done using the microphone and speakers built into your Mac or by connecting an external microphone and speakers.
- *Action Buttons.* Add action buttons to your slides, such as Home, Help, Information, Previous Slide, and Next Slide.
- *Action Settings.* Adjust the actions that take place in conjunction with the action buttons incorporated into a presentation.
- *Custom Animation.* Add or modify the animation in each slide. PowerPoint has dozens of unique and visually appealing animations to allow content in slides to appear, disappear, and move around.

– *Transitions*. Add or modify slide transitions, the animations used to move from one slide to the next. There are dozens of animations built into PowerPoint.

– *Hide Slide*. This command hides the active slide from the main screen, but does not delete it.

◆ *Window*. The functions under this menu allow you to zoom, minimize, and arrange the PowerPoint program window as well as other windows displayed on your Desktop. All of the open presentations are listed under this menu option, so you can quickly switch between presentations with a click of the mouse.

◆ *Help*. Access the Help features available for PowerPoint. For additional help with specific commands and features, you can also click on the question mark icon (surrounded by a purple circle) on the left side of the Toolbar.

◆ *Automator Workflows*. Available only in certain versions of PowerPoint, this menu offers access to AppleScripts and Automator Workflows that can be used in the program.

## ⏻ Mac Tip

If you're new to using PowerPoint, one of the best ways to figure out all this program can do is to download and view some well-designed presentations created by other people. This allows you to see firsthand how information is communicated effectively using slides and how different presenters use features like animations and transitions to add impact to their presentations.

# Ten Tips for Creating High-Impact and Visually Appealing Slides Using PowerPoint

The following ten tips will help you create slides for your presentation that will communicate effectively without distracting your audience:

1.  Open your presentation with a title slide that states the purpose of the presentation as well as your name.

2.  Use a design template to ensure that all slides in your presentation have a consistent look.

3.  Use colors within your slides that work well together and won't distract the audience. The colors used should be visually appealing. Make sure the colors you use for text, for example, are readable when the slides are projected using an LCD projector. Colors may appear darker on your Mac's screen.

4.  Be consistent when using animations and effects, and don't overuse them. Overuse of animations or transitions is distracting and takes away from your message.

5.  Limit the number of slides you use for a presentation. Each slide should remain viewable for between 30 seconds and 2 minutes, depending on the content.

6.  Use each slide to communicate only one important message or bit of information.

7.  Keep the number of words used on a slide to an absolute minimum. The entire script for your presentation should not be displayed on your slides.

# Ten Tips for Creating High-Impact and Visually Appealing Slides Using PowerPoint,
*continued*

8.  Use uppercase and lowercase text on your slides, and choose a font and typestyle that's easy to read.

9.  Be consistent with your use of bullets and numbered lists. There is no need to use full sentences on your slides.

10. Be sure to spell check the content of your slides, and ensure that all numbers, statistics, facts, figures, charts, and tables are accurate and appropriately placed in the presentation.

 **Mac Tip**

As a general rule, when creating slides for a presentation that will be used in conjunction with a live speaker, less is often more. In other words, only use slides to convey basic concepts, showcase vital graphics, or communicate important ideas that the speaker will embellish. Don't distract the audience by cramming too much information onto the slides themselves. The Microsoft website (microsoft.com/atwork/getworkdone/presentations.mspx) offers tips for creating better presentations using PowerPoint in conjunction with other Office applications. Additional tips for creating an effective presentation can be found at psyche.uthct.edu/shaun/SBlack/slides.html or presentationsoft .about.com/od/powerpointinbusiness/tp/bus_pres_tips.htm.

# Scheduling and Contact Management: Microsoft Entourage 2008

Although your Mac comes bundled with iCal, Address Book, and Mail, easy-to-use and reasonably powerful applications for managing your schedule, to-do lists, contacts, and e-mail, some businesspeople don't find their functionality robust enough to handle their needs. Entourage 2008 meets those needs. Bundled with Office 2008, Entourage 2008 picks up where Microsoft Outlook 2007 (for the PC) left off. It offers a complete solution for schedule management, keeping track of to-do lists, maintaining a contact database, and handling all of your e-mail, all in a single application.

As you'd expect from a scheduling application, you can view your appointments individually, look at a full day's worth of appointments, or see weekly or monthly views of your schedule. The My Day module of Entourage 2008 is an additional tool to help you develop and then stick to your schedule to make the most out of your time.

In addition to keeping track of scheduled events in your life, Entourage 2008 incorporates a comprehensive to-do list management application, allowing you to manage all aspects of multiple e-mail accounts, organize your text-based notes and files, and manage projects from start to finish.

Entourage 2008 is fully compatible with all of your existing Outlook 2007 data, and you can easily synchronize all of your data with your Mac's Address Book, iCal applications, and the Mobile Me service. And if you're already familiar with Outlook on the PC or the Address Book, iCal, and Mail applications on your Mac, learning to use Entourage 2008 requires little more than discovering how to access the program's many features and commands.

## Navigating in Entourage 2008

Remember, Entourage 2008 is really several unique applications in one, all designed to work together to keep you organized and working at peak efficiency. Even though it has many uses, you don't have to use each and every one to make your computing life easier. As you'd expect from any Mac application, the Menu bar (located at the top of the Desktop) offers pull-down menus that give you access to many of the program's key features and functions. All of these same commands, however, can be accessed from the program's Toolbar (found in the Entourage 2008 program window) as well as through the use of keyboard shortcuts.

The program window on your Mac will be different depending on what you're using Entourage 2008 for at any given moment. Each module, however, is designed to work seamlessly with the others. For example, if you access the Mail module of Entourage, you'll see the program's mail management screen (your Inbox, Drafts, Outbox, Sent Items, Deleted Items, Junk Mail folder, etc.). If you're using the Calendar module, the information displayed in the program window is based on which schedule view you have selected.

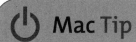

**Mac Tip**

One nice feature of Entourage 2008 is the My Day feature, which opens a separate program window and allows you to view your schedule and to-do items without having the Entourage 2008 program window open.

## *The Menu Bar*

The commands and features available from the Menu bar at the top of the Desktop (as well as by using keyboard shortcuts in many situations) vary based on which Entourage module is active. Many menu options are similar to those on other Mac applications, so what's described in the following sections are the commands that are most useful or unique to each module of Entourage 2008.

### THE MAIL, NOTES, TASKS, AND PROJECT CENTER MODULE'S MENU BAR

- *Apple.* This pull-down menu remains constant, regardless of the program(s) you're running. See Chapter 3 for details.

- *Entourage.* Under this pull-down menu are several options needed to fully utilize this program, including:

- *Preferences.* Set the default options for a wide range of features in the program relating to the address book, to-do lists, calendar, font selection, notifications, sync services, reading e-mails, and composing e-mails. From Preferences, you can personalize the application.
- *Account Settings.* Add and modify e-mail accounts accessible through Entourage as well as News and Directory Service accounts. In many cases, Entourage can automatically set up your POP or Exchange Server e-mail account.
- *Turn On/Off Office Reminders.* Adjust how and when you'll be reminded of appointments, meetings, deadlines, and scheduled events.
- *Switch Identity.* This feature shuts down all Entourage-related accounts and databases and re-opens the application for a new user, while simultaneously loading accounts and databases.
- *Hide Entourage.* Without quitting the application, the Hide feature will make the program window(s) associated with Entourage disappear from the Desktop.
- *Quit Entourage.* Use this command to quit and exit the application.

⚫ *File.* As with any Mac application, the commands under this pull-down menu are for creating, opening, saving, printing, and importing/exporting data. Some of the commands you'll use from this menu include:

- *Project Gallery.* Access templates for creating specialized calendars, e-mails, and other documents.
- *New.* Create a new Mail message, Calendar Event, Task, Note, Contact, Group, News Message, Post, Folder, or Subfolder in any Entourage module. The New command offers a submenu allowing you to choose what you'd like to create.
- *Open Message.* Use this command to open and read a highlighted e-mail message. The keyboard shortcut for this command is Command (⌘) + O.
- *Close.* Use this command to close a highlighted e-mail message.
- *Import.* This command allows you to use a special wizard that makes importing data from an earlier version of Entourage (for the Mac), from another application, or from a text file a quick and easy process.

- *Export.* Use this command to execute a wizard that allows you to export Entourage data so that it can be used by other people on other computers (using other programs). This command can also be used for creating an archive of your Entourage data for backup purposes.
- *Subscribe to a Project.* If you're sharing Entourage information with multiple users or managing a multiperson project with this application, you'll use this command to share data.
- *Page Setup.* Set the printer options you use when working with Entourage. You can choose a specific printer, the paper size, print orientation, and adjust other settings.
- *Print One Copy.* Print a single copy of the e-mail, file, or data you're currently working with within Entourage.
- *Print.* This Print command gives you extra printing-related options before a file or data is sent to a printer.

 *Edit.* In addition to the commands you'd find under the Edit pull-down menu when using almost any Mac application (such as Undo, Redo, Cut, Copy, Paste, Paste from Scrapbook, Clear, Find, Advanced Search, and Select All), some of the Entourage-specific commands you'll find under this pull-down menu include:
  - *Duplicate Message.* Make an exact copy of an e-mail message.
  - *Delete Message.* Delete the e-mail message that's highlighted or that you're currently reading.
  - *To Do.* Access your current to-do list(s). You can choose to see today's lists, tomorrow's lists, this week's lists, all items (regardless of due date), or choose a specific date range. You can also add a reminder or mark a to-do item as completed.
  - *Categories.* Sort your e-mail and other Entourage data into categories to better organize all of your information. Each category can be given a unique name and be displayed using a separate color. Default options include Family, Friends, Holiday, Junk, Personal, Recreation, Travel, and Work, and you can create and manage your own custom categories.

- *Projects.* Use this command to create and manage a new Project.
- *Share Item.* Share specific Entourage data with another user.

- *View.* Some of the commands found under this pull-down menu can be used to access and sort your e-mail. Other commands allow you to hide, customize, or reveal the Toolbar and other menus typically displayed in the program window. A few of the more commonly used commands you'll find here include:
  - *Previous.* Open and read the previous e-mail.
  - *Next.* Open and read the next e-mail.
  - *Hide Toolbar.* Makes the Toolbar at the top of the program window disappear.
  - *Customize Toolbar.* Allows you to determine which command icons will appear in the Toolbar and in what order.
  - *Preview Pane.* Determine whether or not the Preview Pane in Entourage will be displayed, and if so, where. The Preview Pane is where an e-mail can be viewed, without opening it in a new window. The default is for the Preview Pane to appear on the right side of the program window.
  - *Arrange By.* Decide how you want to sort and view your incoming, outgoing, sent, deleted, or junk e-mails.
  - *Unread Only.* Allows you to display only e-mail messages that have not yet been read.
  - *Flagged Only.* Allows you to display only e-mail messages that you have flagged.
  - *Expand All.* Displays more information in each section of the program window.
  - *Collapse All.* This command reduces the amount of data displayed in each section of the program window, thus creating a visually less cluttered screen. Information that is not displayed, however, does not get deleted.

- *Message.* The majority of commands under this pull-down menu are used for creating, editing, replying to, flagging, marking, and sorting your e-mail messages. Some of the commands available include:
  - *Resend.* If you receive an error while sending an e-mail message, this command allows you to resend it.

- *Receive Entire Message*. Instead of just accessing the first few lines of an e-mail (for preview purposes), this command allows you to download and read an entire e-mail message, complete with embedded graphics, if applicable.
- *Edit Message*. Edit an e-mail message.
- *Reply*. Reply to an incoming e-mail message. Your reply will only be sent to the sender of the message, not other recipients.
- *Reply to All*. Reply to the sender and all other recipients of an e-mail message your receive.
- *Reply to Sender*. Allows you to send a reply only to the sender of an incoming message.
- *Forward*. Use this command to forward an incoming e-mail message to others.
- *Forward as Attachment*. Use this command to forward an incoming e-mail message to others. However, the incoming e-mail to be forwarded will be attached to a new e-mail message you create for the recipient you're forwarding the original e-mail to.
- *Redirect*. Use this command to redirect incoming e-mail(s) to other recipients that you designate. This is useful if you go on vacation and want your important e-mails to be automatically forwarded to your colleagues or any alternate e-mail address.
- *Mark as Read*. Use to mark an incoming message has having been read.
- *Mark as Unread*. Similar to a Keep as New command, use this command to read a message, but leave it in your Inbox as a new and unread message.
- *Mark All as Read*. Use this command to mark all new (incoming) e-mails as having been read.
- *Mark as Junk*. Move an incoming e-mail to your Junk folder and add the sender's e-mail address to your spammers list.
- *Mark as Not Junk*. If an e-mail automatically gets forwarded to your Junk inbox, but it's not spam, use this command to move the message(s) to your regular Inbox. Because important e-mails sometimes get automatically forwarded to your Junk inbox by accident, it's important to manually check this mailbox regularly.

- *Block Sender*. Use this command to block e-mails from a specific sender's e-mail address. This is one tool available to you to help stop the influx of spam many computer users receive.
- *Priority*. Set the priority of an incoming or outgoing e-mail message. Options include Highest, High, Normal, Low, or Lowest. This is yet another way to better manage the inflow of e-mail that you must contend with on a daily basis.
- *Save All Attachments*. Use this command to automatically save attachments associated with an e-mail to your Mac's Hard Drive (to a folder or subfolder you determine).
- *Remove All Attachments*. Strip e-mails of attachments before opening them. This is one way to prevent the spread of viruses if you receive e-mails with attachments from unknown senders.
- *Remove Unsafe Attachments*. If Entourage determines that an e-mail attachment may contain a virus, spyware, or malicious data, this command will allow you to read the incoming e-mail message, without opening the attached file. On a Mac, spyware and viruses are not too much of a concern; however, this is a huge concern for PC users to whom you forward e-mails.
- *Apply Rule*. Set rules for accessing, sorting, and managing e-mails, and then apply those rules as you're using Entourage.
- *Move To*. Choose a folder or subfolder where you want to move specific Entourage data or information, such as e-mails.
- *Add to Address Book*. Add contact information from an incoming or outgoing e-mail to your address book.
- *Internet Headers*. Access information in the header of an e-mail. For more advanced web surfers, this is one way to determine where an e-mail came from and its legitimacy.
- *Source*. For more advanced web surfers, this is another way to determine where an e-mail came from and its legitimacy.

 *Format*. Use the commands under this pull-down menu to select fonts, typestyles, font colors, font sizes, alignment, number list formatting, bulleted list formatting, background colors, indents, and other formatting-related information as you compose new e-mails.

- *Tools*. The commands under this pull-down menu are used to manage your e-mail account(s). In addition to executing a send and receive command related to your e-mail account(s), you can also access the spell checker, thesaurus, and other reference tools from this menu. Additional commands available include:
  - *Run Schedule*. Use this command to send and/or receive e-mails from your various accounts and to set up schedules to handle this task automatically. For example, you can set Entourage to check for new e-mails every five minutes.
  - *Send & Receive*. Manually send and receive e-mails from one or more of your e-mail accounts, without waiting for a preset schedule to run.
  - *Open Links*. You can link an incoming e-mail with an upcoming scheduled event or a contact in your Address Book. After you link an e-mail or another piece of Entourage data with other data, you can view what links have been created.
  - *Link to Existing*. Create a link for an incoming e-mail message to an existing address book contact, a calendar event, another e-mail message, a note, or a group. This command helps you link together related information and quickly gain access to all relevant information as you work.
  - *Link to New*. This command allows you to link an incoming e-mail message to a new Address Book contact, a calendar event, another e-mail message, a note, or a group that you're about to create.
  - *Toolbox*. Access Entourage's Toolbox to gain access to the Object Palette (a database of clip art images, symbols, and your own photos), as well as References Tools, and your Scrapbook (which is accessible from all Office applications).
  - *Junk E-Mail Protection*. From the Junk E-Mail Protection window, you can determine what constitutes junk mail and better manage the incoming e-mails that get automatically placed in this folder. You can also block specific spammers and choose to automatically receive all e-mails sent from a specific domain.
  - *Mailing List Manager*. Create and manage a customized mailing list for sending out personalized group e-mails.

- *Newsgroup Settings*. If you utilize internet newsgroups, the commands available here allow you to add and manage those newsgroups.
- *Rules*. Use the commands available in this window to further customize Entourage's e-mail functionality. These tools can help you sort your incoming e-mails and automatically categorize them, for example.
- *Signatures*. Create and manage an unlimited number of e-mail signatures (the text that appears at the end of your outgoing e-mails, such as your name and contact information).
- *Schedules*. Set and manage schedules related to when and how often Entourage will send and receive your e-mails, for example.
- *Accounts*. Add, edit, or manage one or more existing e-mail accounts that Entourage will access.

- *Window*. Use this command to adjust the information that Entourage displays at any given time. You can also quickly switch views, between your incoming e-mails and your calendar(s), for example.
  - *Progress*. Determine what functions are pending or are being currently executed by Entourage (such as sending and receiving e-mail).
  - *My Day*. Access the My Day module of Entourage, allowing you to view your Calendar and To Do lists in a separate window.
  - *Cycle through Windows*. Quickly switch between multiple windows such as the Address Book, Calendar, and To Dos.
  - *Bring All to Front*. Opens all Entourage-related windows simultaneously on the screen.

- *Help*. Access the Help features of Entourage. Use the blue Search field to quickly find how-to information about any feature or command in the program. You can also access online help, visit the Microsoft website, or check for program updates.

## THE ADDRESS BOOK MODULE'S MENU BAR

The Menu bar options will change slightly when you use the Address Book module of Entourage. Available commands will include:

- *Apple*. This pull-down menu remains constant, regardless of what program(s) you're running on your Mac. See Chapter 3 for details.

◆ *Entourage*. Under this pull-down menu, you'll find several additional options needed to fully utilize this program. The commands under this pull-down menu remain constant, no matter which Entourage module you're using.

◆ *File*. As with any Mac application, the commands under this pull-down menu are for creating, opening, saving, printing, and importing/exporting data. You can also access the Project Gallery from this menu.

◆ *Edit*. In addition to the commands you'd find under the Edit menu when of any Mac application (Undo, Redo, Cut, Copy, Paste, Paste from Scrapbook, Clear, Find, Advanced Search, and Select All), some of the Entourage-specific commands you'll find here include:

  – *Duplicate Contact*. Make a copy of a contact record in your Address Book.

  – *Delete Contact*. Delete a contact from your Address Book.

  – *To Do*. Access your current to-do list(s). You can choose to see today's lists, tomorrow's lists, this week's lists, all items (regardless of due date), or choose a specific date range. You can also add a reminder or mark a to-do item as completed using the commands under this menu.

  – *Categories*. Sort your e-mail and other Entourage data into categories to better organize all of your information. Each category can be given a unique name and be displayed in a separate color. Default options include Family, Friends, Holiday, Junk, Personal, Recreation, Travel, and Work, but you can also create and manage your own customized categories.

  – *Projects*. Use this command to create and manage a new Project.

  – *Share Item*. This command will allow you to share specific Entourage data with other users.

  – *Find*. This command is an alternative to using the Search box found in the upper-right corner of the Entourage program window. Use it to quickly find any data related to the application, for example, your Address Book for any data or specific entries.

  – *Advanced Search*. Search your Address Book database, for example, based on any criteria, such as name, company, work phone, or e-mail address.

⬢ *View.* Some of the commands found under this pull-down menu can be used to access and sort your individual contacts in the Address Book. Other commands allow you to hide, customize, or reveal the Toolbar and other menus typically displayed in the program window. A few of the more commonly used commands you'll find here include:

  – *Previous.* Move to the next contact in your Address Book.

  – *Next.* Move to the previous contact in your Address Book.

  – *Go To.* Instead of clicking on one of the module icons in the upper-left corner of the program window, use these commands (or a keyboard shortcut) to switch between Entourage program modules:

    · *Mail.* Command (⌘) + 1

    · *Address Book.* Command (⌘) + 2

    · *Calendar.* Command (⌘) + 3

    · *Notes.* Command (⌘) + 4

    · *Tasks.* Command (⌘) + 5

    · *Project Center.* Command (⌘) + 6

  – *Preview Pane.* Display or hide the Address Book Preview Pane in the Entourage program window.

  – *Columns.* Determine which Address Book fields will be displayed in the Preview Pane for each contact entry. You have dozens of options, including Name, Company, Job Title, Work Phone, Home Phone, Mobile Phone, E-Mail Address, and so on.

  – *Expand All.* This command displays more information in each section of the program window.

  – *Collapse All.* This command reduces the amount of data displayed in each section of the program window, thus creating a less cluttered screen. Information that is not displayed, however, does not get deleted.

⬢ *Contact.* The commands under this pull-down menu allow you to use the information in your Address Book database. Some of the available commands include:

  – *New Message To.* Choose any entry in your Address Book and create (and send) a new e-mail message to that person.

  – *New Invite To.* Choose any entry in your Address Book and create (and send) a new invitation to that person.

- *Send Instant Message to Corporate Account.* Use Windows Messenger to send an Instant Message (IM) to someone's corporate account. Select the recipient from your Address Book.

- *Send Instant Message to Personal Account.* Use Windows Messenger to send an Instant Message (IM) to someone's personal account. Select the recipient from your Address Book.

- *Forward as vCard.* Forward information about a contact in your database to someone else in the form of a universally readable vCard.

- *Map Address.* Automatically use Microsoft's MapPoint website (when your Mac is connected to the web) to access and view a detailed map related to a specific contact's address.

- *Driving Directions from Home.* Select any entry in your Address Book and quickly access detailed driving directions from your location to his location using the Microsoft MapPoint website (when your Mac is connected to the web).

- *Driving Directions from Work.* Select any entry in your Address Book and quickly access detailed driving directions from your work address to her location using the Microsoft MapPoint website (when your Mac is connected to the web).

- *Format.* Use the commands under this pull-down menu to select fonts, typestyles, font colors, font sizes, alignment, number list formatting, bulleted list formatting, background colors, indents, and other formatting-related information as you create and manage Address Book entries.

- *Tools.* Even from the Address Book (or another module), the commands under this pull-down menu are used to manage your e-mail account(s). In addition to executing a send and receive command related to your e-mail account(s), you can access the spell checker, thesaurus, and other reference tools from this pull-down menu option

- *Window.* Use this command to adjust the information that Entourage displays at any given time.

- *Help.* Access the Help features of Entourage. Use the blue Search field to quickly find how-to information about any feature or command in the program. You can also access online help, visit the Microsoft website, or check for program updates.

### THE CALENDAR MODULE'S MENU BAR

The Menu bar options will change slightly when you use the Calendar module of Entourage. Available commands will include:

- *Apple.* This pull-down menu remains constant, regardless of what program(s) you're running on your Mac. See Chapter 3 for details.

- *Entourage.* Under this pull-down menu, you'll find several options needed to fully utilize the program. The commands here remain constant, no matter which Entourage module you're using.

- *File.* As with any Mac application, the commands under this pull-down menu are for creating, opening, saving, printing, and importing/exporting data. You can also use it to access the Project Gallery.

- *Edit.* In addition to the commands in the Edit pull-down menu in most Mac applications (Undo, Redo, Cut, Copy, Paste, Paste from Scrapbook, Clear, Find, Advanced Search, and Select All), you'll find Entourage-specific commands in this pull-down menu when using the Calendar module:
  - *Duplicate.* Use this command to copy a calendar event to another day/time.
  - *Delete Calendar.* Delete data in your calendar(s).
  - *Share Item.* Use this command to share data with others in your calendar(s).

- *Calendar.* The commands under this menu allow you to determine how you'll view your calendar data. As you'll discover, a variety of options and views are available, including:
  - *Previous.* Move to the previous day, week, or month when viewing your calendar.
  - *Next.* Move to the next day, week, or month when viewing your calendar.

- *Go To.* Instead of clicking on one of the module icons in the upper-left corner of the program window, use these commands (or a keyboard shortcut) to switch between Entourage program modules:
  - *Mail.* Command (⌘) + 1
  - *Address Book.* Command (⌘) + 2
  - *Calendar.* Command (⌘) + 3
  - *Notes.* Command (⌘) + 4)
  - *Tasks.* Command (⌘) + 5
  - *Project Center.* Command (⌘) + 6
- *Go to Today.* No matter which calendar view you've chosen, use this command to switch to the current day.
- *View Date.* No matter which calendar view you've chosen, use this command to jump to a specific day or date.
- *Day.* Change the view of your calendar to see one specific day, such as today.
- *Work Week.* Change the view of your calendar to see an entire week at a time. In Entourage, you can preset your Work Week or a regular, seven-day week. Your Work Week can accommodate any specific days and times you work, and display that information accordingly.
- *Week.* Display an entire week's worth of calendar events (see Figure 8.6).
- *Month.* Display an entire month's worth of calendar events. (See Figure 8.7.)
- *List.* View the scheduled items in your calendar (appointments, meetings, events, etc.) as a single list, rather than a calendar format.
- *To-Do List.* In the right side of the program window, this command opens a viewing pane that displays your To Do lists in conjunction with whatever calendar view you're looking at.
- *Arrange By.* Use this command to rearrange your To Do lists by due date, start date, category, project, priority, or folder. This makes managing large and unrelated To Do lists easier.

◆ *Event.* The commands available in this pull-down menu allow you to manage your calendar events and share them with others. Some of the more commonly used commands include:

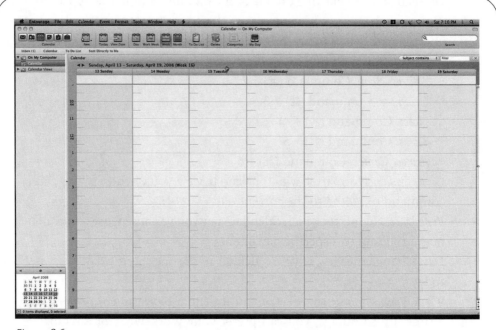

*Figure 8.6*
Shown here is the Week View available to Entourage users using this program to manage their schedule.

- *Send Invitation Now.* Invite others (such as co-workers) to participate in a scheduled event, such as a meeting.
- *Send Invitation Later.* At a later time, invite others to participate in a scheduled event.
- *Check Names.* Manage the names of people on your "invite" list.
- *Status.* Check the status of events or information on your calendar.
- *Time Zone.* Adjust your time zone. This is a useful feature when traveling.
- *Request Responses.* Use this command to communicate with co-workers, for example, and solicit specific types of responses to invitations or other requests.
- *Private.* Set information in your calendar to private so it will not be shared with others.

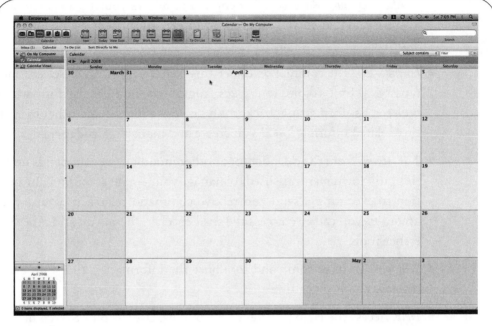

*Figure 8.7*
When using Entourage 2008, you can view and print your schedule in any of several different formats. Shown here is the Month View.

- *Signature.* Create and manage an unlimited number of e-mail signatures (the text that appears at the end of your outgoing e-mails, such as your name and contact information).
- *Priority.* Set, edit, or manage the priority of a calendar entry.
- *Add Attachments.* Use this command to add one or more attachments to a calendar entry, such as relevant e-mails, Address Book contacts, Notes, or To-Do list items.
- *Remove All Attachments.* Use this command to remove any attachments added to a calendar entry.
- *Move To.* This command is used to move a calendar entry from one time/date to another.
- *Copy To.* This command is used to copy a calendar entry from one time/date to another. The original entry will remain active.

- *After Sending, Move To.* This command allows you to categorize and store calendar entries and related information after it is shared with others.

- *Format.* Use the commands under this pull-down menu to select fonts, typestyles, font colors, font sizes, alignment, number list formatting, bulleted list formatting, background colors, indents, and other format-ting-related information as you create and manage calendar entries.

- *Tools.* Even from the calendar (or another module), the commands under this pull-down menu are used to manage your e-mail account(s). In addi-tion to executing a send and receive command related to your e-mail accounts, you can also access the spell checker, thesaurus, and other ref-erence tools.

- *Window.* Use this command to adjust the information that Entourage displays at any given time.

- *Help.* Access the Help features of Entourage. Use the blue Search field to quickly find how-to information about any feature or command avail-able in the program. You can also access online help, visit the Microsoft website, or check for program updates.

## The Entourage 2008 Toolbar

The Toolbar is found at the top of the Entourage 2008 program window. It includes command icons (which are customizable in terms of which icons appear and their order). In the upper-left corner of the program window (below the red, yellow, and green dots for maximizing, minimizing, and zooming the program window), you'll find six icons representing each module in Entourage, including (from left to right): Mail, Address Book, Calendar, Notes, Tasks, and Project Center.

The icon-based command found toward the upper center of the Entourage program window changes, based on which module is active. These icons will represent the most-used commands and features available in an Entourage module.

- When Mail is active, the commands in the center of the Toolbar include: New, Reply, Reply All, Forward, Delete, Junk, To Do, Categories, My Day, and Send/Receive. Figure 8.8 shows what the Toolbar will look like when using the Mail module of Entourage.

- When Address Book is active, the commands in the center of the Toolbar include: New, E-Mail, Invite, Chat, Delete, To Do, Categories, and My Day.

- When Calendar is active, the commands in the center of the Toolbar include: New, Today, View Date, Day, Work Week, Week, Month, To-Do List, Delete, Categories, and My Day. The majority of these commands will impact the view used to see your scheduled items, appointments, and tasks.

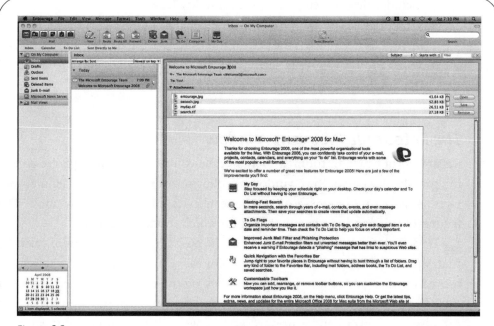

*Figure 8.8*

From the Mail module of Entourage 2008, you can manage all of your incoming and outgoing e-mails from multiple accounts.

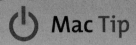

## Mac Tip

In the upper-right corner of the Toolbar is the Search field, which is available throughout the application. By entering any piece of text, such as a name, date, or any piece of information, you can instantly find all instances of that search phrase in your Entourage data files (which includes your Address Book, schedule, to-do lists, notes, and e-mails). This is a handy feature for finding information quickly when using this application.

- When Notes is active, the commands in the center of the Toolbar include: New, Delete, Categories, and My Day.
- When Tasks is active, the commands available in the center of the Toolbar include: New, Status, Due Date, Delete, To Do, Categories, and My Day.
- When Project Center is active, the commands available in the center of the Toolbar include: New, Delete, and My Day.

### The Entourage Program Window

Regardless of which Entourage 2008 module you're using, unless you're accessing the My Day or Toolbox window(s), all of your information (schedule, contacts, e-mails, to-do items, etc.) will be seen in the main program window. The format of this window changes based on which module is active.

By default, in the lower-left corner of the program window is a mini-calendar that shows the current month. This mini-calendar view can be removed, or moved forward or backward simply by clicking the mouse on the left (back) or right (forward) arrows above it, to view calendars for past or future months. You can also raise this calendar upward and allow multiple mini-calendars (up to five) to be displayed simultaneously along the left side of the program window.

While using Entourage may seem a bit confusing at first, because so much information can be displayed and accessed at any given time, you can customize the various displays and views to show only information that you deem important and relevant. And, once you become comfortable navigating in the program using the various pull-down menus, Toolbar command icons, and keyboard shortcuts, you'll find the design and layout of each of Entourage's modules to be relatively intuitive and similar to Outlook on the PC.

Anytime you're having trouble finding important data, the Search field in the upper-right corner of the Toolbar will be an essential tool. You can also access the Help pull-down menu from the Menu bar to learn about any features, commands, or functions built into Entourage 2008.

If you have co-workers who use either Entourage 2008 on a Mac or Outlook 2007 on a PC, you'll find that you can easily communicate with them, synchronize your data and schedules, and manage projects that involve multiple people in your organization. This is one of the most useful features offered by Entourage 2008. The program is equally useful for managing separate schedules for each person in your family.

## Online Chatting: Messenger for Mac

Messenger for Mac is used for sending Instant Messages (IMs) to others. What's nice is that this program is compatible with several different IM systems, including corporate networks, Windows Live, AOL, AIM, MSN, Yahoo! Messenger, and iChat, so you can use this one online chatting application to communicate with a wide range of people in real time. While you're chatting, you can also transfer files or send/receive e-mails with people you're communicating with and manage multiple conversations at once.

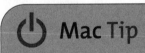

**Mac Tip**

Using Messenger, you can set up both personal and corporate accounts to keep your communications separate.

## Downloadable Office Templates and Extras

As seen in Figure 8.9, from the Mactopia website (microsoft.com/mac /default.mspx) or the downloads area of the Apple website (apple.com/down loads/), you can download additional Office 2008 templates, add-ons, and artwork

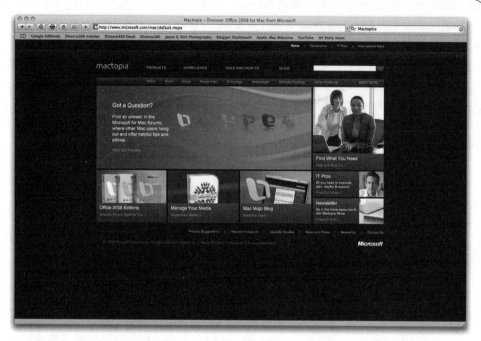

*Figure 8.9*

The Mactopia website is designed by Microsoft to be a clearinghouse for information and downloads for Microsoft Office 2008 for Mac.

(clip art, images, etc.) that will further enhance the functionality of the various applications within this popular suite of applications. In many cases, these templates, artwork assets, and add-ons are offered free of charge, but some third-party software developers do charge for what they offer. For example, there are many companies that offer additional, high-quality, themed PowerPoint templates for a fee.

## Office Compatibility Issues Between the PC and Mac Editions

Much of Microsoft's hype around Office 2008 for Mac and Office 2007 for Windows revolves around the fact that these application suites for different hardware platforms are now 100 percent compatible. So, a Word document created on a Mac, for example, can be accessed with Word on a PC, without any compatibility issues (such as loss of formatting).

Well, the good news is that this compatibility does exist, but there are limitations. For example, both the Mac and PC users must have the latest versions of the various Office applications, and their documents and files must be saved in the proprietary XML file format.

So, if you're using Office 2008 on your Mac, but you want to e-mail a Word file to a PC user using an older version of Word, you must use the Save As command (found under the File pull-down menu in Word) to save the file in the appropriate Word format for the recipient, such as Word 97–2004 (.doc), Rich Text Format (.rtf), Plain Text (.txt), or .pdf. Using some of these formats, however, the formatting within the document itself could be lost altogether or corrupted.

If you and the intended recipient both have versions of Acrobat Professional, for example, you can create editable PDF files of your printable documents and files to ensure all formatting remains intact as you migrate files between newer and older versions of Office applications, and between Macs and PCs.

In a nutshell, if you're using Office 2008 on your Mac, you can easily send and receive files from other Office 2008 for Mac users knowing the files will be fully compatible. If you're sending or receiving files from a PC user running Office 2007, as long as the files are saved using the XML format, they should be fully compatible (but should be checked carefully). Unless one of these two scenarios exists, you'll need to use the Save As command to save your Office files and documents in an older format to help ensure compatibility (which may or may not work properly, depending on the application and complexity of the formatting, fonts, and functionality within the application that's used).

# The iWork '08 and OpenOffice.org Productivity Suite Alternatives

For business professionals and entrepreneurs, Office 2008 is definitely a must-have application suite. There are, however, less costly, yet equally functional alternatives. In Chapter 9, you'll learn all about iWork, Apple's suite of business applications that includes word processing, spreadsheet management, and presentation software.

While iWork offers the same basic features as Office, the cost of this software is considerably less. However, if you'll be importing and exporting files between Macs and PCs, some compatibility issues might arise, depending on the complexity of your files from a formatting and page layout standpoint. Ultimately, whether you adopt Office or iWork as your primary suite of work-related applications will be based on personal preference and what's required to ensure file compatibility with your co-workers, clients, and business associates.

If the cost of adding software to your computer is prohibitive, yet you require word processing, spreadsheet, and presentation software, yet another alternative is to download the OpenOffice.org Productivity Suite for Mac. As the title of this suite of applications suggests, OpenOffice.org is open-source software for word processing, spreadsheets, presentations, graphics, and database management. What this means is that the full working version of this software is available free of charge with absolutely no strings attached! Simply download the software and start using it.

The latest version of OpenOffice.org Productivity Suite for Mac can be downloaded from OpenOffice.org. It's the result of more than 20 years' worth of software engineering by a team of dedicated programmers who have volunteered their time and efforts to create this comprehensive suite of applications for both PC and Mac platforms.

## ⏻ Mac Tip

OpenOffice.org is both the name of the software product (OpenOffice.org Productivity Suite) and the name of the open-source project that designs, develops, maintains, translates, tests, documents, supports, and promotes the suite (known as the OpenOffice.org Community). The project is comprised of more than 5,000 individuals.

One of the best things about Open Office.org Productivity Suite is that if you're already familiar with any similar application suites, such as Microsoft Office 2007 (for PC), Microsoft Office 2008 (for Mac), or iWork '08, you'll have no trouble whatsoever learning to use the programs that are part of OpenOffice.org Productivity Suite.

OpenOffice.org Productivity Suite is comprised of five main applications, including:

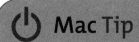

**Mac Tip**

Versions of OpenOffice.org Productivity Suite support more than 70 languages and 100 language localizations. Each version of the suite is stable, reliable, and robust.

1. *Writer.* A full-featured word processor and page layout application that runs on all popular computing platforms, including Windows, GNU/Linux, Sun Solaris, and Mac OS. It's fully compatible with commercial applications, such as Microsoft Word or iWork's Pages '08.
2. *Calc.* This is a powerful spreadsheet management tool that offers the features and functionality you'd expect from Microsoft Excel or iWork's Numbers '08 application. It's compatible with these applications.
3. *Impress.* When it comes to creating professional-quality presentations using 2D or 3D graphics, text, and special effects to get your message across to your audience, this application can do pretty much anything that Microsoft PowerPoint or iWork's Keynote '08 can do.
4. *Draw.* This is a useful graphics development tool that's ideal for creating diagrams, flowcharts, organizational charts, network diagrams, and other simple or complex graphics.
5. *Base.* If your work requires you to create or maintain databases, two popular commercial applications for the Mac are Bento and FileMaker Pro (see Chapter 10). However, part of the OpenOffice.org Productivity Suite of applications is Base, which allows you to easily create and modify tables, forms, queries, and reports while managing your fully customized database. No programming is required to create database applications because Base comes with a variety of wizards and templates that are ideal for novice and advanced users alike.

## ⏻ Mac Tip

OpenOffice.org Productivity Suite can be downloaded and used for free with no strings attached. However, to ensure the future expansion and success of this application suite, users are encouraged to contribute back to the Open Source community, by donating their time or making an optional financial contribution.

Just as with Microsoft Office and iWork, the programs within the OpenOffice.org Productivity Suite work seamlessly together, so data and files can quickly and effortlessly be transferred between documents. Thus, a graph or chart created using Calc or Draw, for example, can be imported into a Writer document or Impress presentation.

Once you've downloaded and installed the OpenOffice.org Productivity Suite from the OpenOffice.org download page (download.openoffice.org), visit the Get OpenOffice.org Extensions page to learn about free add-on applications designed to improve the features and functionality of various OpenOffice.org applications. From this page, you can also download and print comprehensive user guides for each application and download free templates, dictionaries, and clip art.

If you have a question about using any OpenOffice.org Productivity Suite application or feature, free technical support is available online at the OpenOffice.org website (support.openoffice.org/index.html). There is also an established network of knowledgeable OpenOffice.org consultants that you can hire (for a fee) to help you get started using this software through one-on-one training. A wide range of published how-to books about this software are available from bookstores everywhere.

The overall goal of OpenOffice.org Productivity Suite and the Open Office.org organization is "To create, as a community, the leading international office suite that will run on all major platforms and provide access to all functionality and data through open-component based APIs and an

XML-based file format." The result is powerful and highly functional, yet easy-to-use software that's as powerful (and in some cases more functional) than similar commercially available applications that sell for hundreds of dollars.

OpenOffice.org Productivity Suite offers an excellent, free alternative to Microsoft Office 2008 and iWork '08. Because this is an ever-evolving suite of applications and new features are constantly being added, you'll definitely want to check for free software updates on a regular basis.

OpenOffice.org can be downloaded directly from the web and installed on your Mac. However, the size of the download is extremely large, so depending on the speed of your internet connection the process could take up to several hours. An alternative is to visit the OpenOffice.org website and order the software on CD from an authorized distributor. A small fee (between $8.95 and $36.95), to cover the cost of CD duplication, manuals, and shipping, will apply.

# More About iWork '08

iWork '08 is a suite of business-oriented applications developed by Apple and available exclusively for the Mac. iWork '08 is sold at Apple Stores nationwide, from authorized Apple resellers, as well as from the Apple.com website. The next chapter offers a detailed overview of this popular and less expensive Microsoft Office 2008 alternative.

# Apple iWork '08, iLife '08, and Mobile Me

I N ADDITION TO MANUFACTURING MAC COMPUTERS, APPLE ALSO PUBLISHES SEVERAL popular software applications and application suites for Macs. Among these many applications, the iWork '08, iLife '08, and Mobile Me services are especially important. iWork '08 was designed by Apple to meet the word processing, spreadsheet, and presentation needs of business professionals and entrepreneurs. iLife '08 is a suite of applications for handling a broad range of computing needs that comes bundled with all new Macs and complements the Mac OS X operating system nicely.

The Mobile Me online service is helpful in backing up critical data, sharing files, and creating blogs or personal web pages.

# iWork '08

Designed to be Apple's alternative to the Microsoft Office 2008 suite of applications, iWork '08 includes three feature-packed applications: Pages '08 (a powerful word processor), Keynote '08 (software designed for creating cinema-quality presentations), and Numbers '08 (a spreadsheet application that allows uses to create stunning 2D and 3D numeric charts).

Available from all Apple Stores, Apple.com, and Apple authorized dealers, iWork '08 is $79 (considerably less than Microsoft Office 2008). Like Office, iWork '08 has several distinctly different applications, yet they work together seamlessly. For example, spreadsheet data or charts created with Numbers '08 can quickly be imported or copied into Pages '08 document files.

To make all three applications in the iWork '08 suite easier to use and enhance the productivity of the user, each program is bundled with dozens of templates. For example, if you're creating a presentation for an important meeting, Keynote '08 allows you to choose from 35 different templates (more can be downloaded from the Apple.com website and other sources). You can then plug in your text, graphics, and data, add any of more than 25 animations, and quickly create a highly professional and visually stunning presentation, even with no graphic design experience.

## Getting Started with iWork '08

Unlike iLife '08, the iWork '08 suite of applications is sold separately from your Mac, although a trial version of the software will be pre-installed in the Applications folder of your new Mac.

Once you've purchased the iWork '08 software, you'll need to install it onto your Mac. To do this on all Mac machines (except for the MacBook Air), insert the program CD into your computer's optical drive. Within a few seconds, the iWork '08 Install CD window appears (See Figure 9.1).

To begin the installation process, click on the Install iWork '08 icon, found on the upper-right side of the iWork '08 Install CD window. Follow the

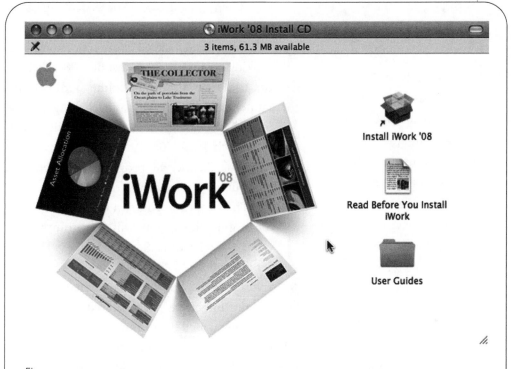

*Figure 9.1*
Upon inserting the iWork '08 CD into your computer's optical drive, you can begin the software installation process by double-clicking on the Install iWork '08 icon, found on the upper-right side of the iWork '08 Install CD window.

on-screen instructions, which include clicking on the Continue icon on several installation information windows that appear. Upon choosing the destination hard drive where you'd like the software installed, you'll need to enter your Mac's system password to continue the installation process.

iWork '08 will take about 5 minutes to install. As this process is occurring, locate the 23-character Product Serial Number in the *Getting Started* manual that's in the software's box. This Serial Number is required to complete the installation process. If you purchase the software online from Apple, your Serial Number will be e-mailed to you.

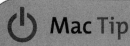

## Mac Tip

Whenever you install any new software onto your Mac, keep the program CD and the software's unique Serial Number someplace safe. At some point in the future, you may need to re-install the software or have to access to the Product Serial Number when seeking technical support from Apple.

When the "Install Succeeded" message appears on your screen, you'll notice three new icons on your Dock. Clicking on the podium-looking icon launches Keynote '08. Clicking on the icon that looks like a 3D graph launches Numbers '08, and clicking on the icon that looks like a pen and ink allows you to launch Pages '08. At this point, you can eject the iWork '08 program CD from the computer's optical drive.

The first time you run one of the iWork '08 applications, you will be prompted to enter your Product Serial Number. The letters in the Serial Number are not case sensitive. Click the Continue icon when the entire serial number has been entered.

Next, you'll be prompted to confirm your Registration Information, including your First Name, Last Name, E-Mail Address, and Country. These fields should automatically be filled out with your personal information; but you can edit this information now, before clicking on the Continue icon. To conclude the installation and registration process, your Mac will connect briefly to Apple's website to transmit your registration information. When the "Thank You" window appears, the installation process is complete.

Before you're ready to begin using the iWork '08 applications, it may be necessary for you to download free software updates from the Apple website. If this is the case, a window will appear on the screen asking for permission to download the necessary updates and the Software Update application will launch. At this point, the three iWork '08 applications are now fully installed, up-to-date, and ready for use.

## Getting Started with Pages '08

First and foremost, Pages '08 is a powerful, feature-filled word processor. However, like Microsoft Word, it's also capable of performing desktop publishing and page layout tasks, so creating full-color, professional-looking reports, newsletters, brochures, and other documents is extremely easy. The software allows you to insert a wide range of graphics into your text-based documents, while also giving you the ability to select your fonts, typestyles, text colors, margins, and other visual elements.

When you launch the Pages '08 application, the Choose a Template for Your Document screen appears (see Figure 9.2) by default. From this window, you can select a document type and template. Or if you wish to create a basic text document or create a fully customized page layout, you can select the Blank option by clicking the mouse on the Blank thumbnail on this screen.

In the future, you can opt for this Choose a Template for Your Document window not to appear when you launch Pages '08. To do this, place a checkmark on the "Don't show this dialog again" option found in the lower-left corner of the window.

To choose a template, use the mouse to highlight the one you want to load, and click on the Choose icon, located in the lower-right corner of the Choose a Template for Your Document window. For this example, the Modern Letter template was selected. Within seconds, a document that uses this template was created and loaded into Pages '08. You can now use Pages '08 word processing features to remove the dummy text incorporated into the template for placeholder purposes and enter your own text and graphics (see Figure 9.3).

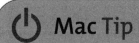

**Mac Tip**

One reason why Mac users opt to use Pages '08 instead of Microsoft Word is because this program is somewhat more intuitive, although equally as powerful. The Help feature is also more robust in Pages '08, so if you're new to word processing, the program is easier to learn and use. iWork '08 is also much less expensive than Microsoft Office 2008.

## Navigating in Pages '08

Like most Mac applications, the commands and functions available to you through the Pages '08 program can be accessed from the pull-down menus at the top of the Desktop,

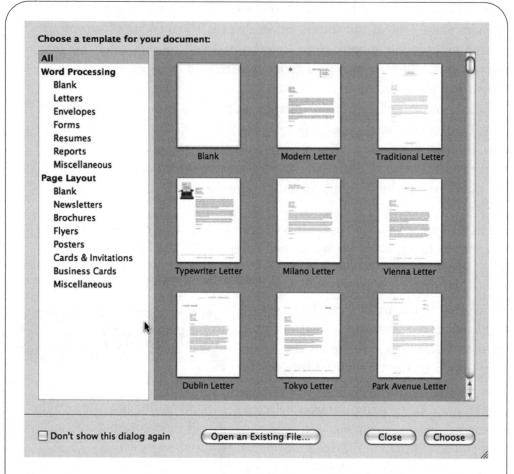

*Figure 9.2*

From the Choose a Template for Your Document window, you can select one of the many Pages
'08 templates that come bundled with the software or you have previously downloaded from
the web. These templates make creating fancy documents, like newsletters, reports, or formal
business letters, easier because all of the formatting for the basic appearance of the document
has been created on your behalf. All you need to do is plug in your own text, and graphics if
applicable.

*Figure 9.3*

Upon loading a Pages '08 template, you can replace the placeholder text and graphics with your own in order to create a professional-looking document without spending the time to do your own page layout or design work.

> ## ⏻ Mac Tip
>
> Throughout this section, detailed descriptions are offered for virtually all of the commands and features available to you when using Pages '08. Many of these commands and features, such as those found under the File, Edit, Window, and Help pull-down menus, are the same as those in other Mac programs, such as Numbers '08 and Keynote '08.

as well as from the icons found at the top of the Pages '08 program window. You also have access to dozens of keyboard shortcuts when using this application.

### The Pages '08 Menu Bar Options

Located in the upper-left corner of the Desktop is the always present Apple icon. To the immediate right of this icon on the Menu bar is the Pages pull-down menu. It offers the following commands:

- *About Pages.* Quickly discover what version of the Pages '08 program you're running and obtain your software's Serial Number. To close this window after viewing the information, click on the red dot in the upper-left corner of the window.
- *Pages Hot Tips.* This command links you to Apple's Page '08 Hot Tips website, which offers more information and tutorials for using the program. Your Mac must be connected to the web to access this feature.
- *Preferences.* Adjust the general preferences and auto-correct options to customize the software. For example, you can select whether the template selection window will appear each time you open a new document.
- *Try iWork.* This option is only selectable if you're using an unregistered version of the software. It will allow you to try the iWork applications for 30 days.

- *Provide Pages Feedback.* This command links you to a website that allows you to e-mail Apple your comments and suggestions about the Pages software. Apple will not, however, respond to comments sent using this site, nor can this site be used to obtain answers to technical support questions.
- *Register Pages.* Use this pull-down menu option to register your purchased copy of the software with Apple.
- *Services.* This pull-down menu will appear when using almost any Mac program. It offers shortcuts to other features and programs available in the Mac OS X operating system.
- *Hide Pages.* Use this feature to temporarily hide the Pages '08 active program window, without shutting down the program.
- *Hide Others.* This feature can be used to hide the program windows from other nonactive applications, folders, or files that are open on your Desktop. It will quickly allow you to eliminate clutter on the screen, without shutting down any of the programs running.
- *Show All.* Causes all hidden windows to be reopened on the Desktop.
- *Quit Pages.* Use this command to quit (shut down) the Pages '08 program. You will be prompted to save your work before executing this command. Quitting the program without saving the document file you've been working on will cause data to be lost.

When each pull-down menu is displayed, on the left side is the command name. On the right is the keyboard shortcut used to execute that command (instead of manually clicking the mouse on the command from the pull-down menu). Most of the keyboard commands require pressing the Apple/ Command (⌘) key in conjunction with

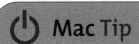

## Mac Tip

If you're already familiar with Microsoft Word on your old PC (or even the Mac version), you'll discover that many of the word processing and page layout commands are identical or extremely similar in Pages '08. This makes learning to use this word processor much quicker.

another key on the keyboard. For example, Command (⌘) + N will allow you to instantly create a new document. You can print the document you're working on by pressing Command (⌘) + P. To save your work at any time, press Command (⌘) + S.

## FILE PULL-DOWN MENU

Moving along the Menu bar located at the top of the Desktop, the File menu is on the right of the Pages pull-down menu. This menu offers the primary commands to create new documents, open existing documents, save documents, export documents, share documents, and print your documents. The commands available on the File pull-down menu include:

- *New*. Create a new document. Depending on how you've customized the program, you'll either see the Template Selection window appear or a Blank document will automatically open.
- *New from Template Chooser*. Create a new document by first accessing the Template Chooser to select the type of document and the specific template you want to customize with your own text and graphics.
- *Open*. Start editing or reviewing an existing Pages '08 file that's stored on your Mac's Hard Disk or on another file storage source, such as a CD or thumb drive.
- *Open Recent*. This command displays the last several documents you've worked with and allows you to quickly re-open any of them in Pages '08.
- *Close*. Close the current document you're working on. Be sure to save the file (and your latest changes) before closing the file. The software will prompt you to do this.
- *Save*. Save the current Pages '08 document you're working on. You should definitely save your file when you're done with it. However, it's also a good idea to periodically save your work in progress. If your computer needs to be rebooted for any reason, you won't lose too much critical data if you've been saving it all along. When saving a file for the first time, a Save window will appear, prompting you to create a file name and to indicate where (in which folder) you want the file saved. The default selection is to save new Pages files in your Documents folder. However,

you can create an unlimited number of subfolders within your Documents folder or choose another save location altogether.

* *Save As.* This allows you to resave the document you're working on in a new file name. In essence, you'll be creating another copy of the document on your Hard Drive, or wherever you opt to save the file, using an alternate file name and perhaps a different file format.

* *Revert to Saved.* This allows you to reload the document you're working on at the point where you saved it last. This will delete any new changes or edits you've made to the document since it was last saved.

* *Export.* Using this command, you can export your Pages document to a PDF file, Microsoft Word-compatible document, or RTF file (Rich Text Format), or save it as a Plain Text file (which can be opened by any word processor or text editor). If you're working with colleagues who use a different word processor, such as Microsoft Word on a PC, you'll need to export your Pages documents to ensure they'll be accessible to users on other machines who are running other word processing or page layout programs. After choosing a file format, you'll be asked to select a file name for your document and choose a location where you'd like the document to be saved.

* *Send to iWeb.* If you're a subscriber to the Mobile Me service (described later in this chapter), sending your files to iWeb is a way to back them up and make them available to others who have access to the internet.

* *Save as Template.* In addition to loading templates created by Apple or other third parties, you can create or modify your own templates and save them as such (as opposed to as Pages documents) using this command.

* *Page Setup.* Set the page attributes, format, paper size, orientation, and scale of the Pages document you're working on. You'll notice that in the lower-left corner of this window, a question mark in a purple circle appears. Anytime you see this icon in any program, you can click on it to access a relevant help screen.

* *Print.* Use this command to send your current document to a printer connected to your Mac. If multiple printers are connected, you'll see a pull-down menu and be able to select which printer you prefer. From the

Print window, you can also create a PDF of the file and preview the file on the screen to see exactly how it will look on the printed page. When you're ready to print, click on the Print icon located in the window's lower-right corner. The keyboard shortcut for printing a document in Pages (and many other Mac programs) is Command (⌘) + P.

## Edit Pull-Down Menu

Along the Menu bar, the Edit menu is located to the right of the File pull-down menu. Here, you'll find commands commonly used when actually doing your word processing, such as Cut and Paste. This pull-down menu also offers the commands necessary for performing spelling checks or for proofreading your document. You'll notice that not every commend under each pull-down menu is available to you at any given time. For example, you can't delete text until you've actually started typing and have created text to delete.

The commands available from the Edit pull-down menu include:

- *Undo.* This command allows you to undo the impact of whatever command you last executed or to delete the last few words you typed.
- *Redo.* This command re-creates anything the Undo command deletes if it's used immediately after using the Undo command.
- *Cut.* Once text is highlighted, you can cut (delete) it from the document using this command. Highlighted text can also be deleted by pressing the Delete key on the keyboard or by pressing Command (⌘) + X.
- *Copy.* Use this command to copy highlighted text into a temporary storage area (referred to as your *scrapbook*). While running Pages or another application, you can then paste that text elsewhere using the Paste command.
- *Paste.* This command allows you to place copied text in another location within the same document or in another document or file altogether.
- *Paste and Match Style.* When pasting text into a document, using this command adjusts the pasted text to match the style of the text surrounding it.
- *Delete.* When text is highlighted, this command deletes (erases) the text highlighted in the document.
- *Delete Page.* If working with a multipage document, this command deletes (erases) the entire current page.

- *Clear All.* This command is used to clear background fill and any style settings added to text.
- *Duplicate.* Use this command to copy any graphics or nontext elements incorporated in a Pages document.
- *Select All.* Quickly select and highlight all text and graphics in a single document.
- *Deselect All.* If you have an entire document highlighted (after using the Select All feature) or if you have several sections of a document highlighted separately, you can remove all selection highlights using this command.
- *Track Text Changes.* If you'll be editing a previously created document and want to keep track of the changes you make (or the changes made by a proofreader, for example), use this command. Once activated, any new text or changes made to the document appear in a different color for easy recognition. On the left side of the program window, a Comments pane appears. In this area, a record of all changes made to the document are automatically kept. Once the changes are reviewed, you can opt to accept or reject them. Rejected changes are deleted, while accepted changes become a permanent part of the document.
- *Merge Address Book Cards.* Use this command to insert data from your Address Book database into any Pages document. This includes contact names, addresses, phone numbers, and e-mail addresses. This function allows Mail Merge capabilities, so you can create personalized form letters.
- *Choose Address Label.* When writing a letter using Pages, you can create an address label for the recipient.
- *Find.* This command allows you to search the entire document for any word or search phrase you enter.
- *Spelling.* This command allows you to manually spell-check a document. You can also (using this command) set Pages to auto spell check as you type. When a spelling mistake is made, the word is automatically underlined on the screen with a red dotted line.
- *Proofreading.* As opposed to just checking spelling, proofreading a document allows the Pages software to review your grammar as well. You can

select the Proofread as You Type command so the software automatically checks and corrects grammar mistakes in real time as you type.

- *Writing Tools*. Choosing this command opens another pull-down menu. From here, you can look up words in a dictionary or thesaurus, or perform a search using Spotlight, Google, or Wikipedia. You can also Show Statistics pertaining to a document. This causes another window that displays details about the document to appear. From this window, you can set the margins of your document, add footnotes, select page number format, create a table of contents for the document, add info about the document's author, and automatically calculate the document's word count, page length, and other details. When it comes to customizing a document, the commands available in this window are extremely useful.

- *Special Characters*. In addition to the regular alpha-numeric characters available on your keyboard, this command allows you to access a vast selection of special characters that can be incorporated into your document(s). These characters include special arrows, currency symbols, punctuation symbols, stars, characters from other languages, and mathematical symbols.

## INSERT PULL-DOWN MENU

Moving to the right along the Menu bar, the Insert pull-down menu is located next to the Edit pull-down menu. The commands you'll find here allow you to add various elements to the document you're working on, such as multiple columns, page numbers, shapes, tables, or charts. You'll find the following commands under the Insert pull-down menu:

- *Sections*. This command allows you to separate your document into separate (you guessed it) sections that incorporate different layouts, numbering, or formatting.

- *Section Break*. Use this command to separate unique sections in a document so alternate numbering or a different layout for formatting can be used.

- *Page Break*. Insert a page break into the document, which causes the text below the inserted page break to begin at the top of a new page.

- *Layout Break*. This command is used to separate a document and incorporate different page layouts in the same document.
- *Column Break*. Use this command to end the flow of text in a column that's defined within the document and then continue the flow of text in another column. Obviously, the command is used when creating or editing a multicolumn document.
- *Date & Time*. Insert the date and/or current time into any document.
- *Page Number*. Insert and format page numbers to be displayed and printed.
- *Page Count*. Allow the document to display its total number of pages, in addition to the individual page numbers. Thus, in the header or footer, it could display "Page 2 of 10."
- *Table of Contents*. Pages has the ability to automatically create a table of contents for a long document, based on headings and subheads you create.
- *Footnote*. Add and format footnotes within your Pages document.
- *Bookmark*. Creating a bookmark allows you to quickly link to a particular location within a document. Use this command when a document will be viewed on a screen (as opposed to in print). A bookmark can be used to mark passages in a document that you want to refer to in other parts of the document.
- *Hyperlink*. Used for documents that will be displayed on the screen (or distributed via a website and viewed using a browser), hyperlinks allow you to create connections to specific pages or content in your document, or link a word or phrase to another document, e-mail address, or website, for example.
- *Address Book Field*. This command is used to import data from the Address Book application
- *Comment*. Create a comment in a document that can be viewed separately from the document itself, but that pertains to a specific portion of the document. On the screen, the comment(s) you add will be seen in a separate comments column displayed on the left side of the Pages program window. Text that's related to your comment will be highlighted on the screen in another color.
- *Text Box*. Create a separate box of text in a document. It can be any size.

- *Shape.* Using this command, you can add a variety of graphical shapes to your document and then customize them accordingly.
- *Table.* Insert a table in a document. A table is a combination of columns and rows that can be used to display numbers, text, or other content in a graphical and more organized manner. You can select the number of columns and rows that will appear in a table and then customize its appearance.
- *Function.* Use this command to automatically perform mathematical calculations on columns or rows of numbers.
- *Chart.* Create and insert a simple chart. To create more elaborate charts in 2D and 3D, you'll want to use Numbers '08 and then import the chart into the Pages document.
- *Choose.* Use this command to insert another Pages document in the one you're currently working on.

## FORMAT PULL-DOWN MENU

The Format pull-down menu, found to the right of the Insert pull-down menu along the Menu bar, offers commands used to control the appearance of your document—what fonts, typestyles, and graphics you'll use. The commands available to you from this pull-down menu include:

- *Font.* Use the menu options found under Font to change between Regular text and **Bold**, *Italic*, <u>Underlined</u>, ~~Strikethrough~~, or Outline text (or any combination of these typestyles). You can also make text bigger or smaller, and adjust other criteria for the appearance of your text. By clicking on the Show Fonts command, for example, you can choose from all of the fonts installed on your Mac. All of the commands found under the Fonts menu option are also available elsewhere in the Pages program.
- *Text.* Adjust the paragraph justification: left justified, centered, right justified, or left-and-right justified. You can also adjust indent levels.
- *Table.* Customize the appearance and format of tables you add to your documents.
- *Chart.* Create simple charts and adjust their appearance and format.

- *Shape*. Choose, edit, and customize the shapes you add to your documents.
- *Text Box*. Customize the appearance of text boxes.
- *Copy Character Style*. Copy the character style (font, typestyle, font color, font size, etc.) from one section of text to another. This process is similar to cutting and pasting text; only the character style is impacted.
- *Copy Paragraph Style*. Copy the formatting of highlighted paragraphs to the formatting of other paragraphs in your document. This process is similar to cutting and pasting text; only the paragraph style is impacted.
- *Paste Style*. Once a style has been copied, it can be pasted (or applied) to other text in the document.
- *Create New Paragraph Style from Selection*. Once text is highlighted, you can create a new paragraph style that is different from the formatting and style selections already in place.
- *Import Styles*. Pull styles from other documents and incorporate them into the document you're currently working on.
- *Mask*. This command is used for cropping a graphic image without permanently altering the original image. The appearance of the image in your document, however, will be altered.
- *Mask with Shape*. This command is used for cropping a shape, without permanently altering the original image. The appearance of the shape in your document, however, will be altered.
- *Instant Alpha*. This feature allows you to take certain colors used in an image and make them transparent. You can adjust the level of transparency to create a wide range of visual effects. It is useful for removing unwanted background colors, for example.
- *Remove Instant Alpha*. Use this command to remove unwanted colors in a document (after the colors are selected).
- *Reapply Defaults to Selection*. If you've made formatting or style changes to a document or a portion of a document that you want to remove, this command lets you revert back to the document's default style settings.
- *Advanced*. This command offers several additional document formatting commands and allows you to set various default options in the Pages application.

## ARRANGE PULL-DOWN MENU

In addition to word processing, Pages '08 is a powerful page layout tool. The commands found under the Arrange pull-down menu (located to the right of the Format pull-down menu, along the Menu bar) include:

- *Bring Forward, Bring to Front, Send Backward, Send to Back, Send Object to Background, Bring Background Objects to Front.* These commands deal with the layers of a document you can create. You can move objects between layers for ease of editing and to create various visual effects where objects overlap each other.
- *Make Background Objects Selectable.* Using this command allows you to manipulate and alter the background graphic or image used.
- *Align Objects.* This command allows you to select multiple objects in a document (including shapes, photos, or graphics) and align them horizontally and/or vertically.
- *Distribute Objects.* This command allows you to position multiple objects in a document (including shapes, photos, or graphics).
- *Flip Horizontally.* Use this command in conjunction with a shape, photo, or graphic to flip it horizontally on the page.
- *Flip Vertically.* Use this command in conjunction with a shape, photo, or graphic to flip it vertically on the page.
- *Lock.* Once an object is positioned perfectly on a page (or in a document) it can be locked to prevent it from accidentally being moved while editing the rest of the document.
- *Unlock.* Use this command to unlock objects that have been previously locked.
- *Group.* Group together two or more objects (photos, graphics, or shapes, for example) to move them or manipulate them as if they're a single object.
- *Ungroup.* Ungroup multiple objects that have been previously grouped together.

## VIEW PULL-DOWN MENU

As you create your documents using Pages '08, you can view the text on-screen using several different views, based on the information you want to see. You can also select what menu options and icons you want visible as you work. The View pull-down menu, located to the right of the Arrange pull-down menu on the Menu bar, offers the following commands:

- *Show Styles Drawer*. This command causes a Paragraph Styles, Character Styles, and List Styles window to appear, providing yet another method for easily changing fonts and typestyles within a document.
- *Show Page Thumbnails*. When this command is turned on, thumbnail images of the pages in your current document are displayed on the left side of the Pages program window. This offers a visual representation of the page layouts in your document.
- *Show Search*. Search for any text or phrase in your current document and see a list of where that text appears. The list is displayed on the left side of the Pages program window. Using the mouse, you can jump directly to any search phrase reference in the document by clicking the mouse on that search results listed.
- *Show Comments*. If comments have been added to a document, the Show Comments command displays the comments on the left side of the Pages program window.
- *Hide Format Bar*. To create more room on your screen to see the actual document you're creating, you can hide the Format bar.
- *Show Layout*. This alters the view of your document seen on the screen. The Show Layout View is used when doing page layout, as opposed to basic word processing. Page layout refers to placing and formatting text, graphics, photos, or other elements on the same page.
- *Hide Rulers*. This command causes the on-screen ruler that's typically displayed below the Format bar to disappear from the screen.
- *Show Invisibles*. In a document there are editing symbols, such as paragraph breaks, that aren't typically displayed on the screen while typing. When formatting a document and doing page layout, seeing these symbols may be useful. Using this command, they can be made to appear on the screen, even though they won't be printed.
- *Zoom*. Adjust the magnification of the document on the computer's screen. This is particularly useful if you're working with a small type size.

- *Show Inspector.* From this window, you can control virtually all of the formatting options available to you in Pages, including making adjustments to the document's margins, layout, object placement, text, lists, tabs, graphics, tables, and charts.
- *New Inspector.* Use this command to adjust the formatting or style used in a specific portion of a document, or if you want to have multiple versions of the Inspector window open at once to adjust different aspects of the document.
- *Show Colors.* This is a color selection and matching tool.
- *Show Adjust Image.* This editing tool is used to adjust photos and images already placed in your document. It has the same functionality you'll be familiar with if you use the iPhoto application.
- *Show Media Browser.* Use this command to find and then import audio, photos, video, or certain other graphic elements into your documents.
- *Show Document Warnings.* This command opens a window that lists any potential problems with a document, such as formatting or compatibility issues.
- *Hide Toolbar.* Create more space on your Desktop by hiding the Pages Toolbar.
- *Customize Toolbar.* Move the graphic icons around on the Pages Toolbar, and add or delete icons to customize your software. When this command is selected, all of the command icons available in Pages are displayed. Using the mouse, you can drag and drop the command icons you want into position on the Toolbar, and customize the look of the Toolbar.

## WINDOW PULL-DOWN MENU

Under the Window pull-down menu, found to the right of the View pull-down menu along the Menu bar, you'll find the following commands:

- *Minimize.* This command minimizes the Pages program window that's active. It serves the same purpose as clicking on the yellow dot in the upper-left corner of the window.

- *Zoom Window*. Change the size of the Pages program window on your Mac's Desktop.
- *Bring All to Front*. Use this command to bring all windows associated with Pages to the forefront on your screen. This command is useful if you have multiple applications running simultaneously and certain windows, like the Inspector window, get buried.
- *[Current File Name] or Untitled*. If multiple documents are open at once, this command lets you quickly switch between open documents.

## HELP PULL-DOWN MENU

The Help menu is on the extreme left side of the Menu bar, to the right of the Window pull-down menu. Anytime you have a question about how to use Pages '08, you can find the answers you need from the options available under this menu. They include:

- *Search*. Quickly search through Pages' Help database using a keyword, command, or search phrase to find references you need to get your question answered.
- *Pages Help*. This tutorial page helps you navigate your way around the Pages Help to find the specific content you're looking for. This is like an interactive user's manual that's searchable.
- *Welcome to Pages*. This command links you directly to Apple's website where online tutorials and additional help information for Pages and other iWork '08 applications can be found.
- *Video Tutorials*. A collection of video tutorials on how to use Pages is offered by selecting this command.
- *iWork Tour*. This interactive Keynote '08 presentation introduces you to the many features of Pages '08, Keynote '08, and Numbers '08. Learn about major application features.
- *Pages User Guide*. Download the Pages '08 or iWork '08 manual from Apple's website. This command provides a direct link to the iWork page of the website.
- *Keyboard Shortcuts*. See a complete list of keyboard shortcuts available to you when using Pages '08.

◆ *Service and Support.* Access Apple's online technical support area for Pages. Your computer must be connected to the internet in order to use this feature.

## The Pages Program Window

Now that you have a basic understanding of the main commands available to you from Pages '08's pull-down menus, let's take a look at the program window and what commands and options are available here. In the upper-left corner of the Pages program window, you'll see the familiar red, yellow, and green dots for closing, minimizing, and expanding the active window. In the top center of this window, you'll see the name of the document you're currently working on. If you've just created a new document and haven't yet saved or named it, the phrase "Untitled (Word Processing)" appears here. In the upper-right corner of the window is the icon that makes the Toolbar appear or disappear. The Toolbar is the horizontal line of command icons found near the top of the Pages program window. By default, the Toolbar contains 12 command icons designed to make using Pages '08 faster and more intuitive. As you become more proficient in Pages '08, you can customize the Toolbar.

## Pages '08's Toolbar Options

Moving from left to right along the Toolbar, the command icons available to you include:

◆ *View.* Change the view of the document you're working on.
◆ *Sections.* Add or modify sections in your document.
◆ *Text Box.* Create and edit a text box in your document.
◆ *Shapes.* Add and modify shapes in your document.
◆ *Table.* Add and customize a table in a document.
◆ *Chart.* Add and customize a chart in a document.
◆ *Comment.* Add and view comments in a document.
◆ *Track Changes.* Keep track of changes and edits made to the original version of a document.

- *Inspector*. Have the Inspector window appear on the Desktop, giving you access to a wide range of formatting options and features.
- *Media*. Find and add various media elements to your document.
- *Colors*. Adjust, add, or change the colors associated with text and graphics in a document.
- *Fonts*. Change fonts and font attributes (including typestyles). Clicking on this command icon causes the Fonts window to appear.

The Format bar is located below the Toolbar in the Pages program window. This offers a series of command options (in the form of icons and pull-down menus) for formatting the document you're working on. The majority of these icons and commands are self-explanatory and are also available from the program's main pull-down menus or by using keyboard shortcuts.

## Pages '08's Format Bar

Along the Format bar, starting from the extreme left, you'll find an icon that allows you to show or hide the Styles Drawer. The next icon allows you to choose a paragraph style. The next icon (moving to the right) allows you to choose a character style, such as **Emphasis** (aka **Bold**), ~~Strikethrough~~, or <u>Underline</u>.

From the Font pull-down menu, you can quickly change between any font that's installed on your computer. The default font when you select a blank document to create is Helvetica, but you'll have dozens more to choose from. You can also download additional fonts, for free, by visiting the 1001Fonts.com website (1001fonts.com).

To the right of the Font pull-down menu, along the Format bar, is another pull-down

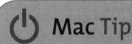

### Mac Tip

If you find yourself switching fonts, typestyles, font sizes, and font colors often when doing your word processing, you can opt to open the Font Panel at the bottom of the type size pull-down menu. This causes a separate formatting window to be displayed on the screen that allows you to quickly change the formatting or appearance of your text.

menu that allows you to select the typestyle for the selected font. Choices include: Regular, *Oblique* (aka Italics), **Bold**, and ***Bold Oblique***. From the pull-down menu to the right of the typestyle pull-down menu, you'll see another pull-down menu for selecting your type size. The default selection (when you create a new blank document) is 12-point type. However, you can adjust this to any size between 9-point and 288-point.

The next icon is the font color icon. The default selection is black, but when you select this icon, all of your text color options are displayed. Click the mouse on the font color you'd like to select to make it the active color. In addition to choosing the font/text color, you can select the background color of your text (which can be different from the background color of the page itself). This can be used to create a highlighted text effect. Click on the "a" icon located to the right of the text color icon along the Format bar.

Next to the Background Color for Text icon are three additional icons that allow you to quickly switch between **Bold**, *Italic,* and <u>Underline</u> text (or any combination of these) as you're typing. When none of these icons are selected, regular text appears when you type. If you highlight the Bold and Italic icons together, the text will appear both ***bold and italicized***. If all three icons are selected, the text you type will appear ***<u>bold, italicized, and underlined</u>***.

Moving again to the right along the Format bar, the next four icons allow you to determine your paragraph alignment. The text you type can either be left justified, centered, right justified, or left-and-right justified. Let's take a look at this paragraph formatted based on each option:

*Left Justified*

Moving again to the right along the Format bar, the next four icons allow you to determine your paragraph alignment. The text you type can either be left justified, centered, right justified, or left-and-right justified.

*Centered*

Moving again to the right along the Format bar, the next four icons allow you to determine your paragraph alignment. The text you type can either be left justified, centered, right justified, or left-and-right justified.

*Right Justified*

Moving again to the right along the Format bar, the next four icons allow you to determine your paragraph alignment. The text you type can either be left justified, centered, right justified, or left-and-right justified.

*Left and Right Justified*

Moving again to the right along the Format bar, the next four icons allow you to determine your paragraph alignment. The text you type can either be left justified, centered, right justified, or left-and-right justified.

Located to the right of the paragraph justification icons is the Line Spacing option. The default is single-spaced text, but you can modify your spacing using this pull-down menu.

To quickly add one, two, three, or four columns to your document, use the pull-down menu to the right of the Line Spacing pull-down menu. The pull-down menu icon found on the extreme right of the Format bar allows you to create bulleted or numbered lists.

## More Pages Commands, Features, and Options

Below the Format bar of Pages '08 is the Ruler. This allows you to visually see the margins on the page and can be used to set tabs, align columns or tables, and serve as a visual cue when setting spacing in your document. If you're working with an 8.5-inch-by-11-inch document, for example, the ruler located along the top of the page will be 8.5 inches wide.

 **Mac Tip**

Pages '08 allows you to easily import and export documents in a Microsoft Word–compatible format (as well as PDF format), so you can easily share your documents with co-workers using Word on either a Mac or PC. If when you open a Microsoft Word document using Pages '08 there are any formatting incompatibilities with the file, you'll be notified and given the opportunity to correct them.

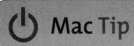

## Mac Tip

In addition to the tutorials and help screens available in Pages '08, you can find additional information and support at the Apple.com website. For Pages '08 help, visit apple.com/support/pages/. For Keynote '08 help, visit apple.com/support /keynote/, and for Numbers '08 help, visit apple.com/support/numbers/.

Along the left side of the Pages program window is the familiar scroll bar for moving up and down (horizontally) within the document. If you're using an Apple Mighty Mouse, you can more easily scroll up and down by moving the center Scroll Ball on the mouse.

As with any other window in the Mac OS X environment, the resizing symbol is in the lower-left corner. The details about the document you're currently working on are located along the bottom of the window. In the lower-left corner, the zoom percentage at which you're viewing the document on the screen is displayed. Next to this information is the number of pages currently in your document and what page number you're currently viewing. If necessary, a horizontal scroll bar will appear at the bottom of the Pages program window.

With a basic understanding of the Pages commands and menu options described within this section, you'll be able to use this program to do all of your word processing, and handle the majority of your page layout and desktop publishing needs. Once you start using Pages '08 as your word processor, you'll quickly discover it offers virtually the same functionality as Microsoft Word.

## Getting Started with Keynote '08

For anyone who needs to create presentations, Keynote '08 is a powerful tool. Like Microsoft PowerPoint (part of Microsoft Office 2008), Keynote '08 allows people to create professional-looking presentations when they have absolutely no graphic design experience. The program comes with more than 35 different templates to help you create customized and visually stunning presentations that can be shown using the computer's screen or by connecting the computer to an LCD projector. Presentations can also be converted into PDF format and/or printed.

Because Keynote '08 is part of the iWork '08 suite of applications, content from one application can easily be incorporated into another. Thus, you can take 2D and 3D charts and graphics created using Numbers '08 and make them part of your Keynote '08 presentation. Within Keynote, you can even add any of more than 25 animated effects to make the presentation more appealing and interesting to your audience.

Now that you know the basics of using Pages '08, you'll quickly discover that the user interface and many commands available to you in Keynote '08 and Numbers '08 are very similar.

## *Navigating in Keynote '08*

When you run Keynote '08 on your Mac, the main program window appears and the Menu bar at the top of the screen changes, giving you access to the main commands and pull-down menus in the program. Many of the pull-down menu commands along the Menu Bar are identical or very similar to those found in other iWork '08 applications. Pull-down menu commands found in Keynote '08 include:

- *Apple*. This pull-down menu remains constant, regardless of what program you're running on your Mac. See Chapter 3 for details.
- *Keynote*. The commands available from this pull-down menu are virtually identical to those available on the Pages pull-down menu.
- *File*. Create a New file, Open an existing file, Close a file, Save a presentation, Export a presentation, Record Slideshow, Choose Theme, Save Theme, Page Set Up, and Print are among the main options available from this pull-down menu. The Record Slideshow command is unique to this application and is used to creating self-running presentations.
- *Edit*. Again, the commands found under this pull-down menu are very similar to what you'll find when using Pages. Commands include Undo,

Redo, Cut, Copy, Paste, Delete, Clear All, Duplicate, Select All, Deselect, Find, Spelling, and Special Characters.

* *Insert.* When creating slides for a presentation, the options available from this pull-down menu allow you to add Column Breaks, Text Boxes, Shapes, Tables, Functions, Charts, Commands, and Text Hyperlinks. Unique to this program are additional commands such as Smart Build (for adding animations to slides) and Web View (for seeing what your presentation will look like if posted on the web). The Choose command allows you to find and add photos, graphics, and other elements to slides that are stored on your computer's Hard Drive.

* *Slide.* When building a presentation, the commands under this pull-down menu include New Slide (for adding an additional slide), Skip Slide, Expand, Expand All, Collapse, Collapse All, and Go To (for moving between slides).

* *Format.* The commands found in this menu (and also in the Inspector window) allow you to adjust fonts, typestyles, tables, charts, shapes, and formatting throughout your presentation.

* *Arrange.* Again, you'll see similarity between the commands found in this pull-down menu and the commands offered in the Arrange pull-down menu in Pages '08.

* *View.* Switch between Keynote '08's various views as you create, research, and present your presentation using this application.

* *Window.* The commands in this pull-down menu and the commands are similar to those offered in the Window pull-down menu in Pages '08.

* *Help.* The commands in this pull-down menu and the commands offered under the Help pull-down menu in Pages '08 are much the same.

Each time you run Keynote '08, the Choose a Template for Your Presentation window appears in the Keynote '08 program window. This Choose a Template for Your Presentation window (Figure 9.4) works exactly like the Choose a Template for Your Document window in Pages '08. Within the window, thumbnails for many different presentations are displayed. Choose the one you like best, or select White, Black, or Gradient to create a presentation from scratch without using a template.

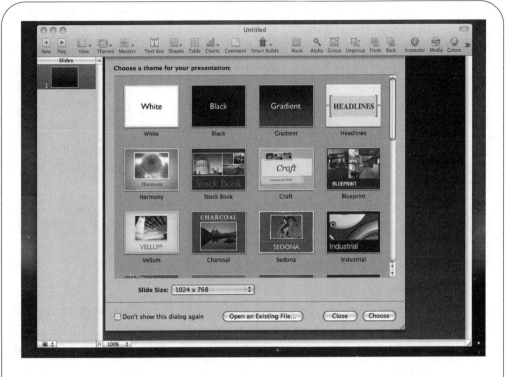

*Figure 9.4*
Each time you start Keynote '08 with the intention of creating a new presentation, you can select the presentation template you'd like to begin using.

Many of the Keynote program window elements are the same as any Mac program, including Pages '08, so the overall look of the menus and interface should be familiar. The Toolbar, found along the top of the Keynote '08 program window, offers the following command icons:

- *New*. Create a new slide to be added to your presentation.
- *Play*. View a slide as your audience will see it, complete with animations.
- *View*. Quickly switch between Keynote '08 views. Choices include Navigator, Outline, Slide Only, and Light Table. You can also adjust on-screen rulers used for formatting purposes.

- *Themes*. Choose a theme for each of your slides based on the templates built into the software.
- *Masters*. This command icon allows you to choose among dozens of pre-formatted slides within each template. For example, there are main title and subtitle slides, bullet point slides, photo slides, title and bullet slides, and blank and photo collage slide formats. For each slide in your presentation, choose a format that is most suitable for the information you're trying to convey, then plug in your own text and graphics.
- *Text Box*. Add a text box to any slide during the slide creation or editing process.
- *Shapes*. Add a shape to any slide during the slide creation or editing process.
- *Table*. Add a table to any slide during the slide creation or editing process.
- *Charts*. Add a chart to any slide during the slide creation or editing process.
- *Comment*. This feature allows you to add a yellow sticky note to any slide. You can use these sticky notes to remind yourself of information or to keep a record of relevant comments or ideas that aren't displayed in the slide itself.
- *Smart Builds*. Add pre-created animations to your slides, such as dissolves, spins, flips, and swaps, to make your presentation visually exciting.
- *Mask*. Used to crop a photo or graphic image for a presentation without actually altering the master graphic file that's stored on your computer.
- *Alpha*. This feature allows you to take certain colors in an image and make them transparent. You can adjust the level of transparency to create a wide range of visual effects. It is useful for removing unwanted background colors, for example.
- *Group*. Group together two or more objects (photos, graphics, or shapes, for example), to move them or manipulate them as if they're a single object.
- *Ungroup*. Ungroup multiple objects that have been previously grouped together.
- *Front*. Move an object forward in a slide you're creating or editing on the screen. This feature utilizes layers.

❧ *Back.* Move an object back within a slide you're creating or editing on the screen. This feature utilizes layers.

❧ *Inspector.* Gives you access to most editing and formatting features available in Keynote '08 in a separate window.

❧ *Media.* Find and incorporate media elements such as photos, audio, or video files stored elsewhere on your computer, into your slides.

❧ *Colors.* This is a color selection tool.

❧ *Fonts.* This command pulls up the Fonts window, which is identical to the Fonts window available in Pages '08. It's used for selecting fonts, typefaces, type size, font colors, and other related options.

❧ *Format Bar.* Use this command to make the Format bar (typically found under the Toolbar) appear and disappear from the screen.

Once again, it's important to understand that each major feature or command available in Keynote '08 can be accessed or executed using one of the command icons along the Toolbar, from a pull-down menu along the Menu bar, using the Inspector window, or using keyboard shortcut commands.

One excellent feature of Keynote '08 is that presentations created using Microsoft PowerPoint can be opened, viewed, edited, and presented using Keynote '08. Due to changes in formatting and minor compatibility issues between these programs, you may need to re-edit your PowerPoint presentation when using Keynote '08 and make some modifications to it.

When creating a presentation, the Keynote '08 program screen will look somewhat similar to PowerPoint and offer much of the same functionality. Use the Inspector menu to handle most of your formatting. On the left side of the screen (as shown in Figure 9.5), you'll see thumbnail images of all slides in your

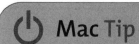

## Mac Tip

If you created a presentation using Keynote '08 that you know will be run using PowerPoint, you'll want to export the file and select the PowerPoint format to help ensure compatibility and then make sure the presentation works properly whether it's run on PowerPoint on a PC or Mac-based computer.

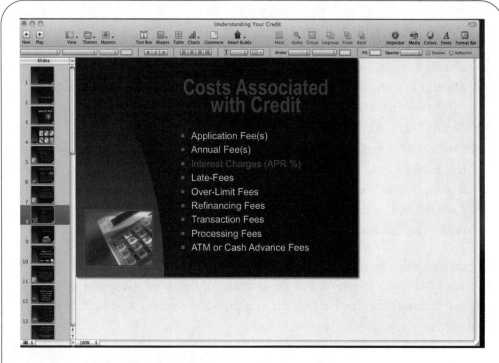

*Figure 9.5*
This is the Keynote '08 screen you'll see when creating each slide for your presentation.

presentation. The main portion of the program window is your work space, displaying the slide you're currently creating, editing, or viewing.

The appearance of the Keynote '08 program window changes when you access different modes. For example, there's the slide creation mode (shown in Figure 9.5). When you switch to the Play Slideshow mode, the entire screen is used to display your presentation, one slide at a time. Using the Rehearse Slideshow command, the current slide is displayed on the left side of the screen, while the next slide in your presentation is displayed on the right side of the screen. Below each slide is a timer, which you can use when rehearsing. The Light Table View (Figure 9.6) allows you to see thumbnails of your entire presentation in the order in which they'll appear. Using the mouse, you can move slides around when in this mode, quickly changing the order of slides.

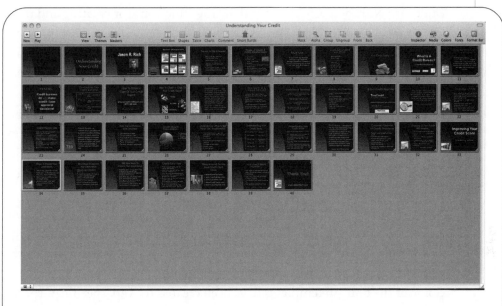

*Figure 9.6*
The Light Table View allows you to see thumbnail images of all of the slides in your presentation, and then use the mouse to move the slides around and reorder them.

As you're creating your slide show, you can add Presenter Notes to be seen by you, the presenter, that will not be displayed on the slide itself. This is handy for creating speaking points or writing out your script.

# Getting Started with Numbers '08

While Pages '08 is used for communicating thoughts and ideas using text and the printed page and Keynote '08 can be used to graphically communicate ideas during a spoken or multimedia presentation, Numbers '08 is a powerful spreadsheet program designed for number crunching and performing complex mathematical calculations. In addition to manipulating numbers, however, this program allows for colorful 2D and 3D charts and graphics to be created with ease so you can communicate numeric-based information graphically.

Built into Numbers '08 are more than 150 functions for creating and managing powerful, compelling spreadsheets with relative ease. The program comes with built-in templates that have mathematical formulas, charts, image placeholders, and filler text already incorporated within them, so all you'll need to do is plug in your own numbers.

Once again, you'll find the user interface of Numbers '08 to be intuitive and very similar to other iWork '08 applications, so you'll be able to get up and running quickly using this program, especially if you're already familiar with Microsoft Excel (the spreadsheet application that comes bundled with Microsoft Office 2008).

When you first start this application, the Choose a Template for Your Document window appears. This allows you to choose from one of the templates built into Numbers '08. You can also opt to open an existing file or create your own spreadsheet without using a template.

Some of the built-in templates have been created for very specific purposes, such as checklists, budgeting, event planning, home improvements, travel planning, loan comparison, mortgages, team organization, invoices, business financials, return on investment calculations, and expense reports.

## Navigating in Numbers '08

After selecting your template, you'll have access to the main Numbers '08 program window. At the top of the screen is the Menu bar. The pull-down menu options available to you, from left to right, include:

- *Apple*. This pull-down menu remains constant, regardless of what program you're running on your Mac. See Chapter 3 for details.
- *File*. Create a New spreadsheet file, Open an existing file, Close a file, Save a spreadsheet, Export a spreadsheet, Choose Theme, Save Theme, Page Set Up, and Print are among the main options available from this pull-down menu.
- *Edit*. The commands found in this pull-down menu are very similar to those you'll find when using Pages. Commands include Undo, Redo, Cut, Copy, Paste, Delete, Clear All, Duplicate, Select All, Deselect, Find, Spelling,

and Special Characters. Exclusive to this program, you'll find also find commands for Deleting Rows and Columns within a spreadsheet.

* *Insert.* When creating a spreadsheet, the commands available from this pull-down menu allow you to add tables, charts, shapes, and text boxes, and assign mathematical functions to be carried out. Under this menu option are additional commands for copying rows and columns, and inserting the time and date, page numbers, comments, hyperlinks, and column breaks into a spreadsheet. The Choose command allows you to import media content, such as photos, or audio, graphic, or video files.

* *Table.* This is one of the primary pull-down menus you'll use to manipulate data in your spreadsheets and to customize the functionality of the spreadsheet by adding or deleting rows and columns, resizing rows and columns, hiding rows and columns, merging cells, splitting rows and/or columns, and handling related tasks.

* *Format.* The commands in this pull-down menu (and also in the Inspector window) allow you to adjust fonts, typestyles, tables, charts, shapes, and formatting used in your presentation. You can also use the Mask and Instant Alpha features of the software from this menu.

* *Arrange.* You'll find similarity between the commands in this pull-down menu and the commands offered in the Arrange pull-down menu in Pages '08.

* *View.* Change the view of the spreadsheet you're working on. You can hide or show various elements of the Numbers '08 program window and access the Inspector window.

* *Window.* You'll find similarity between the commands in this pull-down menu and the commands offered in the Window pull-down menu in Pages '08.

* *Help.* You'll find similarity between the commands in this pull-down menu and the commands offered in the Help pull-down menu in Pages '08.

## Exploring the Numbers '08 Toolbar

At the top of the Numbers '08 program window is the Toolbar, which contains the following command icons:

- *View*. Adjust the on-screen view of the spreadsheet you're working with.
- *Sheet*. Create a new separate section in the spreadsheet you're working with.
- *Tables*. Add and manipulate numeric tables in your spreadsheet.
- *Function*. Assign mathematical tasks to be done between various cells, rows, and/or columns of your spreadsheet. Options include: Sum, Average, Minimum, Maximum, Count, More Functions, and Formula Editor. It's from this command icon that you program the spreadsheet and perform calculations and number crunching.
- *Sort & Filter*. These commands and features are also used for number crunching and handling calculations within your spreadsheets.
- *Charts*. Choose from a variety of 2D and 3D charts that can be created from your spreadsheet data.
- *Text Box*. Add or edit a text box in your spreadsheet.
- *Shapes*. Add or edit a shape in your spreadsheet.
- *Comment*. Add a yellow sticky note comment to any cell, row, column, or element of your spreadsheet. These notes can contain ideas or information you want displayed on the screen, but they will not appear in the spreadsheet itself.
- *Inspector*. Gives you access to editing and formatting features available in Numbers '08 in a separate window.
- *Media*. Find and incorporate media elements such as photos, and audio or video files stored elsewhere on your computer, into your spreadsheet.
- *Colors*. This is a color selection tool.
- *Fonts*. This command pulls up the Fonts window, which is identical to the Fonts window in Pages '08. It's used for selecting fonts, typefaces, type size, font colors, and other related options.

Below the Toolbar is the Format bar, which gives you access to most of the same formatting commands and options available in the Inspector window or by using keyboard shortcuts.

Much of the functionality built into Microsoft Excel is also available in Numbers '08, only Numbers was designed exclusively for the Mac, and its price is considerably lower. Of course, spreadsheet files created using Excel can be easily imported into Numbers '08, and spreadsheets created using Numbers '08 can be exported for use with Excel (being run on either a PC or Mac).

# iLife '08 Enhances the Personal Computing Capabilities of Your Mac

As the title of this software suite suggests, iLife '08 is a collection of applications designed to enhance your personal computing experience on your Mac by allowing you to fully utilize your personal photos, home videos, creative abilities, and even musical skills. Unlike iWork '08 (Figure 9.7) which is sold separately, iLife '08 (Figure 9.8) comes bundled with all new Macs. It includes the following applications:

## iPhoto '08

iPhoto is a digital photo album that allows you to organize all of your personal photos by date or event. You can also utilize the software's powerful image editing tools to easily enhance your photos, giving them a more professional look. For example, with a few clicks of the mouse, the all-too-common problem of red-eye can be eliminated.

*Figure 9.7*
iWork '08 is a suite of business-oriented applications that's sold separately from the hardware. The popular application suite includes word processing, spreadsheet, and presentation software. *Photo courtesy of Apple.*

*Figure 9.8*
The iLife suite of applications is bundled with all new Macs. It enhances the personal computing functionality of the computer, especially when it comes to managing photos, videos, music, and other types of created content. *Photo courtesy of Apple.*

Because iPhoto keeps your photos organized, the Search feature allows you to quickly find the single image you're looking for using a keyword search based on the image's file name, date, or other criteria.

Once fully edited, photos can be shared by creating slide shows, or by using the Mobile Me Web Gallery service (membership to Mobile Me required), you can create online galleries to share your images online with friends and family.

iPhoto also offers the tools to create unique and personalized photo gifts that can be ordered online using the software. Your images can be turned into calendars, photo books, mouse pads, T-shirts, mugs, and many other items.

Unlike other photo editing and organizational tools, iPhoto is easy to use and highly intuitive, and allows you to enhance your personal photos to give them a more professional and appealing look. When you attach your digital camera or a memory card (via a memory card reader) to the computer, iPhoto automatically imports and organizes your photos, making the transfer process quick and effortless.

Once you start using iPhoto, you'll never look at your family or vacation photos the same way again!

## GarageBand '08

GarageBand gives you the ability to transform your Mac into a power-packed, multitrack, digital recording studio with many of the same features used in professional recording studios. Easily record instruments or vocals, record and edit your performances, adjust the EQ of the recordings, add effects, and then burn your finished songs to CDs. GarageBand is relatively easy to use and a must-have application for singers and musicians.

## iMovie '08

Millions of people have video cameras and shoot countless home videos of their kids, vacations, and life experiences. Using iMovie, it's possible to better organize and share your video content; add special effects, graphic transitions, music, and titles to your movies; and then share them with friends, family, or total strangers on Mobile Me Web Gallery or YouTube.

In addition to organizing your home video files and allowing you to enhance the footage, iMovie allows you to easily transfer your video files to your iPod, iPhone, iPod Touch, or Apple TV. It's the perfect companion software to iDVD '08, which allows you to burn videos to DVD, right from your Mac.

## iWeb '08

Without any programming required, iWeb '08 allows you to use the Mobile Me service to create simple and highly personalized web pages that can incorporate your own text, graphics, photos, videos, or audio. In other words, virtually anything you create using iLife '08 can be published on the web as a personal web page relatively easily.

iWeb '08 is excellent for blogging as well and you can add "web widgets," which allow you to pull live and ever-changing content from other sites, like headline news, videos, or stock tickers. You can also add Google AdSense ads and Maps into your personal web pages, and create online photo albums that look professional.

When creating web pages, iWeb '08 allows you to choose from a handful of themed templates, so all you need to do is drop in your own content. Creating a web page takes just minutes, and you can even use your own unique domain name so people will have no trouble finding and experiencing your site.

iWeb '08 isn't powerful enough to create web pages for work or commercial purposes, and there are other blogging options out there. But few other options allow you to create simple web pages with your personalized content so quickly and easily with no programming knowledge.

### iDVD '08

Picking up where the functionality of iMovie '08 leaves off, iDVD '08 allows users to take video and digital photographic content and create DVDs that can be viewed on any DVD player. Using the software, DVDs can be given animated menus. The software can also be used to create DVD-based slide shows comprised of photos.

## Share Your Creations and More Using the Mobile Me Online Service

For an annual fee of $99, becoming a member of the Mobile Me online service operated by Apple has some useful advantages, especially for avid iLife '08 users. All content created using iLife '08 applications can easily be shared online using Mobile Me to create web galleries (for sharing photos) or personal web pages.

Formally known as .Mac, the new Mobile Me online service from Apple also offers a powerful online email system that allows users to send and receive e-mails from any computer that's connected to the web. Users are provided with a unique e-mail address.

If you own or use multiple Macs, the Mobile Me Sync feature allows you to sync your Address Book and iCal database with multiple computers automatically. Safari bookmarks, keychains, Widgets, and Mobile Me e-mail can also be synced.

Every member of Mobile Me is provided with at least 10GB of online storage space and the ability to utilize iDisk, which can be used for backing up important files remotely (a topic covered within Chapter 11). Using Mobile Me, it's also possible to form and manage online groups (interactive web pages) and maintain a personal blog.

One of the features Mobile Me offers that's definitely of interest to business users is Back to My Mac. This secure, password-protected service allows users to access their Macs remotely via the internet from any other Mac (located any-where in the world) that's also running the Mac OS X Leopard operating system.

So if you have an iMac or Mac Pro at home or the office, by using Back to My Mac, you can access files from that computer's Hard Drive using your MacBook, MacBook Pro, or MacBook Air from a remote location. For more information on how to use this service, visit apple.com/dotmac/backtomy mac.html.

## Additional Software and Add-Ons Are Just a Few Mouse Clicks Away

Microsoft, as well as other third-party developers, offers hundreds of Microsoft Office 2008 templates you can download, and many are offered free of charge. Apple and its third-party developers also offer a wide range of add-on templates you can download to enhance the functionality of the iWork '08 software by allowing you to customize templates created by professionals. For example, for Pages '08, you can download additional templates for business letters, envelopes, forms, resumes, reports, newsletters, brochures, fliers, posters, cards, invitations, and business cards.

Beyond downloading additional templates, the Download section of the Apple.com website (apple.com/downloads/) offers literally thousands of addi-tional Mac applications you can download and install. Some of these applica-tions are freeware, meaning they're offered free of charge. Other software available from this site is shareware, which means there's a small fee associated with purchasing the software, but before making the purchase, you can down-load and install the software and use it for a free trial period.

In the Download area of the Apple.com website, you'll also find download-able demos of commercially available software. As you read the description of each available program, it will state whether it's freeware, shareware or a demo.

In addition to the software you've already read about, Chapter 10 features detailed information about 14 additional must-have software applications for the Mac that will appeal to businesspeople and entrepreneurs.

# Additional Mac Software Ideal for Business Professionals

ALTHOUGH MACS HAVE BEEN EMBRACED BY STUDENTS, ARTISTS, GRAPHIC DESIGN-
ers, videographers, and other creative professionals for years,
they were not taken seriously by business professionals until
recently. This change of attitude occurred for a variety of reasons. Businesspeople have discovered that not only are Macs as powerful (and in some cases more powerful) than their PC–based,
Windows-running counterparts but they're also easier to use. Also,
many of the software developers responsible for publishing popular

business applications have begun developing Mac versions of software that's in demand by business users.

Furthermore, great strides have been made in making Macs more compatible with office networks, allowing files such as word processing documents, spreadsheets, graphic files, financial data, and e-mails to be transferred seamlessly between PCs and Macs.

In cases where a businessperson must run an application that hasn't yet been adapted to the Mac, all of the latest Macs now also run Windows XP or Windows Vista applications, virtually ensuring that businesspeople who migrate to Macs will be able to interact easily with co-workers and clients still embracing PC technologies.

Of course, the capabilities of your computer to help you do your work, be more productive, organize your life, and compete in today's business world are also dictated by the software you install and use. You already know about the variety of applications bundled with your Mac (such as Address Book and iCal). The iLife, iWork, and Microsoft Office suites of software (covered in Chapters 7, 8, and 9) are all useful to business professionals for handling common tasks like word processing, spreadsheets, presentations, and the editing and viewing of graphics. This chapter focuses on additional business-oriented software from well-known third-party developers that can help you get the most out of your new computer and expand its capabilities. The 14 applications you'll read about are, of course, just a sampling of the applications available.

You'll find literally thousands of freeware, shareware, and commercial software applications for your Mac by visiting the

 **Mac Tip**

Many of the applications available from the Apple.com website's Download area offer a free, 30-day trial period, allowing you to download and install programs onto your Mac and then use them for a full month before having to pay for and register the software. If you're not sure which financial package, word processor, or database management program will best fit your needs, download and try several before making your final decision.

## ⏻ Mac Tip

If you're about to start using a Mac version of a program you're already famil-iar with from your days as a Windows PC user, chances are you'll discover sub-tle changes and/or enhancements in the Mac version of the program, so be prepared to invest a little time becoming familiar with the new version and how you'll interact with the software using Apple's one-button mouse. On your PC, many applications use a right mouse button, which isn't available on the Mac. Thus, menu options and other commands may be slightly different when using the Mac version of popular software applications. Often, when using your Mac, pressing Control + mouse button simulates a right mouse button click on a PC.

Downloads section of the Apple.com website (apple.com/downloads/). In addi-tion to being able to download the latest updates to software you already have, this site also allows you to learn about, preview, purchase, and download many third-party applications.

One drawback to purchasing and downloading commercial software from the web is that the user's manual for the program must also be downloaded and then read on your computer screen or printed on your computer's printer. (A typical user's manual can be hundreds of pages.) If you buy the software from a retailer, it'll be distributed on a CD, and a printed user's manual will typically come with the software. Having a user's manual on hand can often make learning to use the new software easier.

# 14 Must-Have, Business-Oriented Software Applications for Your Mac

No matter what application(s) you want to run on your new Mac, chances are you'll find what you're looking for and be able to fully utilize your computer in

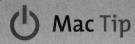

## Mac Tip

New and updated versions of these programs, plus other programs designed to handle similar tasks, may now be available. Visit each software developer's website for information about the latest version of an application that's available. Then, once the software is installed on your computer, use the Check for Updates feature of the software to download new updates.

much the same way as you used your old PC. By learning about some of the more popular business-oriented applications available, chances are you'll also discover new ways you can use your Mac to better serve your business and personal computing needs.

In addition to Microsoft Office or Apple's iWork '08, the following are 14 must-have software applications that businesspeople and entrepreneurs will appreciate having available to them on their Mac.

## 1. Adobe Acrobat 8 Professional

*Publisher*: Adobe

*Price*: $299 (Standard Version)/$449 (Professional Version)

*Availability*: Online (downloadable) or from Apple Stores nationwide

*Phone*: (800) 585-0774

*Website*: adobe.com/products/acrobat/

*Notes*: A free 30-day demo version of the software is available from Adobe's website and from the Apple.com Downloads website. The Adobe Reader software, which allows the computer to open and display PDF files, is available as a free download.

Whether you use a Mac or PC, chances are you've already encountered the need to create PDF files in business. Using Adobe Acrobat 8 Professional (see Figure 10.1), any type of document or data that can be printed can easily be transformed

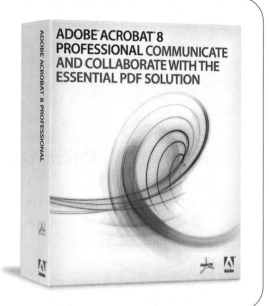

*Figure 10.1*

"Invented by Adobe Systems and perfected over 15 years, Adobe Portable Document Format (PDF) lets you capture and view robust information—from any application, on any computer system—and share it with anyone around the world. Individuals, businesses, and government agencies everywhere trust and rely on Adobe PDF to communicate their ideas and vision ... More than 200 million PDF documents on the web today serve as evidence of the number of organizations that rely on Adobe PDF to capture information." *Source: Adobe.*

into the widely recognized PDF file. This allows documents to be saved, copied, e-mailed, printed, faxed, and distributed electronically yet always maintain their exact appearance and formatting, no matter what type of system or what size screen the document is viewed on.

Acrobat Reader is a free program that allows your computer to display PDF files. However, to create PDF files efficiently, you'll want to use Adobe Acrobat 8 Professional. With this software, not only can you create .PDF files, you can also take existing PDF files and edit them.

In addition to creating PDF files from any program capable of printing data or files, using Acrobat 8, paper-based documents can be quickly scanned and saved as .PDF documents for storage or to be used as e-mail attachments, for example.

"Hundreds of millions of users of Acrobat and Adobe Reader have established PDF as a trusted format that enables documents to flow between companies and across the gap between digital and print," said Tom Hale, senior vice president, Knowledge Worker Business Unit at Adobe. "With Acrobat 8, Adobe is enabling knowledge workers to use next generation electronic documents to easily collaborate with people, ideas and information, regardless of all-too-common operating system or platform constraints."

Acrobat 8 is a powerful and easy-to-use application that's ideal for anyone who needs to share or archive paperwork, printed data, or documents. It's truly become an indispensable software application for countless business users.

## 2. Bento and FileMaker Pro 9

*Publisher*: FileMaker, Inc.

*Price*: $49 (Bento)/$299.99 (FileMaker Pro 9)

*Availability*: Online (downloadable) or from Apple Stores nationwide

*Phone*: (800) 325-2747

*Website*: filemaker.com

*Notes*: A free 30-day demo version of these software packages is available from the
FileMaker website and from the Apple.com Downloads website.

Anyone with the need to maintain any type of customized database in order to keep track of, sort, search through, share, and/or archive important information will benefit from using either Bento or FileMaker Pro 9.

Bento, whose packaging is shown in Figure 10.2, is an inexpensive, easy-to-use, yet extremely powerful database management application designed to help users organize all kinds of information in one place. Designed exclusively for the Mac, Bento makes managing contacts (shown in Figure 10.3), coordinating events, tracking projects, prioritizing tasks, and cataloging data an extremely easy process. The software comes with database templates for a wide range of applications, but also allows users to create their own templates to meet specific needs. Absolutely no programming is required to create and manage a database that can incorporate many different types of data, including text, photos, and audio or video files.

Bento works seamlessly with Address Book, iCal, and iTunes, for example, so data already stored on your computer can be accessed and incorporated into a much more powerful database. Just one potential use of Bento is to transform your Mac into a powerful contact management tool (as opposed to

*Figure 10.2*

Bento is an inexpensive, yet powerful database management tool designed exclusively for the Mac. It works seamlessly with applications like Address Book, iCal, and iTunes.

an electronic address book). The template to do this and to import your Address Book data is built into the Bento software.

Other templates bundled with Bento allow for project management, inventory control, time billing, event planning, file archiving, to-do list management, expense tracking, issue tracking, customer mailing list management, membership list management, and vehicle maintenance file management.

Bento utilizes a straightforward, graphic user interface that has a short learning curve, allowing you to create and manage almost any type of database within minutes. No matter what type of data or information you need to organize, Bento makes the process efficient and cost-effective.

For more advanced database management needs, FileMaker Pro 9 is available for both PCs and Macs. This program can be used to manage all kinds of information about people, projects, or assets, for example. FileMaker Pro 9 is compatible with a wide range of applications, so importing data into a customized database from Microsoft Excel, for example, can be done with a few clicks of the mouse.

*Figure 10.3*
Bento comes bundled with dozens of database templates, so you can get started using the
software in minutes.

Designed to handle much more robust database needs than Bento,
FileMaker Pro 9, whose packaging is shown in Figure 10.4, is a true business
application that comes bundled with 30 ready-to-use, "starter" templates.
Without any programming expertise, the user can customize the look and
functionality of his database and then share his data across the Mac or PC platforms.

As you'll see in Figure 10.5, photos, logos, and other graphic elements can
easily be incorporated into a database, the user has total flexibility when it
comes to editing or manipulating that information. For example, it can be
printed in fully customized reports. Photos, logos, and other graphic elements

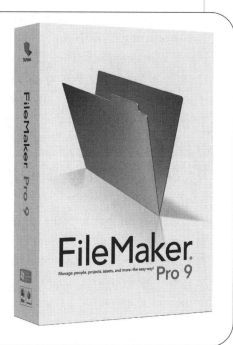

*Figure 10.4*
FileMaker Pro 9 is one of the most powerful and flexible database management applications available for the Mac.

*Figure 10.5*
Every aspect of a database created and maintained using FileMaker Pro 9 can be custom-configured with ease.

can easily be incorporated into database entries, and multiuser support allows co-workers to collaborate with ease. Database files can also be shared via the web, translated into PDF files, or converted for use within Microsoft Excel.

FileMaker Pro 9 is an ideal database management solution for business professionals, especially those working with collaborators and co-workers still using Windows-based PCs.

## 3. Endicia Postage Solutions

*Publisher*: Endicia

*Price*: $15.95 per month for the software and service/$199.95 (Includes Dymo LabelWriter 400 printer, Endicia software, and seven months of service)/$299.95 (Includes Dymo LabelWriter Twin Turbo Printer, four rolls of postage stickers, Endicia software, and seven months of service)

*Availability*: Online

*Phone*: (800) 576-3279

*Website*: endicia.com/Products/Mac/

*Notes*: Used for printing U.S. postage stamps, this software package must be used with a compatible printer, such as the Dymo LabelWriter 400, and a computer with access to the internet.

For anyone who operates a small business and has a constant need to visit the U.S. Post Office in order to buy postage stamps, obtain shipping forms, and send letters or packages via First Class, Priority Mail, or Overnight Express Mail, life will get much easier and more efficient when you start using Endicia Postage Solutions' service in conjunction with your Mac. This software is ideal for online and home business operators and small offices that spend between a few hundred and several thousand dollars per month on postage and shipping services through the U.S. Postal System (USPS).

Once you download the Endicia software and set up an account, you can purchase postage stamps online and print stamps, and professional-looking shipping labels, directly from your Mac using any compatible printer, such as the Dymo LabelWriter 400. Sheets of stamps can be printed using virtually any printer.

The Endicia software does much more than just allow you to purchase and print U.S. postage stamps, however. The software has its own contact database, but it also imports data seamlessly from Address Book so you can custom print address labels (and postage).

With a few clicks of the mouse, you can determine how a letter or package will be sent (First Class Mail, Priority Mail, or Overnight Express Mail), add services like Delivery Confirmation, Signature Confirmation, Certified Mail (with or without Return Receipt), and/or Insurance or International Customs forms, and automatically complete all necessary shipping forms in seconds.

You can even design and print your mailing labels and postage. The Endicia software keeps track of your mailing history so you can track expenses, and it allows you to instantly purchase additional postage online with a few clicks of the mouse.

The software becomes more powerful when you connect an optional postage scale to your Mac (via the USB port), allowing the software to automatically calculate postage rates for anything and everything you ship via the USPS. There are no forms to manually fill out. And services like Delivery Confirmation (which the USPS typically charges extra for) are included free when you ship a letter or package via Priority Mail using Endicia. Once shipped, packages can quickly and easily be tracked using the Endicia software, without having to re-enter shipping confirmation numbers or tracking numbers.

The Endicia Postage Solution for Mac is priced at $15.95 per month, plus the cost of whatever postage you use. This is significantly cheaper than renting a postage machine from Pitney Bowes, for example. From the company's online store, you can purchase money-saving bundles, which include one of several different label printers, rolls of compatible shipping and postage labels, several months' worth of Endicia service, plus the software, all for a flat fee, starting at $199.95.

Whether you ship a few letters or packages per day or several hundred, you'll save time and be more efficient and productive when you use Endicia Postage Solutions to handle your USPS shipping needs. The software takes just minutes to set up and is extremely easy to use.

## *4. iTunes*

*Publisher*: Apple

*Price*: Free

*Availability*: Online (downloadable)

*Phone*: (800) 275-2273

*Website*: apple.com/itunes/download/

*Notes*: iTunes is free software that allows Mac users to purchase, download, listen to, view, and store music, video, and other multimedia content. To purchase music and videos (or rent videos), an account must be set up. This software is also used for syncing content and data with an iPod, iPod Touch, or iPhone.

For millions of iPod, iPod Touch, and iPhone users, not to mention Mac users who want to download, watch, and listen to audio and video content they've obtained from the web, iTunes is Apple's one-stop shop for purchasing and downloading music, as well as purchasing or renting movies and a vast assortment of other video content. iTunes is also used to catalog and play back your own music or video library, and offers the tools necessary to convert audio CDs into digital MP3 files.

To use iTunes on your Mac with your own music library is free of charge. The software comes bundled with all new Macs and it can be downloaded from the iTunes website. If you opt to purchase and download music, music videos, episodes of TV shows, or movies, however, you'll need to establish an iTunes account using a major credit card (or debit card), or purchase prepaid iTunes Gift Cards (available from a wide range of retailers nationwide).

iTunes has teamed up with virtually all of the major record labels, television networks, and movie studios to offer a vast selection of content for purchase or download through the service. Each downloaded song costs just $.99, but special money-saving deals are offered if you opt to purchase and download an artist's or group's entire album. Downloading a single episode of a popular TV show costs $1.99, but full seasons of episodes can be purchased at a discount.

Renting a movie through iTunes cost $3.99. This allows you to store the movie on your computer's Hard Drive (or on your iPod Touch or iPhone) for up to 30 days. However, once you start watching the movie, the rental period lasts just 24 hours. You can, however, purchase the movie in digital form for slightly less than the cost of purchasing a DVD of that same movie. As you can see in Figure 10.6, music videos and other video content are also available from iTunes. Fees may apply for downloading this content, but content like movie trailers is for offered for free.

One really nice feature of iTunes is that new songs and certain TV show episodes are offered free each week, giving people the opportunity to sample a new artist or show. Special deals have also been worked out with *American Idol*, for example, giving iTunes users a chance to hear or view exclusive content from the show's contestants that isn't available elsewhere.

*Figure 10.6*

From the iTunes Store, you can purchase music and TV show episodes and rent down-loadable movies. *Photo courtesy of Apple.*

Through a partnership with Audible, thousands of audiobooks are also available for purchase and download through iTunes, while millions of podcasts are available free of charge. Just a sampling of the free daily or weekly audio podcasts available include broadcasts of *This American Life,* NPR's *Fresh Air, The Economist,* NPR's *Car Talk,* Onion News Network, ESPN, *60 Minutes* (CBS), the BBC, ABC News, CNBC, BusinessWeek, *The New York Times, Slate* magazine, and *The Wall Street Journal.*

While iTunes isn't a business application per se, but if you travel a lot for business, loading your computer, iPod, iPod Touch, or iPhone up with new music, TV shows, or movies allows you to customize your entertainment on airplanes or during your commute to and from work.

In addition to providing an ever-growing online source of downloadable audio and video content, iTunes is a full-featured tool for managing your personal audio and video digital library, all of which can be enjoyed on your Mac. To learn about all of the features packed into iTunes, check out the online video tutorials at apple.com/itunes/tutorials/.

## 5. Mac Speech Dictate

*Publisher:* MacSpeech Inc.

*Price:* $149.99

*Availability:* Online, Apple Stores nationwide, and from other software retailers

*Phone:* (603) 350-0903

*Website:* macspeech.com

*Notes:* This voice recognition software package comes bundled with a Microsoft headset and requires access to the internet.

Back in the 1960s, the television series *Star Trek* featured computers that required no mouse or keyboard because they understood the human voice and were able to respond to vocal commands. Well, what was once science fiction is now available to Mac users. One of the Mac OS X's built-in features is Text to Speech (using an application called Voice Over), with the ability to recognize your speech to execute specific commands. These capabilities can be turned on and customized by accessing the Mac OS X's System Preferences menu, and then selecting Speech.

Taking this functionality to the next level is MacSpeech, which offers MacSpeech Dictate. According to the company, when using this software you no longer need to spend hours typing at your Mac, proofreading, or correcting errors. Now, all you need to do is speak into the microphone headset (that comes with the software) when using many popular Mac applications, including word processing, chat, and e-mail.

Once the MacSpeech software is "trained" to recognize your voice, it will understand almost every word you say, allowing you to issue vocal commands to your computer. You can also dictate text into your word processor instead of typing. "MacSpeech Dictate empowers Mac users to create documents with their voice instead of typing," explained Andrew Taylor, president and CEO of MacSpeech Inc. "MacSpeech Dictate delivers fast set-up, quick command recognition, high accuracy, and increased productivity."

This is an ideal application for people who don't consider themselves to be computer savvy and who haven't fully developed their typing skills. It's also excellent for business professionals who prefer to dictate letters, memos, e-mails, and documents, or for people who'd be more productive issuing vocal commands to their computer because they're slower remembering keyboard shortcuts and getting to pull-down menu options.

## 6. MacJournal 5

Publisher: Mariner Software

Price: $34.95

Availability: Online (downloadable) or from Apple Stores nationwide

Phone: (612) 529-3770

Website: marinersoftware.com

Notes: A free 30-day demo version of the software is available from the Mariner Software website and from the Apple.com Downloads website.

Most people are so busy in their everyday lives that they can't remember what they did yesterday, much less what they experienced or achieved days, weeks, or months earlier in their personal or professional lives. To help people keep track of their life experiences and create entertaining and informative blogs (if they opt to share their personal opinions, thoughts, and experiences with others online), Mariner Software created the MacJournal 5 application.

As its title suggests, at its core MacJournal 5 is a function-filled digital diary program that encourages people to quickly create personal journal entries that can incorporate any type of digital content, including text, video, audio, and photos. Journal entries can be password protected for privacy or quickly formatted into a blog.

If you prefer not to type your journal entries, you can create video or audio entries with ease using your Mac's built-in iSight camera and/or microphone.

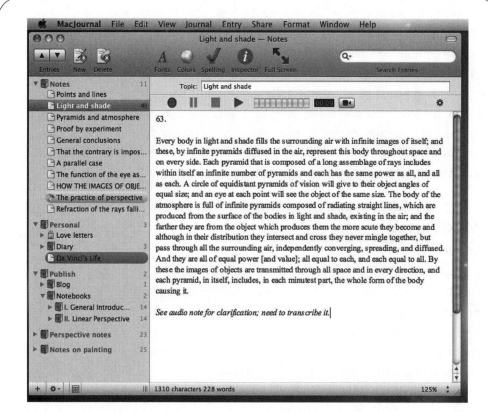

*Figure 10.7*

The MacJournal 5 software is great for keeping a digital diary of your life, or you can create a blog and share your experiences and thoughts with the world.

If you opt to share your journal entries in the form of a blog, the MacJournal 5 software is compatible with many popular online blogging services, including Mobile Me, Blogger, WordPress, and LiveJournal. Thanks to its powerful search capabilities, you can quickly find past entries or content in old journal entries.

Shown in Figure 10.7, while MacJournal 5 can be used to maintain a personal journal or blog, it also can be used by businesspeople looking to keep track of work-related thoughts, ideas, and brainstorms. The software also provides powerful tools for creating blogs that can be used to promote yourself as an expert in your field or help you communicate with customers, clients, co-workers, or business prospects using text-, audio-, or video-based entries. The work-related uses of this software are limited only by your ingenuity.

MacJournal 5 is a well-priced, extremely powerful, easy-to-use, and nicely designed application that offers much more functionality than a traditional diary, day planner, or generic word processor.

## 7. Neat Receipts for Mac

*Publisher*: NeatReceipts
*Price*: $179.95
*Availability*: Order online or purchase from computer retailers nationwide
*Phone*: (866) NEAT-REC
*Website*: neatreceipts.com
*Notes*: This software for storing and organizing receipts comes bundled with a specially designed scanner.

Whether you're an independent entrepreneur running your own business, or a successful businessperson with an expense account who works for a large corporation, chances are you have to keep track of your expense receipts, especially from business trips. NeatReceipts has developed a high-tech yet simple way to sort, calculate, and archive receipts associated with both personal and business-related expenses.

Combining highly accurate and function-filled software with a portable, sleekly designed scanner, the NeatReceipts system for the Mac captures all of the text from your paper-based receipts regardless of their size and shape, and translates the relevant information into a digital format.

To reduce paper clutter, the receipts themselves are archived in digital PDF format. You can print them, e-mail them, store them, and refer to them later, yet always view them as they originally appeared. These archived receipts can be sorted and stored in separate folders, so you can easily separate personal and business-related expenses, expenses from specific trips, or divide your expenses up by day, week, or month.

The information from newly created digital data from receipts can be seamlessly imported into a spreadsheet format, so it can be incorporated into expense reports created using popular programs like Microsoft Excel, Intuit's Quicken, or Intuit's QuickBooks. After scanning a paper receipt, the software is able to automatically pick out important data, like the date, amount, name of the vendor, payment type, and sales tax.

Using this same technology, business users can organize business card files, tax records, invoices, contracts, and a wide range of other financial documents. The NeatReceipts scanner weighs less than one pound and measures 10.8 inches by 1.6 inches by 1.3 inches, and is powered and connected to your Mac using a USB cable. The scanner fits into a typical briefcase or notebook computer case.

## 8. PageSender

*Publisher*: Smile on My Mac, LLC
*Price*: $39.95
*Availability*: Online (downloadable)
*Phone*: (408) 884-2320
*Website*: smileonmymac.com/pagesender/index.html
*Notes*: This software transforms your Mac (that's connected to the internet) into a full-featured fax machine.

If you find yourself on the road a lot and traveling for work, you'll probably rely heavily on your MacBook, MacBook Pro, or MacBook Air. By installing the PageSender software to any Mac, the computer is instantly transformed into a feature-packed fax machine, capable of sending and receiving faxes via the internet. Basically, this program allows you to fax or e-mail anything you can print from your Mac. Instead of sending the file to a printer, however, the software allows you to send it as a fax, simply by entering the recipient's fax number. You can also attach additional files (such as Word documents, PDF files, or images) to what's being faxed.

The software allows you to import contact information and phone numbers from your Address Book or Entourage, and automates the process of sending multiple faxes. When connected to the internet, PageSender allows you to receive faxes and view them on your Mac's screen (or send them to a printer). To do this, you'll need to subscribe to a web-based service, like eFax, jConnect, EasyLink, or MaxE-mail (and a low monthly fee will apply), or you can purchase the optional fax modem accessory for your Mac.

To enhance the professionalism of the faxes you send, you can create fax cover pages. The PageSender software even maintains a complete log of all faxes sent and received. This feature comes in handy and saves you money, especially when staying at hotels that may charge up to $3 per page to send or receive faxes. It also allows you to send or receive faxes from anywhere you have an internet connection, such as airports, cafés, home, or your office.

## 9. PersonalBrain Pro

*Publisher*: The Brain Technologies Corporation
*Price*: $149 (Core Edition)/$249.95 (Pro Edition)
*Availability*: Online (downloadable)
*Phone*: (310) 751-5000
*Website*: thebrain.com
*Notes*: A free 30-day demo version of the software is available from the company's website.

Whether your job requires you to constantly brainstorm new and innovative ideas, or you simply need to keep track of hundreds or thousands of random thoughts, bits of information, project details, facts, or figures, using brain mapping software might prove to be a more useful solution than trying to organize your information into a structured database, spreadsheet, or text-based document.

PersonalBrain Pro is extremely powerful mind mapping software that allows you to keep track of all kinds of information, connect random facts or ideas together, and attach any type of file (audio, video, photo, graphic, text, website URL, spreadsheet, etc.) to each piece of information entered.

As you'll see in Figure 10.8, the software is designed to help people organize and visualize information associatively, instead of separating pieces of information into lists or folders. PersonalBrain Pro enables users to link together files, web pages, and ideas as "thoughts." Each thought can represent

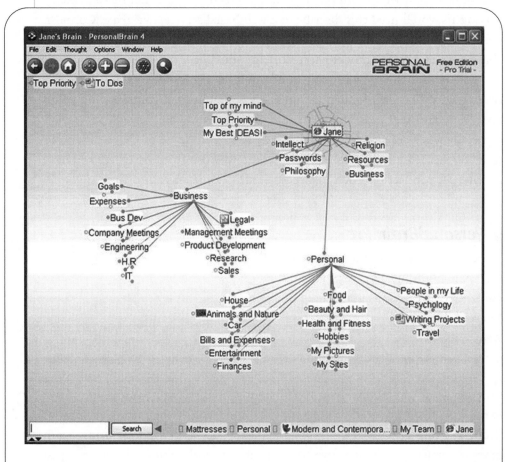

*Figure 10.8*
PersonalBrain Pro will help you organize your thoughts and ideas.

any type of digital information. Clicking on a thought will reveal all connected or related thoughts, which when seen visually will simulate human thinking and enhance the creative thinking and organizational process.

PersonalBrain Pro allows for users to document and organize using a free flow of ideas. "PersonalBrain Pro helps you to organize all your ideas, files, and web pages the way you think, capturing your unique perspective and thought process," boasts the company's website.

When using mind mapping software, the process begins with a single "thought." As you use the software, you can keep adding additional thoughts, connect those that are related, and develop an interactive mind map that can take on any size or shape and be shared with others.

The user interface created for PersonalBrain Pro is extremely visual, allowing you to drag and drop information and navigate using your mouse or keyboard shortcuts. Information in your mind map can be located in seconds using the search feature, and at any time, you can add detailed notes or attach related files or documents for each individual idea.

PersonalBrain Pro allows you to see and capture your thinking so as to make more effective decisions. It will help you organize your thoughts, create detailed to-do lists, manage large detail-oriented projects with greater efficiency, and keep a vast amount of information organized and at your fingertips. All of the information entered into your "brain" can be viewed visually, edited, and manipulated with ease, allowing you to move well beyond traditional hierarchical data storage. When you want to access information stored in your "brain," there's never a need to search through separate files, folders, or directories.

Designed for personal or business use, PersonalBrain Pro is available for the Mac, PC, and Linux, and all data files are fully compatible. So information can be exchanged with co-workers easily, regardless of what type of computer PersonalBrain Pro is being run on.

Due to the extreme flexibility and functionality of this unique software, businesspeople and entrepreneurs have discovered a wide range of uses. PersonalBrain Pro has been used to create customer service knowledge databases, develop sales and marketing support materials, used as a tool for problem solving, as a way to gather and organize business intelligence, as well as for decision support and project management.

PersonalBrain Pro is designed for people who need to analyze, brainstorm, organize, and synthesize a wide variety of information both on their computer and the internet. The software allows users to express key relationships across all information sources, so underlying thinking and key ideas become instantly visible. "The software represents a major advancement for personal knowledge management and dynamic mind mapping," explains Harlan Hugh, CEO of TheBrain Technologies. "The latest version for the Mac offers more than 60 new features, including a smart user interface, zoomable icons and images, HTML export, and total personalization."

PersonalBrain Pro is already in use by hundreds of companies, of all sizes and in many different industries. While the software is designed with ease of use in mind, it takes time to become comfortable and proficient organizing your thoughts and information in such a totally different way. Once you've completed the learning curve associated with this software, you'll probably discover it can save you time and make you more efficient, productive, and organized, while allowing you to enhance your own creativity and brainstorming abilities. The time you invest learning to use this unique software will be well rewarded.

## 10. Photoshop CS3 and Photoshop Elements 6

*Publisher*: Adobe

*Price*: $89.99 (PhotoShop Elements 6)/$649 to $999 (PhotoShop CS3)

*Availability*: Online (downloadable) or from software retailers nationwide

*Phone*: (800) 585-0774

*Website*: adobe.com

*Notes*: A free 30-day demo version of the software is available from the Adobe website.

To view, edit, and store your personal photos, iPhotos, part of the iLife '08 suite of applications bundled with your Mac, is a perfect solution. However, if your photo or graphic editing needs are more advanced, Photoshop CS3 is the software used by professional photographers, graphic artists, and website designers. It's perhaps the most powerful photo and graphic editing application on the market, for both PCs and Macs.

## ⏻ Mac Tip

Photographers, graphic artists, and website designers often find working with Photoshop CS3 easier if instead of using a mouse, a graphics tablet is connected to the computer. Wacom's Intous line of graphic tablets (wacom.com) offers an inexpensive, yet powerful option, starting at just $79. The Intous 3 tablet is used by many professionals. The 6 inch-by-8 inch table is priced at $329.95, while the 12 inch-by-19 inch tablet is $749.95.

Photoshop CS3, whose packaging is shown in Figure 10.9, is a complex program with a rather significant learning curve, but once you become proficient using this tool, your ability to edit photographs and graphics is limited

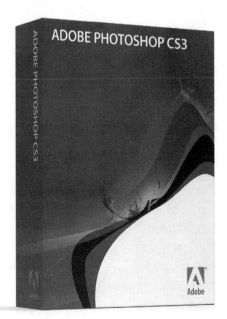

*Figure 10.9*
Adobe Photoshop CS3 is an extremely popular and powerful tool for editing photos and digital images.

## ⏻ Mac Tip

Apple has its own software designed to rival Photoshop CS3 in terms of functionality. Its Aperture 2 gives amateur and professional photographers alike a wide range of tools to manage massive image libraries, speed through photo edits, make essential editing adjustments, and deliver photos online and in print. The price of Aperture 2 is $199. It's available from Apple Stores, the Apple.com website, and wherever Apple software is sold.

mainly by your own creativity. People use Photoshop CS3 for a wide range of professional jobs. According to Adobe, Photoshop CS3 is, "the essential software for perfecting your images. It now offers productivity and workflow enhancements, powerful new editing tools, and breakthrough compositing capabilities." The Mac version of Photoshop CS3 has been designed especially with the Mac OS X Leopard operating system in mind. At the time this was being written, Adobe planned to release an all-new version of Photoshop, called Photoshop CS4, sometime in late–2008 or early–2009.

Some of the key photo editing functionality built into Photoshop CS3 has been scaled down into a user-friendly, consumer-oriented application, called Photoshop Elements 6. This package offers more editing functions than iPhoto, but is much easier to use than Photoshop CS3. Photoshop Elements 6, whose packaging is shown in Figure 10.10, offers an easy way to view, organize, edit, and share photos in imaginative and creative ways. For archiving purposes, photos can be associated with keyword tags. Using the editing functions, special effects can be added to images, and enhancement of images is easy. Fixing red-eye in an image is simple and requires just a few mouse clicks.

While Photoshop Elements 6 is ideal for creating scrapbooks, photo books, slide shows, cards, and CD or DVD labels, for example, if your job involves creating professional-looking brochures, websites, advertisements, reports, or other documents that use photographs or graphics, you'll want and need the power and capabilities of Photoshop CS3.

*Figure 10.10*

For most casual and amateur photographers who don't need all of the professional features built into Photoshop CS3,
the less expensive and scaled-down
Photoshop Elements 6 program is ideal.

## ⏻ Mac Tip

One of the easiest ways to learn how to use Photoshop CS3 is to invest in a
video training program or to take a class. Dozens of how-to books are available,
and there are annual workshops and symposiums, called Photoshop World,
that are held annually in major cities across America. *Photoshop User* magazine
(available at newsstands, photoshopuser.com) is also a must-read for people
who use this popular application. At the time this book was being written,
Adobe was hard at work developing Photoshop CS4 for the Mac, although no
release date for this software upgrade was announced.

## 11. QuarkXPress 7

*Publisher*: Quark

*Price*: $799

*Availability*: Online (downloadable) and from software retailers nationwide

*Phone*: (303) 894-8888

*Website*: quark.com

*Notes*: A free 30-day demo version of the software is available from the Quark website.

When Microsoft released Office 2008 for Mac, powerful desktop publishing and page layout features were integrated into this suite of business-related applications, allowing users to transform basic text documents into profes-sional-looking documents using the built-in tools and templates. The desktop publishing and page layout tools offered in Microsoft Office 2008 are more than adequate to meet the basic publishing and document design needs of many individuals and small businesses.

## ⏻ Mac Tip

In the publishing industry and in corporate America, after QuarkXPress, the most popular alternative software for graphic designers, publishers, and other publishing processionals is Adobe's InDesign CS3 (CS4). It offers the profes-sional page layout and desktop publishing tools needed to create a wide range of documents, reports, publications, and other printed materials. This software is designed to work seamlessly with popular word processors as well as its Adobe products, allowing users to incorporate text, graphics, photos, and visual effects into their published documents. If you're already familiar with other Adobe products and have a basic understanding of page layout and design, InDesign offers a slightly more user-friendly experience than QuarkXPress, yet provides the same robust features and functionality. For more information about InDesign, visit adobe.com/products/indesign/.

For high-end desktop publishing and page layout needs, however, the power and capabilities of a dedicated desktop publishing program are required. Two of the most popular applications for this are Adobe InDesign CS3 (adobe.com/products/indesign/) and QuarkXPress 7 for the Mac.

QuarkXPress 7 is page layout software created specifically for design and publishing professionals. It allows users to combine text and graphics to create visually stunning printed materials in the highest-quality output possible. Among graphic designers and publishing professionals, QuarkXPress is an industry-standard tool capable of handling even the most complex page layout requirements, and much more.

## 12. Quicken for Mac and QuickBooks Pro

*Publisher*: Intuit

*Price*: $69.99 (Quicken)/$199.95 (QuickBooks Pro)

*Availability*: Online (downloadable) or from Apple Stores nationwide

*Phone*: (877) 683-3280

*Website*: quicken.intuit.com or quickbooks.intuit.com

*Notes*: Free 30-day demo versions of these software packages are available from the Intuit website.

When it comes to managing all aspects of one's personal finances, there's no better program than Quicken, shown in Figure 10.11. Offering a graphic interface and all of the built-in functionality necessary to manage bank accounts, credit cards, investments, and other assets, Quicken helps millions of people manage their money, perform online banking, and live comfortably within their financial means. The software also makes preparing tax returns easier.

Using Quicken requires some basic bookkeeping and accounting knowledge, but dramatically cuts the time it takes to maintain up-to-date and accurate personal financial records. The program allows users to automatically import bank account, credit card, and investment data from banks, financial institutions, and other sources, so the chances of errors as a result of manual data entry are greatly reduced.

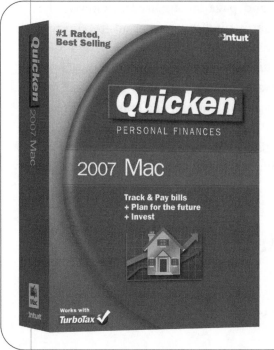

*Figure 10.11*
When it comes to managing personal finance, there's no more popular program than Quicken for Mac. If you used Quicken on a PC, your data files can be easily imported into this Mac version.

For small businesses, QuickBooks takes the power and functionality of Quicken and expands it to provide a complete bookkeeping and accounting solution capable of managing a business's finances, accounts payables, and accounts receivables. Invoicing, inventory management, credit card processing, and other functionality are also integrated into this program.

In its most basic form, QuickBooks Pro for Mac allows users to print checks, pay bills, track sales, and manage expenses. It also offers the capability to create estimates, invoices, purchase orders, and reports, as well as integrate tools for tracking employee time and managing payroll. Tracking inventory and managing credit card transactions are among the other capabilities of this full-featured and extremely popular software.

Data from QuickBooks can easily be exported to Excel, and data can be synchronized from Address Book, Outlook, iCal, and Mobile Me. Each feature built into QuickBooks is designed to save the user time, be better organized, and maintain an accurate and timely overview of company finances. A working knowledge of bookkeeping and accounting practices and principles is definitely required to properly use this software.

Whether you use Quicken to manage your personal finances or rely on QuickBooks to handle accounting and bookkeeping tasks associated with your small business, there are no better financial management programs available that are as chock-full of features and so user-friendly. Files from the PC version of Quicken or QuickBooks can easily be imported into the Mac version, and vice versa.

## 13. Stox

*Publisher:* JoeSoft

*Price:* $49.95

*Availability:* Online (downloadable) or from Apple Stores nationwide

*Phone:* (877) 477-6763

*Website:* joesoft.com

*Notes:* A free 30-day demo version of the software is available from the company's website and from the Apple.com Downloads website.

For anyone who manages her own investment portfolio, or at least wants to keep tabs on a portfolio being managed on her behalf, the Stox software from JoeSoft offers a suite of research, tracking, and analysis tools using an interface that's as user-friendly as the Mac itself.

By utilizing many different online resources, Stox compiles color-coded charts, plus gathers market-specific news items that cater to the detailed trade parameters created by the user/investor. Part of the research the software compiles are easy-to-understand, graphical performance reports that showcase minute-by-minute performance.

Create and track complete portfolios, or focus your attention on one specific stock, mutual fund, or investment opportunity. At any given time, Stox informs you of your profits and losses, and allows you to track portfolio performance from a single on-screen window that's clutter free and easy to access.

Bundled into the software are a handful of features, like user-customizable alarms, the ability to print many different types of reports, and a customizable (animated) ticker. "Stox is an in-depth analytical stock management tool that helps you research and track your stock portfolio," said Greg Brewer, CEO of Prosoft Engineering Inc., the parent company of JoeSoft. "It really is the next generation of portfolio management software which is suited for both novice users and seasoned investors alike."

Stox requires internet access in order to handle its various functions. The software offers a nice addition to the many other free and fee-based tools available on the web for novice and experienced investors.

## 14. Skype

*Publisher*: Skype Limited
*Price*: Free (You pay for certain landline calling services)
*Availability*: Online (downloadable)
*Phone*: (866) 446-0831
*Website*: Skype.com
*Notes*: This is a free software download that allows users to make phone calls from their computer over the internet. To make calls from the internet to landlines or to make international calls, very low fees apply. Computer-to-computer calls are free. Users must set up an account to use this software.

These days, making telephone calls within the United States is an inexpensive proposition, whether you use a landline phone or cell phone. However, making international calls from the United States, or when traveling, making calls from overseas back to America, can become extremely costly. Trying to call home when visiting Europe, Mexico, or virtually any other country could easily cost $2 to $4 per minute, whether you use a hotel phone, cell phone, or public payphone.

For businesspeople, Skype offers the ideal tool for making international phone calls for mere pennies per minute. This is an internet-based phone service that, as long as you have a strong (and high-speed) internet connection wherever you happen to be, allows users to make domestic or international calls right from their computer.

Because Macs have built-in speakers and a microphone, the Skype software transforms the computer into a fully functional speaker phone that's capable of calling anyone, anywhere, anytime. The software links with Address Book, so finding phone numbers to your contacts is easy. The software even knows when to dial international prefixes and country codes, so there's no confusion about dialing the wrong combination of digits.

For more personal phone calls, Skype and several third-party companies offer telephone handsets that connect directly to the computer via the USB port. These handsets work just like a traditional telephone, except when using Skype, all phone calls initiate from the internet instead of traditional phone lines.

When communicating with millions of other Skype users, all internet-to-internet (computer-to-computer) calls are always free. There is no per-minute rate. You'll only pay for service when using your computer to call landlines. The rates, however, are a fraction of what traditional phone companies charge.

Upon downloading the Skype software, you'll be prompted to set up a Skype account, at which time you can prepay for calling services. Depending on the type of account you set up, you can be provided with a unique Skype phone number and voice mail service. When communicating with other Skype users via the web, you can also take advantage of your Mac's built-in iSight camera to experience decent-quality, real-time videoconferencing (which is a free service). Sending and receiving text massages via Skype is also part of the service's functionality.

The best thing about Skype is the extremely low cost; however, users also appreciate the easy-to-use interface that makes calling or receiving calls a snap. Many of Skype's services are free, and you won't find a better deal for making overseas calls or calling back to the United States from overseas. International calls start at less than two cents per minute. Depending on your needs, the Skype Pro or Skype Business services are ideal for businesspeople and entrepreneurs.

## Backing Up Your Data Is Essential

Once you've customized and personalized your Mac and have installed the software you plan to use on a regular basis, the next major consideration is how you'll protect your important data against a wide range of problems and disasters. The best way to do this is to be prepared for what could happen by creating and maintaining a backup of your computer's primary Hard Drive, including all of the personal and work-related files, folders, databases, and data you create and use on your Mac. The next chapter focuses on how to back up your data and the various backup options available to you.

# CHAPTER 11

# Backing Up Your Critical Data

A S THAT AGE-OLD SAYING IMMORTALIZED ON A BUMPER STICKER SO ACCURATELY states, "SH*T HAPPENS!" No matter how careful and diligent you are in terms of caring for your Mac and backing up your data, at some point, something will most likely go wrong and you'll run the risk of losing critical data.

Regardless of what type of computer you use (Mac or PC), just some of the things that could go wrong with a your desktop or notebook computer and cause data loss include:

## ⏻ Mac Tip

According to Mozy Inc., 6 percent of all personal computers will suffer an episode of data loss in any given year. It's essential that you protect yourself to avoid the hassle, frustration, and cost associated with losing essential data and having to recover or reconstruct it.

- The computer gets stolen.
- The computer gets dropped.
- The user spills a drink on his computer.
- The hard drive crashes (mechanical failure).
- A virus infects the computer and deletes data.
- An electrical surge damages the computer.
- A hacker steals, deletes, or alters essential data.
- The user accidentally deletes or overwrites one or more important data files.
- The computer is damaged by fire or flood.

If you're a Mac owner and you invest in the AppleCare service plan at the same time you purchase your new computer, for three years any repairs your computer requires will be handled free of charge by Apple. This plan, however, covers the hardware only—not your data. It also does not cover you if the computer is lost or stolen. Thus, it's entirely your responsibility to back up your programs and data, and keep those backups safe and secure so you can quickly restore your information should anything go wrong.

While it's virtually impossible to protect your computer and data against every possible scenario, by regularly creating backup copies of your data you'll have the piece of mind knowing that if and when something does go wrong, you'll be able to retrieve your data with little or no negative impact.

When it comes to backing up your Mac's data, you have a variety of options at various price points. Ideally, you should consider backing up your data to an external hard drive (or to CDs or DVDs) locally and maintaining some type of remote backup system. Each backup option has pros and cons.

If the worst happens and your computer's Hard Drive crashes or is somehow compromised and you don't have a recent backup of your data, there is still hope of recovering your data if you hire a data recovery service, but the costs will be high (hundreds or thousands of dollars). And based on why your data was lost, the ability to retrieve all of your data is not guaranteed. So to save yourself a lot of time, money, and aggravation, develop and implement a plan for maintaining backups of your data using one or more of the methods described in this chapter.

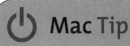 **Mac Tip**

Depending on how sensitive your data is, consider utilizing password security and data encryption to protect your information against thieves and hackers. This security should be used on your primary data, as well as your backups.

**Mac Tip**

In the past, creating backups of data was a time-consuming and confusing process that many computer users avoided, all the while maintaining the hope that nothing would ever happen to their computer or essential data. The various data backup options now available for your Mac are easy to use, require virtually no time, and provide reliable backups of your data. Implementing at least one of the data backup strategies described in this chapter is truly essential, especially for business users.

## Your Primary Backup Options

The options available for backing up your data fall into two main categories: local backup and remote backup. Local backup involves connecting an external hard drive to your computer and automatically having your Mac make a duplicate copy of your important data onto this external data storage device. This is the easiest and least expensive backup option, because thanks to the Time Machine software built into Mac OS X Leopard, the backup process can be done completely automatically.

An alternative to saving your data to an external hard drive is to manually copy your important data files to another external media format, such as data CDs or DVDs. This involves either using backup software on your Mac or manually copying files from one location to another.

While a local backup option is definitely worthwhile, this method does not protect your data if your computer (and the connected external hard drive) are stolen or damaged by fire, flood, or another disaster. Using a remote backup option (preferably in addition to a local backup process) allows your Mac to use the internet to send a copy of your data to a server at another location altogether. This process is password protected, the data is encrypted for security purposes, and the remote backup can be created automatically using software provided by the remote backup service.

The majority of remote backup services charge a monthly or annual fee, based on the amount of data storage space required. Using this option, if your computer gets destroyed in a fire, for example, you can restore your data from the remote server using another computer.

## Apple's Time Machine Software

Bundled with the Mac OS X Leopard operating system is a powerful data and software backup application called Time Machine. On your Dock, this application has a green-and-silver circular icon. When used with an external hard drive, Time Machine automatically creates and constantly maintains a backup of your entire primary Hard Drive (files, photos, Address Book contacts, iCal scheduled events, data, applications, movies, account preferences, Safari bookmarks, etc.).

As the title of this software suggests, Time Machine allows you to go back in time, almost literally. It maintains detailed information about your computer's data and configuration on a day-by-bay basis. So, at any time, you can restore your computer to exactly how it was a day, week, or even a month earlier, and at the same time, restore any lost or corrupted data.

When you first start using Time Machine (which should be at the same time you start using your new Mac), the software will copy the entire contents of your computer to an external backup drive. Thus, it's essential that the backup drive you connect to your Mac have more storage capacity than the primary Hard Drive built into your Mac. The external hard drive can connect to your Mac via USB or Firewire cable, or have a wireless connection (like Apple's Time Capsule, described later in this chapter).

Once the initial backup is created, as you start using your computer, creating new files, and modifying existing files, Time Machine will make regular backups of all new or changed files. This process happens on an hourly basis, so you'll never lose more than one hour's worth of work (or data) if your computer suddenly crashes or you accidentally erase or overwrite an important file.

After you set up the Time Machine software, which takes just minutes using the on-screen prompts, everything happens in the background. If you power down your computer while a backup is being made, Time Machine will simply continue the backup when the computer is turned back on. For this software to work on an ongoing basis, however, it must remain connected to an external hard drive. For a desktop computer, this isn't a big deal. For a MacBook, MacBook Pro, or MacBook Air user, your computer will not be able to make backups. Thus, when you return to your office, or in the evening, attaching a pocket-size external hard drive and allowing Time Machine to do its thing is an excellent idea.

The default is for Time Machine to maintain a backup of your Mac's entire main Hard Drive. However, you can use the Options feature in the Time Machine Preferences window to determine exactly what files should be backed up and how often backups should be made.

If a worst case scenario happens and your current Mac gets damaged or destroyed, but your external hard drive with your Time Machine backup data remains intact, when you acquire a replacement Mac you can use Apple's

Migration Assistant software (built into the Mac OS X operating system) to restore your most essential programs and data from your Time Machine backup. Simply choose "Restore System from Time Machine" when running Migration Assistant. While the restoration process is relatively straightforward, this is something that an Apple Genius at any Apple Store can do on your behalf to ensure it's done correctly and you regain full access to your data.

At any time, you can access Time Machine by double-clicking on the program icon found on your Mac's Dock. You can also use Finder to access the Applications folder and double-click on the Time Machine icon within the folder. Once Time Machine is active, however, a second icon appears in the upper-right corner of your Desktop, near the clock and AirPort (Wi-Fi) icons. Clicking the mouse on this icon reveals a menu that lists the date and time when the last Time Machine backup was made. You'll also be given the following three menu options:

1. *Back Up Now*. Create a backup using Time Machine anytime you wish by clicking on this command.
2. *Enter Time Machine*. This command launches the Time Machine application and allows you to restore your data after selecting an exact restore point. To exit out of this application, simply press the Escape (ESC) key on the keyboard, or click on the Cancel icon in the lower-left corner of

 **Mac Tip**

If a file is created and then deleted within the one-hour period that Time Machine conducts its automatic incremental backup, that file will probably be lost forever, unless the software used to create the file also creates automatic backups. Remember, this software only works when an external hard drive is connected to the Mac. The Time Machine software must also be turned on, which can be done from the Time Machine Preferences window.

the screen. When Time Machine is active, the Mac's Desktop is replaced by a space background. A timeline is on the right side of the screen. In the center of the screen is the Finder window, and at the bottom of the screen are the Cancel and Restore icons (on the extreme lower-left and lower-right side of the screen, respectively). In the lower-center portion of the screen is the time and date of the backup showcased in the center of the screen in the Finder window. By clicking the mouse on the silver arrows next to the window in the center of the screen, you can move back in time to determine your exact restore point. From the Finder window, you can then select which file(s) you wish to restore.

3. *Open Time Machine Preferences.* From this window, you can customize the Time Machine application by determining what files will be backed up and how often backups will be created.

# Apple's Time Capsule

Designed to be a companion product for Time Machine, Apple's Time Capsule (sold separately and shown in Figure 11.1) is a wireless 500GB or 1TB hard drive on which data can be stored without having to connect your Mac to an external hard drive using a USB or Firewire cable. This drive is designed to work over your home or office's wireless network. Time Capsule also serves as a high-speed AirPort Extreme (Wi-Fi) Base Station, and is $299 for the 500GB version. The 1TB version sells for $499.

Using Time Capsule, not only will your Mac notebook or desktop be able to maintain a constant backup of its files and data, the unit can also be used to share printers between multiple Macs, and can be used to create a wireless internet hotspot that's compatible with the iPhone or iPod Touch. It can also be used by others as a backup storage device for Windows-based PCs in an office environment, for example.

Once the Time Capsule is plugged in and becomes part of your home or office network, linking it up with one or more Macs and having the Macs use it to store backup data involves just a few clicks of the mouse to set everything up. After that, all backups are made automatically and in the background.

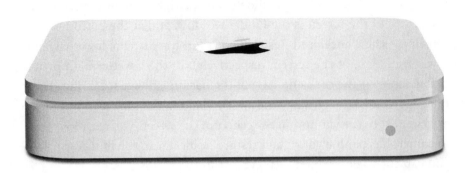

*Figure 11.1*
For most Mac users, the Time Capsule is the perfect companion to the Time Machine software
and an ideal solution for creating complete, ongoing, and reliable backups of all your programs
and data. *Photo courtesy of Apple.*

The Time Capsule unit itself is designed to resemble the iMac in appearance, with a sleek, modern, all-white appearance. It measures 7.7 inches long by 7.7 inches wide by 1.4 inches high, and weighs just 3.5 pounds. The Time Capsule must remain plugged into an electrical outlet to be functional. Included with the unit are all the software and cables needed to get the unit operating within minutes as part of a wireless network. On the back of the Time Capsule unit, you'll find the power plug, one USB port (used for plugging in a printer), one WAN port (used to plug in your cable modem), three Ethernet ports (to plug in up to three computers via an Ethernet cable as opposed to using a wireless connection), and a security slot.

Time Capsule is available from Apple Stores, from Apple authorized resellers, and from the Apple.com website. For anyone who is concerned about protecting his data and who is not overly technologically savvy, this backup system offers ease of use, a low price point, plus the added functionality of being used as a multiport, wireless internet hub and a device that makes sharing printers by multiple Macs easy and cable free.

# Backing Up to an External Hard Disk

Apple's Time Capsule was developed specifically for Macs running the Mac OS X Leopard operating system, but any external USB or Firewire hard drive can be used with the Time Machine backup software or to manually back up data. These drives are available at computer stores, office supply superstores, and consumer electronics stores, and range in price from under $100 to over $500, depending on the drive's physical size, capacity, and speed.

When you connect an external hard drive to your Mac via a USB cable, for example, an icon for that drive will appear on the Desktop, meaning it's ready to be used and that files can be written to or read from it.

If you're going to be backing up the entire contents of your Mac's internal hard drive, the external drive you connect and use with Time Machine must have a greater storage capacity. When shopping for an external hard drive, you'll find literally hundreds of options on the store shelves (not to mention what you can order online or via mail).

Start by shopping for a well-known and established hard drive brand. This will help ensure the reliability and stability of the unit over time. Companies like Western Digital, Iomega, SimpleTech, Maxtor, and Seagate are established brands. Next, think about capacity. How much storage space will you require (80GB, 100GB, 160GB, 250GB, 500GB, or 1TB)? The more storage capacity, the more expensive the unit will be. Whatever you believe your storage needs currently are, add 50 percent to that number when choosing your hard drive.

Once you know what size hard drive you're looking for in terms of capacity, consider the physical size of the drive itself. If you're using the drive with an iMac, for example, portability of the drive might not be

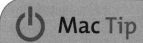

## Mac Tip

An unlimited number of external hard drives can be connected to your Mac. Thus, in addition to using one drive solely for backup purposes using Time Machine, you could also connect a second hard drive to your Mac for the sole purpose of archiving your photos, music files, or videos.

a priority. If, however, you'll be using the drive with a MacBook or need to transport the drive between your home and your office, for example, you'll want a unit that is powered by the computer's USB port, so it does not need to be plugged into an electrical outlet. You'll also want a unit that fits in the palm of your hand or in a purse or briefcase.

You'll need to choose if you want your external drive to connect to your Mac via a USB cable or a Firewire cable. Firewire is the faster option for transferring data, but it is often a more costly option as well. All Macs are equipped with a Firewire port. If you go with the USB option, make sure the drive is USB 2.0 compatible (which will be the case for newer drives).

The final consideration is the speed of the drive. This refers to how quickly data can be sent from your Mac and stored on the drive itself. If you look at the technical specifications of the external hard drive, look for a seek time of less than 10 milliseconds. Ideally, you'll also want a drive with a buffer size of at least 4MB, although a 2MB buffer is more common. In terms of the drive's rotational speed (measured in rpms), the higher this number, the better. Go with a drive with at least a 5,400rpm. A drive with a speed of 7,200rpm or 10,000rpm is more desirable. You'll definitely notice the difference in speeds if you transfer large files (data, music, video, or photos) between your Mac and the external drive.

After you've done your comparison shopping at traditional retail stores and have done your online research (and have read consumer and editorial reviews of the various hard drive products), to save money, consider visiting a price comparison website, such as Nextag.com, and doing a lowest price search for the specific hard drive make and model you've selected. This will help you find the lowest price possible for the drive you're looking to purchase. Before making the actual purchase, consider going online and reading consumer or editorial reviews of the hard drive unit.

## Backup Software Solutions

If you visit the Apple website's download area and do a search for "backup software," you'll find several options. These programs allow you to pick and choose which files and folders on your Mac's primary Hard Drive you'd like to back up on a regular basis and the destination drive you'll use for storage purposes. Instead of using an external hard drive, you could use backup software to save your important data to CDs or DVDs, depending on the type of optical drive that's built into your Mac (or connected to it).

Once you've selected which files and folders you want to back up on a regular basis, backup software allows you to determine the interval at which the automatic backups take place. (If you're backing up data to CDs or DVDs, the software will remind you when a backup needs to be done, but you will manually need to insert blank CD or DVD media into the computer's optical drive as needed.)

One of the easiest-to-use backup software applications available was developed by Apple for use with all Macs and the Mobile Me online service. The software, simply called Backup, comes bundled with the Mobile Me service's program CD. While the software allows your most important data to be backed up to the Mobile Me service on a remote server, it also allows you to set an alternate destination, such as an external hard drive.

While Time Machine is used to back up your entire main Hard Drive, the Backup software is best suited to back up only specific data files, such as your key chains, Safari bookmarks, Word documents, iCal and/or Address Book files, or other critical data. For more information about this software, visit apple.com/support/dotmac/backup/.

To find similar data backup software applications from third-party developers, visit apple.com/downloads/macosx/system_disk_utilities/. iBackUp (grapefruit.ch/iBackup/) is just one example of third-party backup software for the Mac. This particular program is offered as freeware for personal use.

# Remote Backup Options

A remote backup solution is a computer with massive storage capabilities located off-site that your Mac links to via the internet. The Mobile Me service described on page 310 (as well as within Chapter 9) is one example of a remote backup service. To utilize these services, your computer will need to be connected to the web via a high-speed connection, and you'll need to pay a monthly or an annual fee.

In many cases, the fee you'll pay relates directly to how much off-site storage space you use, whether it's 10GB or 500GB. When you subscribe to a service, you'll be provided with special software that allows automatic backups of specific files at predetermined intervals.

One key benefit to maintaining an off-site backup of your data is that if something happens to your computer (it gets lost, stolen, or damaged), your data is safely and securely stored in a separate location. These services use both password protection and data encryption to protect your data and files.

## Mozy

Mozy (877-669-9776/mozy.com/mozy/mac) is one of the premier third-party remote data backup services available to Mac users. The "personal" edition of this service is available for $4.95 per month for unlimited storage. MozyPro (a remote backup solution designed for small businesses) is $3.95 per month plus $.50 per gigabyte (GB).

## iBackUp

Another third-party remote backup solution for Mac users is available from iBackUp (800-949-3555, ext. 114/ibackup.com/ibackup-for-mac/index.html). As you'd expect, this service offers 128-bit SSL encryption of all data, plus data compression to speed up backup and data restore time. This service charges a

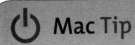

## Mac Tip

One potential drawback to using a remote data backup service is that you must keep paying ongoing monthly or annual fee to maintain the backup. If your membership to the service expires, your backup data is lost. So, if you decide to use one of these services, plan on its being an ongoing expense.

monthly fee, based on the amount of storage space required. For example, 10GB of storage is priced at $9.95 per month (or $99.50 per year), while 50GB of storage is $49.95 per month (or $499.50 per year). If you need 100GB of remote storage space, it'll cost you $99.95 per month, (or $999.50 per year). What the company refers to as "Enhanced Backup Plans" cost slightly more per month and offer a Snapshots feature, which provides historical views of data.

## Carbonite

Carbonite is one of the most popular and cost-effective remote backup solutions for PC users. Unlimited storage is offered to PC users for $49 per year. While Mac compatibility with this service had been announced by the Carbonite company, no date for the service's launch or pricing had been released at the time this book was being written. For details about Carbonite, visit carbonite.com or call (877) 665-4466.

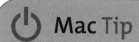

### Mac Tip

There are many free remote backup services designed exclusively for archiving photos and graphic images. Some of these services are Shutterfly (shutterfly.com), Flickr (flickr.com), Snapfish (snapfish.com), Kodak Gallery (kodakgallery.com), Photobucket (photobucket.com), and Google Picasa (picasaweb .google.com).

## Microsoft Office Live Workspace

If you're a Microsoft Office user, Microsoft has created a remote backup service for all Office applications, called Office Live Workspace. At the time this book was written, the service was available to Office users free of charge. It allows files and data created using Office to be stored online and shared with other users to whom you grant access to your files. Each Office Live Workspace account is given 500MB of online data storage space. The service allows backup of individual files up to 25MB. For more information about this remote backup solution for Office applications, visit workspace.office live.com.

**Mac Tip**

If you've spent hours creating an important file and don't have the ability to create a backup onto a CD, DVD, or thumb drive, a quick and easy alternative is to use the Save As command in the application to create a copy of the file and then e-mail that file to yourself. This way, a copy of the file will be stored on a remote e-mail server as well as on your laptop computer.

## The Mobile Me Backup Alternative

Designed specifically for use by Mac users, the Mobile Me online service offers a variety of functions and features that were described in Chapter 9. The Mobile Me service requires an annual membership fee of $99.95 per year. That includes a total of 10GB of online storage space. For 20GB or 30GB of online storage space, you pay an additional $49.95 or $99.95 per year, respectively.

In terms of backing up data, Mobile Me members can use Apple's Backup software to automatically back up important data and files. You can also use the iDisk feature of Mobile Me to maintain backups and share online access to your important files. More information about Mobile Me can be found at apple.com/support/dot mac/, or by visiting any Apple Store. Membership can also be purchased by phone (800-MY-APPLE) using a major credit card.

## Creating Backup CDs or DVDs

Even without specialized backup software, you can manually create backup CDs or DVDs (depending on the type of optical drive installed on your Mac). To do this, simply insert a blank (writable or rewritable) CD or DVD into your Mac's optical drive. Use Finder to open a window for this drive on your Desktop. Again using Finder, open the folder(s) you'd like to copy to CD or DVD. With the mouse, drag the files from the original Finder window to the destination window (or use the Copy and Paste feature pull-down menu options or keyboard shortcuts).

When all of the files have been copied to the blank destination CD or DVD, click on the Burn icon to save the files. As soon as the copy and burn process is

## ⏻  Mac Tip

If you're a MacBook, MacBook Pro, or MacBook Air user and you've created an important file while on the go—a report, a presentation, a spreadsheet, an updated schedule, or new contacts to your Address Book database—it's an excellent strategy to travel with a small thumb drive (at least 1GB capacity) and create a manual backup of the files as you create them. Keep the thumb drive in your pocket, on a keychain, or in a purse—separate from the computer itself. Thus if anything happens to your notebook computer, the critical files will still be on hand should you need them. Depending on their capacity, thumb drives cost between $30 and $100. They're very small and are sold at office supply stores, computer stores, consumer electronics retailers, and even at airport or hotel gift shops. Thumb drives are also referred to as flash drives.

complete, check to make sure the data transferred properly, and then eject the disc and store it in a safe location. The drawbacks to this backup method are that it must be done manually, it's time consuming, and you run the risk of losing or damaging the backup CDs or DVDs.

## Data Restoration Services and Software

When and if the worst case scenario happens and your computer's primary Hard Drive crashes, you accidentally delete a file (and empty the Trash), or your data somehow becomes corrupted, seek professional assistance immediately to reduce the chance that the data is lost forever. Reputable data recovery services are able to extract data from damaged or erased hard drives, but there's typically a high fee associated with these services.

Ideally, you should find a data recovery or data restoration service in your local area so you don't have to ship your computer to a distant location.

Carefully pack up the computer and hand-deliver it to the data recovery service (unless the service is willing to make a house call).

After an initial evaluation of your computer's Hard Drive, the service will be able to determine if your data is recoverable, and if so, at what cost. Maintaining a reliable backup of your data is a much better and cheaper alternative than having to rely on a data recovery service.

These companies are listed in the Yellow Pages, or can be found online using any search engine. Enter the search phrase "Data Recovery, [Your Home City]" or "Data Restoration, [Your Home City]" to find a company in your area. Ideally, you should seek a referral to ensure the company you use is reliable and experienced, and will keep your recovered data secure and private.

For less serious data loss or corruption issues, there are Mac software packages designed to help recover lost, deleted, or corrupted data. Techtool Pro from Micromat Inc. (800-829-6227/micromat.com) offers a $98 suite of tools for diagnosing and repairing computer hardware issues, optimizing hard drives to obtain peak performance, and handling basic data recovery. Techtool Pro is available wherever Mac software is sold, or it can be purchased and downloaded from Micromat's website.

## Mac Tip

Tech Restore (888-64-RESTORE/techrestore.com) is just one company based in California that specializes in data recovery for Macs as well as Mac upgrades and repairs. Overnight data recovery service is available, as is overnight shipping to and from the repair facility.

Another third-party software application designed to recover lost data is FileSalvage from SubRosa Soft (510-870-7883/subrosasoft.com). This software, which sells for $89.95, can be used to undelete files from your Hard Drive, digital camera, or iPod, in many cases, even if the Hard Drive has been formatted or corrupted. FileSalvage can be purchased and downloaded online from the company's website, or a program CD version can be purchased wherever Mac software is sold.

## Final Thoughts

For the first few times you use your new Mac, chances are you'll encounter situations that are confusing or frustrating simply because you're unfamiliar with the Mac OS X's user interface or you're still in the habit of using incompatible Windows keyboard shortcuts. Once this basic learning curve passes, you'll probably realize just how enjoyable, hassle-free, reliable, and intuitive using a Mac is, compared to running similar applications on a PC.

As you move forward, stay up-to-date with all of the latest Mac OS X operating system updates, make sure you download updates to whatever applications you use, maintain a regular backup of your most critical data, and look for ways to utilize your Mac's built-in features and functionality to make your personal and professional life easier, more productive, and more organized.

For example, even if you'll be using your Mac primarily for business purposes, during your spare time you can use the computer (along with iPhoto, for example) to store, edit, and enjoy all of your personal photos. You can also use the computer to edit and present your home movies in a more entertaining way, and better manage your personal finances. Of course, like any computer, your Mac is also capable of playing a wide assortment of fun and challenging games, which many people find entertaining as well as relaxing.

Thanks to iTunes, your Mac can also become your own personal entertainment center, allowing you to store, organize, and listen to all of your favorite songs and audio CDs, and to download movies and TV show episodes, which you can watch on your computer's screen. If you prefer interactive entertainment,

## ⏻ Mac Tip

The Apple website (apple.com) serves as a clearinghouse for all news and information relating to your Mac, new applications, updates to the Mac OS X operating system, and anything and everything else you'll need to know as a Mac user. In Chapter 1, a list of independent Mac-oriented magazines and websites is listed. From these resources, you can obtain unbiased news and product reviews, and learn all about new product announcements related to your Mac.

iChat offers instant messaging, online chatting, and videoconferencing using any of several popular online services. And you can tap your creativity to develop and manage a personal web page or blog and share your thoughts and opinions with the world.

As you'll discover, your Mac is capable of handling a wide range of business-oriented applications, but it's also a powerful personal computing tool with thousands of uses that are limited only by your interests and imagination. When you connect your Mac to the internet, the possibilities increase dramatically. So as you start using your new Mac, look for fun and creative ways to make full use of your new Apple notebook or desktop computer.

# Record-Keeping Worksheet

I F YOU REQUIRE TECHNICAL SUPPORT OR REPAIR SERVICES FROM APPLE OR A THIRD-PARTY software publisher, you will be required to provide information about your computer and software, including the date of purchase and a Serial Number. The following worksheet will help you keep detailed records on your Mac and its software.

## Apple Contact Numbers and Websites

- *Apple Technical Support.* (800) 275-2273/apple.com/support
- *Apple Online Store.* (800) MY-APPLE/store.apple.com
- *Find a Local Apple Store.* apple.com/retail

## Mac System Configuration Information

To obtain this information, click on the Apple icon in the upper-left corner of your Desktop and select the About This Mac command. When the About This Mac window appears, click on the More Info icon.

Mac Model: _____

Computer Serial Number: _____

Processor Name and Speed: _____

Amount of RAM: _____

Hard Drive Capacity: _____

Optical Drive Type: _____

Date of Purchase: _____

Location Where the Original Purchase Receipt Is Stored: _____

Purchase Location: _____

Local Apple Store Phone Number and Address: _____

_____

## Printer Information

Printer Make/Manufacturer: _____

Printer Model: _____

Ink Cartridge(s)/Toner Cartridge(s) Product Numbers: _____

_____

_____

Printer Drum Model/Product Number (for laser printers):_____

Specialized Printer Label or Specialty Paper Product Number(s):_____

_____

## Apple Account Information

(Created when setting up your Mac using the Setup Assistant.)

Account Name: _____

Account Short Name: _____

Password: _____

Admin Account Name: _____

## Apple ID Information

(Created when registering your computer with Apple online.)

Apple ID: _____

Password: _____

## AppleCare Information Protection Plan

(Website: apple.com/support/register)

AppleCare Product Purchased:_____

Registration Number: _____

Name, Address, Phone Number, and E-Mail Address Used When Registering With AppleCare: _____

———————————————————————————

———————————————————————————

———————————————————————————

Registration Date: _____

(Your AppleCare plan will expire three years from the registration date.)

## Software Information

For each commercial program you install on your Mac, keep a record of the software's Serial Number and related information.

Software Package Title: _____

Version Number: _____

Product ID (if applicable): _____

Serial Number: _____

Date Purchased: _____

Location of Original Program CD(s): _____

Software Package Title: _____

Version Number: _____

Product ID (if applicable): _____

Serial Number: _____

Date Purchased: _____

Location of Original Program CD(s): _____

Software Package Title: _____

Version Number: _____

Product ID (if applicable): _____

Serial Number:_____

Date Purchased:_____

Location of Original Program CD(s): _____


Software Package Title: _____

Version Number: _____

Product ID (if applicable): _____

Serial Number:_____

Date Purchased:_____

Location of Original Program CD(s): _____


Software Package Title: _____

Version Number: _____

Product ID (if applicable): _____

Serial Number:_____

Date Purchased:_____

Location of Original Program CD(s): _____


## Internet and E-Mail Account Information

E-Mail Address: _____

E-Mail/Internet Service Provider Name: _____

Phone Number: _____

Account Number: _____

Username: _____

Password: _____

Incoming (POP) Mail Server: _____

Outgoing (SMTP) Mail Server: _____


E-Mail Address: _____

E-Mail/Internet Service Provider Name: _____

Phone Number: _____

Account Number: _____

Username: _____

Password: _____

Incoming (POP) Mail Server: _____

Outgoing (SMTP) Mail Server: _____


## Mobile Me Membership Information

(Website: mac.com)

Member Name: _____

Password: _____

Account E-Mail Address: _____@mac.com

Registration Date: _____

Personal Mobile Me Website URL(s): _____

Personal Mobile Me Web Gallery URL(s): _____

## Remote Data Backup Service

Service Name: _____

Website: _____

Phone Number: _____

Account Number: _____

Username: _____

Password: _____

Notes: _____

## Favorite Websites

Website URL: _____

Username: _____

Password: _____

Notes: _____

Website URL: _____

Username: _____

Password: _____

Notes: _____

Website URL: _____

Username: _____

Password: _____

Notes: _____

Website URL: _____

Username: _____

Password: _____

Notes: _____


Website URL: _____

Username: _____

Password: _____

Notes: _____

# Mac-Compatible Apple Alternatives

O NE BIG COMPLAINT MANY PEOPLE HAVE WHO ARE CONTEMPLATING GIVING UP their PC and migrating to the Mac is the cost of genuine Apple Mac computers. With Apple Mac system configurations starting at $1,099 for a MacBook and $1,199 for an iMac, this is somewhat more costly than a comparably equipped PC-based computer that runs Windows. The low-end Mac Mini is priced starting at $599, but you still need to figure in the cost of a monitor, mouse, and keyboard.

Added to the base cost of a new Mac, you'll probably want to invest in the AppleCare service plan, which is priced starting at $249, but could be higher, depending on the Mac you purchase. AppleCare provides three years' worth of support and repair coverage for the computer and is a worthwhile investment.

Until recently, if you wanted a computer to run the Mac OS X operating system and all Mac applications, you had to purchase a genuine Apple Mac computer. Well, that's starting to change. As of April 2008, a company called Psystar Corporation was selling what it called the Open Computer, with a price starting at just $399.99. This desktop computer is a PC that works just like a Mac and runs the genuine version of the Apple Mac OS X Leopard operating system (and all compatible Mac software applications).

The slightly upgraded $549 configuration for the Open Computer includes a 2.2GHz processor, 2GB of RAM memory, a 250GB hard drive, a GeForce 8600 graphics card, and the Mac OS X operating system pre-installed. The computer's CPU has four USB ports and includes a dual layer DVD+/–R burner that is equal to Apple's own SuperDrive optical drive unit. While the base unit does not include a Firewire port, one can be added for a small additional fee. This configuration is more than adequate for running most Mac applications or even multiple applications simultaneously.

According to Psystar, the Open Computer is less expensive than the Mac Mini, Apple's entry-level Mac computer, but significantly more powerful than most of the higher-end Macs currently on the market. The Open Computer is available from the Psystar website (psystar.com) or can be ordered by calling (888) 456-7801.

It's important to understand that Apple in no way endorses or supports the Open Computer, nor have the claims made by the company in regard to its 100 percent compatibility with genuine Macs been proven by Entrepreneur Press or this book's author. In fact, industry analysts were predicting that Apple would soon be filing lawsuits to stop the sale of the Open Computer. However, at the time this book was being written, the computers were available for sale.

Another company, Axiotron (310-426-2670/axiotron.com), has licensed the rights from Apple to create an officially sanctioned tablet-based computer that runs the Mac OS X Leopard operating system and all Mac applications. The ModBook was announced back in 2007, but only recently became available. It is the only Mac-based tablet computer on the market. The ModBook has a 13.3-inch widescreen LCD display and comes with Mac OS X Leopard pre-installed, as well as the company's award-winning Inkwell handwriting recognition software. The unit also has a built-in GPA system and a system configuration that rivals any genuine Apple Mac system currently on the market.

According to Axiotron, the ModBook was designed for mobile users, artists, design professionals, and photographers who need enhanced precision and control when drawing or writing directly on a portable tablet computer screen. The suggested retail price of the basic ModBook is $2,290.

Both the Open Computer and ModBook offer alternatives to purchasing genuine Apple Mac computers. They are able to run the Mac OS X Leopard operating system and/or Microsoft Windows XP or Windows Vista.

# Glossary
# 100 Mac-Related Terms You'll Want to Know

WHEN YOU EVALUATE THE SYSTEM SPECIFICATIONS AND CONFIGURATION OF any computer, including all Macs, you'll come across terminology that describes the technology and its capabilities. Later, when you start using various Mac applications on your new computer, you'll repeatedly encounter additional computer-related terms you'll need to understand.

This glossary will help you understand 100 common Mac and general computer-related terms used throughout this book. As a (soon to be) former PC user, chances are you're already familiar with much of this vocabulary. Many of the definitions provided here, however, relate to how these terms are used in conjunction with a Mac OS X–based computer.

**Acrobat Reader**. A free program from Adobe that allows a computer to open and display PDF files. Adobe Acrobat Professional (described in Chapter 10) is a commercial application that allows users to create, edit, display, and manage PDF files.

**Address Book**. An application built into the Mac OS X operating system that allows users to maintain an electronic address book (contact database). Address Book data can be shared with other Mac applications.

**AirPort Extreme**. This is Apple's solution for making its computers Wi-Fi (wireless internet) compatible.

**Apple Remote**. Because Macs are capable of allowing users to watch TV shows and movies, plus listen to music (thanks to iTunes and any media users insert into their computer's optical drive), each Mac computer comes with an Apple Remote, which works the same way as a traditional TV or stereo remote control to play, pause, fast forward, or rewind the video or audio content you're listening to or watching. The Apple Remote is a wireless device that fits in the palm of your hand.

**AppleCare Protection Plan**. An optional, three-year, comprehensive technical support and repair service available directly from Apple that covers any Mac system. This service does not, however, protect against theft or loss of equipment or software.

**Bluetooth**. This is a wireless technology that allows a computer to communicate with peripherals and/or accessories, such as a printer, without using cables. To learn about the many uses for this technology in regard to computers and cellular telephones, visit bluetooth.com.

**Built-In Wireless (Wi-Fi)**. This is the wireless technology that allows a Mac computer (or any computer for that matter) to connect to the internet without the use of an Ethernet cable or dial-up modem. For this type of internet connection to work, the computer must be within range of a Wi-Fi hotspot (within 100 feet or so of a wireless internet hub).

**CD-ROM Drive**. This type of optical drive allows the computer to read and often write from standard CD digital media. The optical drive's capabilities may be defined using terms like "CD-R," or "CD-RW," which means that data cannot only be read from the CD-ROM drive at a high speed (such as 8x, 16x, or 24x), it can also be written to the CD for backup or data storage purposes. A CD-R disc can be written to just once (the data is stored on that CD permanently). A CD-RW drive allows CD data to be erased and rewritten, meaning that same CD can be used repeatedly to store different data at different times.

**Command Key**. This key on the keyboard (found next to the Space Bar), which also displays the Apple logo, the word "Command," and/or the "⌘" symbol, allows keyboard shortcuts to be executed when using almost any Mac application. A keyboard shortcut typically involves pressing the Command key in conjunction with one or two additional keys, such as Command (⌘) + Q to quit/exit an application.

**CPU**. This is the computer's Central Processing Unit, the brains of the computer. Mac-based computers offer different CPU processing speeds at different price points. The processor speed of the Intel Core 2 Duo chipset, for example, which runs most Mac-based computers (as of mid–2008), can have a processing speed of between 1.6GHz and 2.5GHz. The faster the processing speed, the better, especially if you're running graphic-intensive programs or software that requires a lot of computing power. If you'll be running multiple programs simultaneously, a faster processing speed is beneficial.

**Dashboard**. The program built into the Mac OS X operating system that allows users to utilize and run Widgets.

**Desktop**. The primary work space on your computer screen when using the Mac OS X operating system. At the top of the Desktop you'll find the Menu bar, while at the bottom of the Desktop you'll find the Dock. In the Desktop, program, file, and folder windows can be opened.

**Display**. This is the screen of the computer. For desktop computers (iMacs) for example, the display and CPU are the same unit. On a MacBook notebook computer, the screen is also built into the system. For a Mac Pro or Mac Mini, you'll need to add a separate monitor or display unit to the computer.

**Dock**. Located at the bottom of the screen (unless you utilize System Preferences to change the default) is a group of program icons. You can customize the order of these icons and place program icons here for your most commonly used Mac applications. (As a PC user, think of the program icons on your Dock as shortcuts that allow you to launch a program with a single click of the mouse.)

**Double-Click**. A common interaction with the mouse that involves pressing the mouse's button two times quickly in order to handle certain tasks, such as launching an application from the Applications folder using Finder.

**Drag**. Involves using the mouse to move a program icon, file, or folder, for example, from one location to another. You can drag an icon on your Desktop to the Trash icon in order to delete it.

**Eject**. The Eject button is used to remove a CD/DVD from the computer's optical drive. It's also necessary to eject an external hard drive, memory card reader (containing a memory card), or a thumb drive/flash drive before removing the USB or Firewire cable connecting it to your computer. This is done by dragging the icon representing the drive from the Desktop to the Trash icon, or by highlighting the icon representing the drive and using the Eject command found under the File pull-down menu along the Menu bar. The keyboard shortcut to Eject a drive is Command (⌘) + E.

**Ethernet**. This is technology that allows a computer to be connected to a high-speed (Broadband, DSL, or FIOS) modem to access the internet. Unless your internet router is wireless, to connect to the internet your computer needs to connect to an internet router via an Ethernet cable that plugs into the Ethernet port built into all Mac-based computers (except for the MacBook Air).

**Expose**. A feature added to the Mac OS X Leopard edition of the operating system that allows you to view all open programs (or all windows related to a program) at once on your screen and quickly switch between them. To access Expose, simultaneously press both side buttons on the Apple Mighty Mouse or press Function + F9 (to show all open program windows) or Function + F10 (to show all open windows within an application).

**External Hard Drive**. An optional hard drive that's connected to the computer using a USB or Firewire cable. It is not built into the computer. An external hard drive can be used for backup purposes in conjunction with the Time Machine application, for example, or it can be used for additional storage space for applications, files, and data.

**File**. a collection of data, programs, or documents stored in a computer's memory or within a storage device under a specific name (its file name).

**Finder**. A feature built into the Mac OS X operating system that is responsible for managing all of your applications, files, folders, discs, network connections, and external devices (such as printers). When your computer is on, Finder is always running (although it's often in the background and unseen by the user, unless it's called upon).

**Firewire**. This is a technology that allows two computers or a computer and a peripheral to be connected via a special cable so data can be transferred at extremely high speeds. If you plan to network two Mac computers, for example, so data can easily be transferred between machines, using a Firewire connection is the fastest option.

**Flash Drive**. See *Thumb Drive*.

**Folder**. A collection of files, data, or documents stored on a computer and grouped together under a single name. A folder is typically represented by an icon (within Finder, for example) that allows a user to access a specific directory that contains related files.

**Font**. A specific style of text that shares a common appearance or design. An unlimited number of unique fonts can be stored in the Fonts folder, allowing the user to customize the appearance of text.

**Force Quit**. The command used when a Mac program crashes, freezes, or hangs. It forces the application to close without having to reboot the computer. This command can be executed using the Force Quit command found under the Apple pull-down menu on the Menu bar.

**Freeware**. This is software available for your Mac that is offered by the programmer(s) or publisher free of charge. Typically, freeware can be downloaded from a website like the Downloads section of Apple.com.

**Genius**. A Mac specialist who works at the Genius Bar in an Apple Store. You can set up a free meeting with a Genius to receive in-person technical support or assistance by setting up an appointment in advance. Each appointment lasts about 15 minutes.

**Gigabyte (GB)**. This is how the amount of memory a computer possesses is measured. It can also refer to how much data can be transferred in one second. One Gigabyte (abbreviated "G" or "GB") contains 1,073,741,824 bytes of data or 1,024 megabytes (MB).

**Hard Drive**. This is the storage device a computer uses to store programs and data. All Mac computers have an internal (built-in) Hard Drive, but additional external hard drives can be added to give a computer additional data storage capacity. These days, hard drive space is measured in gigabytes. A basic MacBook Hard Drive might be 120GB, while a souped-up Mac Pro might have a 320GB or larger Hard Drive. The larger the storage capacity, the more programs and data that can be stored. When evaluating a Hard Drive, you want to consider its size (memory capacity) as well as the rate at which it transfers data between the drive itself and the computer.

**Height, Width, Depth, and Weight**. This refers to the physical dimensions of the computer. Apple provides these specifications in inches and pounds, as well as centimeters and kilograms.

**Hide**. This command closes a window that's open on your Desktop (removing it from view) but does not close or quit the application or place a temporary icon representing that window on the Dock.

**iCal**. The application built into the Mac OS X operating system used for scheduling, time management, and creating/managing to-do lists.

**iChat**. The application built into the Mac OS X operating system used for communicating online with other computer users via Instant Messaging or online-based videoconferencing. Once you're communicating with a specific person, files can also be transferred between users using this software. iChat is compatible with Mobile Me, AOL/AIM, and other popular Instant Messaging services.

**iLife**. This is a suite of first-party Apple software that comes bundled with all Mac computers. It allows users to perform a variety of tasks, such as download and listen to music (via iTunes), watch DVD movies, as well as edit and store digital photographs.

**iMac**. An Apple Mac desktop computer suitable for most casual computer users.

**Instant Message (IM)**. A method of sending text-based messages to other computer users via the web in order to communicate in real time using a service like AIM (America Online Instant Messenger).

**Intel Core 2 Duo (or Extreme) Processor**. Intel is the manufacturer of the computer processor chips now used to power Mac-based computers. The Intel Core Duo is capable of running both the Mac OS X Leopard and Windows XP or Windows Vista operating systems, and the chipsets come in several different configurations, which determine overall processing speed. At least once per year, Intel announces significant upgrades to its chips, which allow for enhanced computing power. So when you purchase your Mac, the chipset might have a different name.

**Internal Hard Drive**. The primary Hard Drive built into your Mac used to store applications, files, programs, and data.

**iPhoto**. The application built into the Mac OS X operating system used to view, archive, and edit digital photos, as well as create slide presentations.

**iSight Camera**. Located at the top of Apple displays on iMacs, MacBooks, MacBook Pros, and MacBook Air units is a tiny video camera, called iSight, which allows still digital images to be taken. It can also be used as a web cam, for example, to handle videoconferencing applications or video blogging.

**iWork**. This is a suite of applications developed by Apple that offers similar functionality to Microsoft Office, including word processing, spreadsheets, and presentation software.

**Keyboard Shortcut**. The ability to execute commonly used commands in a program by pressing two or more keys on the keyboard simultaneously, as opposed to using a pull-down menu command, for example. Most keyboard shortcuts use the Command (⌘) key, in conjunction with one or two additional keys on the keyboard. Some keyboard commands are unique to specific applications, while others work when using almost any Mac program.

**Keyword**. A term or phrase used in a search field to find specific data, text, or files. For example, keywords can be used to locate files or information when using Finder.

**Lithium-Polymer Battery**. The rechargeable battery used by the MacBook, MacBook Pro, and MacBook Air notebook computers.

**Mac Mini**. The "economical" Mac that does not come bundled with a monitor or keyboard.

**Mac OS X Leopard**. The operating system used by all newer Apple computers and those older Macs that have been upgraded.

**Mac Pro**. The higher-end Apple desktop computers. These Macs typically have a faster processor, larger Hard Drive, and better optical drive than the lower-end iMac desktop computers. The Mac Pros are more suitable for "power users" and businesspeople who need additional computing and processing power, as well as better performance.

**MacBook**. The basic Apple notebook computer suitable for most users. It comes in several different system configurations.

**MacBook Air**. The thinnest and lightest of Apple's notebook computer offerings.

**MacBook Pro**. This is Apple's most powerful notebook computer. Customers can choose between two screen sizes and among a variety of different options when selecting their computer's system configuration, especially if they order from Apple.com. This is Apple's higher-end notebook computer that's most suited to power users and business professionals.

**MagSafe Power Adapter**. The unique power adapter that connects the MacBook line of notebook computers to the electrical outlet.

**Mail**. The e-mail management application built into the Mac OS X operating system. It's designed to work in conjunction with Address Book and iCal.

**Megabyte (MB)**. A measurement of computer memory equal to one million bytes.

**Memory**. Refers to how much RAM (Random Access Memory) is built into a computer, which impacts its overall performance as well as how much data or information can be stored. Memory can also refer to the storage capacity of a computer's hard drive, for example.

**Memory Card**. A data storage device that can be used by a digital camera, for example, to store images. By connecting a memory card reader to a Mac, the computer can read data from a memory card and import it. There are many different formats of memory cards, which also come in a variety of different storage capacities.

**Menu Bar**. This is the main selection of pull-down menus available when using any program running under the Mac OS X operating system. The Menu bar is found at the top of the Desktop. Pull-down menu options change, however, based on what application is currently active.

**MHz (Megahertz)**. Refers to the clock speed of the computer's processor. The faster the processing speed, the better in terms of the computer's power and performance. An iMac, for example, might have a processing speed of 2.33 GHz (gigahertz).

**Microsoft Office 2008**. The popular suite of business-related applications created by Microsoft and available for the Mac. A version of Office is also available for Windows-based computers. This suite includes Word (word processing), Excel (spreadsheets), PowerPoint (presentation software), and Entourage (e-mail, scheduling, and contact management).

**Mighty Mouse**. This is Apple's ergonomically designed mouse. The corded version comes with all iMacs and Mac Pro desktop computers. A corded or cordless version of the Mighty Mouse can also be connected to any Mac notebook or desktop computer and can be purchased separately. This mouse has one main button, a Scroll Ball, and two side buttons.

**Minimize**. A command used to remove a program or folder window from the Desktop, without exiting the application. A minimized window will appear on the Dock in the form of an icon. To minimize a window, click on the yellow dot in the upper-left corner of a window, or select the Minimize Window command found under the Window pull-down menu on the Menu bar. The keyboard shortcut for this command is Control (⌘) + M.

**Mobile Me**. Formerly known as .Mac, this online service created and maintained by Apple offers a variety of tools and services for Mac users, including remote file backup capabilities and online-based applications for creating and hosting a personal website.

**Mouse Click**. A single press of the mouse button when using any Mac application.

**Multitouch Trackpad**. Instead of a Mighty Mouse, all Mac notebook computers utilize a trackpad, which allows you to control the on-screen cursor using your index finger and thumb (to press the trackpad button). The Multitouch Trackpad is available on the MacBook Air and MacBook Pro, and provides added functionality, such as the ability to zoom, rotate, and pinch.

**Open Source Software**. Applications created by a team of programmers that are offered to users for free. OpenOffice.org Productivity Suite is an example of open source software. This suite of applications rivals Microsoft Office or iWork for the Mac, but can be downloaded and used for free.

**Optical Drive Formats Reads/Writes (DVD+R, DVD-R, DVD-RW, CD-R, CD-RW, CD)**. The media drive built into a Mac can read and write to a variety of different formats of CDs or DVD-based media, based on the specifications of the drive. While most can play (or read data from) CDs or DVDs, a computer user will also want an optical drive capable of writing data to these media formats.

**Overwrite**. This is a process of copying a newer version of a file, while at the same time deleting (or replacing) the older version of that file (as opposed to creating a newer version of the file, but maintaining the older version as well). This term is often used when dealing with the synchronization of data between two devices or folders, for example.

**PDF File**. Created by Adobe Systems, Adobe Portable Document Format (PDF) lets computer users capture and view information—from any application on any computer system—and share it with others, regardless of what computer platform (operating system) they're using.

**Preferences**. The commands available in a Mac application that allow you to customize the program to better meet your needs. Most programs allow you to adjust various preferences by selecting the Preferences command from the Menu bar's pull-down menu that has the active program's name. For example, if you're running Microsoft Word, you'll find the Preferences menu option under the Word pull-down menu on the Toolbar.

**Preview**. The program built into the Mac OS X operating system that allows users to view various types of graphic files and digital images, including PDF files, photos, and clip art graphics.

**Printer**. A peripheral that can be connected to the computer in order to print out files, data, graphics, and documents. Many different types of printers are available. Most can connect to a Mac using a USB cable or via a wireless Bluetooth connection. Many printers can also be accessed by a Mac connected to a network or via a Firewire cable.

**Processor**. The chips within a computer (the central processing unit) that handle the actual computing tasks and calculations within a computer. A processor's performance is measured by its speed (in Gigahertz). The faster the processor, the better. For example, a 2.6 GHz processor will perform better and faster than a 1.6 GHz processor.

**Program Window**. Each application running on a Mac will operate in at least one active program window displayed on the Mac OS X Desktop. Each window will house one application. So when multiple program windows are displayed on the screen, multiple applications are running simultaneously. The user can quickly switch between active program windows.

**RAM (Random Access Memory).** The memory available within a computer that allows data to be stored and retrieved, without saving it to a hard drive or another media format, for example. The more RAM a computer has built in, the more computing power it'll have and the easier it will be to run multiple applications simultaneously. For most Mac applications, a computer equipped with 2GB of RAM is suitable. If you're running complex applications or graphics-intensive applications, such as PhotoShop CS3 or a game, 4GB of RAM gives the computer much better performance capabilities.

**Resolution.** Refers to the quality of what's displayed on the computer's screen or within a printout (hard copy). For example, a MacBook with a 13.3-inch display has a native screen resolution of 1280 by 800 pixels. The 20-inch screen of an iMac has a digital resolution of 1920 by 1200 pixels. The better the resolution, the more detailed the picture quality or graphics quality will be.

**Safari.** The built-in application in the Mac OS X operating system used for surfing the web. This is Apple's premier web browser software, and offers similar functionality to Microsoft Internet Explorer or Mozilla's Foxfire.

**Save.** The command used in almost every Mac application to save (store) the file or data you're currently working with. In most cases, in addition to saving a file using a file name you create, you must also select the location (in what folder of your Hard Drive, for example) the file will be stored.

**Save As.** The command used to create a new version of a file or document you're working with in an application. Using this command, you can create an alternate file name and/or select an alternate save location for the file or data.

**Screen Saver.** An application built into the Mac OS X operating system that kicks in after the computer has not been in use for a predetermined number of minutes. In addition to helping to protect the monitor from displaying the same stagnant image for hours at a time, a screen saver can also be decorative and/or display some type of data. Screen savers can be created and/or customized by the user, and thousands are available for download from sites like Apple.com.

**Setup Assistant**. When a new Mac is purchased, the first application a user runs is the Setup Assistant, which guides the user through the computer's initial setup procedure step by step.

**Shareware**. This is software that is offered to a potential user for free on a trial period basis (usually 30 days), after which the software can be purchased and used indefinitely, or deleted from the computer. Shareware allows users to test software on their computer before paying for it. In most cases, a shareware edition of a program is identical to the full commercial version. In other cases, shareware editions of software have key features deactivated until the software is purchased. Thousands of Mac compatible shareware applications can be downloaded from the Downloads section of the Apple.com website.

**Shut Down**. The process of turning off a Mac. The Shut Down command is found in the Apple pull-down menu on the Menu bar. Shutting down the computer is the same as turning it off.

**Spaces**. A program in the Mac OS X operating system that allows users to quickly switch between applications.

**Subfolder**. Within a data folder on a Mac, a user can create an unlimited number of subfolders to better organize data in a hierarchical system. Folders and subfolders can be accessed (or created) using Finder as well as specific Mac applications.

**SuperDrive**. A type of optical drive that Apple bundles with many of its Macs. It's capable of reading and writing to a variety of optical disc formats, including CDs and DVDs.

**Synchronize**. The process of transferring data between two or more computers or devices, such as a Mac and an iPhone, between a Mac and a PC, between two or more Macs, or a Mac and an iPod, for example. When data is synchronized, the files match on multiple computers and/or devices.

**System Preferences**. The functionality within the Mac OS X operating system that allows users to customize their computing experience and how they interact with their Mac. The System Preferences applications can be found within the Applications folder of any Mac.

**Thumb Drive**. A portable storage device that can be plugged into the USB port of any computer. These tiny devices are ideal for backing up data or transferring a small number of files between computers. A thumb drive can have a storage capacity of between 16MB and 8GB (or more). A thumb drive is also referred to as a portable flash drive.

**Time Capsule**. The optional peripheral designed for use with Time Machine for maintaining a backup of a Mac's internal Hard Drive. This device uses a wireless connection to a Mac, and allows multiple computers to share a printer. It also serves as a Wi-Fi base station (wireless internet router).

**Time Machine**. The backup software built into the Mac OS X Leopard operating system that is designed to maintain a constant and up-to-date backup of a Mac's entire Hard Drive. To use this software, an external hard drive must be connected to the Mac.

**Toolbox**. In all Microsoft Office applications (Word, Excel, PowerPoint, etc.), this is a separate window from the main program window that gives users quick and easy access to a variety of commands and features used in each application.

**Trackpad**. See *Multitouch Trackpad*.

**Trash**. This icon, found along the Dock, is used for deleting files and programs from the Mac. Items can be copied to or dragged to the Trash. When the Trash is later emptied, all files and data in it are permanently deleted. When the Trash window is open (by clicking on the Trash icon), select the Empty Trash command found under the Finder pull-down menu to delete the contents of the Trash.

**Typestyle**. This refers to the appearance of any font or text. A typestyle can be regular, **bold**, <u>underlined,</u> *italic,* or ~~strikethrough,~~ or customized in a variety of other ways, depending on the application. Text can also be displayed using combinations of these criteria, such as ***<u>bold, underlined, and italicized</u>***.

**USB (Universal Serial Bus)**. A "plug-and-play" technology used for connecting various devices and peripherals such as a mouse, keyboard, printer, or thumb drive to a computer. When such a device is connected to a computer, the computer automatically detects it and configures the appropriate drivers without the user's intervention.

**Widget**. A small, downloadable program that's used in the Dashboard application. Widgets can collect and convey information, or perform simple tasks or functions. Thousands of Widgets are available for free from the Apple.com website.

**Window**. An area of the computer's display in which an application can be run or data can be displayed. On a Mac's Desktop, an unlimited number of windows can be displayed simultaneously, although the user can only actively use one at a time. There are several ways to quickly switch between windows using the Mac OS X operating system.

**Windows XP/Windows Vista**. Refers to two versions of Microsoft's Windows operating system, which is favored by the majority of PC users. Many people who switch to a Mac do so to get away from the Windows operating system.

**XML File Format**. An open source file format adopted by Microsoft Office, iWork, and other applications and software suites that helps to ensure file compatibility when files, data, and/or documents are transferred between computers and across computing platforms (from Mac to PC, or vice versa).

# Index